MW01517998

l

e
a

Annotated translation
by Jun Fang and Lifang He
of
Reminiscences of the Plum-shaded Convent
(*Yingmeian Yiyu* 影梅庵憶語)
by Mao Xiang (1611-1693)

Proverse Hong Kong
2019

The Romance of a Literatus and his Concubine in Seventeenth-century China is an annotated translation of **Reminiscences of the Plum-shaded Convent** (*Yingmeian Yiyu* 影梅庵憶語), written by China's prominent essayist and poet Mao Xiang 冒襄 (1611-1693) in memory of his concubine Dong Xiaowan 董小宛 (1624-1651). Critically acclaimed by generations of Chinese commentators, this memoir presents a vivid image of a young woman who determinedly pursued the goal of escaping from her former life as a courtesan and calmly dealt with all the difficulties she encountered in the last decade of her short life. It also reveals the political and social vicissitudes of Chinese society and the life of its élite during the tumultuous Ming-Qing dynastic transition. (The "Plum-shaded Convent" refers to the place where Dong was buried.)

Working on both the Daoguang edition of the original text printed in the early 19th century and the identical version, published in the early twentieth century under the editorship of Mao Xiang's descendant, the erudite scholar Mao Guangsheng (1873-1959), and drawing on the translators' previous research on Mao Xiang and the late Ming literati, this book offers a truthful rendition of the Chinese masterpiece. It identifies essentially all the historical figures who appear in the memoir and provides ample explanatory notes. To help readers understand the context of the book, the translators have provided photographs of some of the places mentioned in the memoir, which they took during their visits to East China in 2018. Also included are examples of Mao Xiang's calligraphy and Dong Xiaowan's painting.

This book is both the first translation of *Yingmeian Yiyu* into English since 1931 and a valuable resource for studying Chinese history, literature, and gender relations in the seventeenth century. **The Romance of a Literatus and his Concubine in Seventeenth-century China** should appeal to a wide readership of students, specialists, and interested laypersons.

Jun Fang 方駿 received his Ph.D. in History and East Asian Studies from the University of Toronto. He is Professor of History at Huron University and Adjunct Research Professor at the University of Western Ontario. Prior to joining the faculty at Huron in 2005 he taught Chinese history at Nanjing University (1987-1989) and the Education University of Hong Kong (1995-2005). He has published twelve books including *China's Second Capital – Nanjing under the Ming*, and is completing a book-length manuscript on "chaste women" in Ming China.

Lifang He 何麗芳 received her Ph.D. in Chinese Linguistics from Shaanxi Normal University and is Assistant Professor of Chinese at Huron University. She taught Chinese language and culture at the Education University of Hong Kong from 1998-2005 and has been teaching Chinese language and cinema at Huron since 2005. She is the author of *Duoyuan Wenhua Yujing Zhong De Hanyu Yuyin Xide* 多元文化語境中的漢語語音習得 (The Acquisition of Chinese Phonetics in the Context of Multiculturalism).

For Tina

The Romance of a Literatus and his Concubine in Seventeenth-century China

Annotated translation
by Jun Fang and Lifang He
of

Reminiscences
of the Plum-shaded Convent
(*Yingmeian Yiyu* 影梅庵憶語)

by Mao Xiang (1611-1693)

Proverse Hong Kong

The Romance of a Literatus and his Concubine
in Seventeenth-century China:
Annotated translation by Jun Fang and Lifang He
of
Reminiscences of the Plum-shaded Convent
(*Yingmeian Yiyu* 影梅庵憶語)
by Mao Xiang (1611-1693).
Alternate edition published in Hong Kong by Proverse Hong Kong
ISBN:978-988-8491-37-7
Copyright © Proverse Hong Kong, April 2019.

Distribution (Hong Kong and worldwide):
The Chinese University Press,
The Chinese University of Hong Kong,
Shatin, New Territories, Hong Kong SAR.
Email: cup-bus@cuhk.edu.hk; Web: www.chineseupress.com

Distribution and other enquiries to:
Proverse Hong Kong, P.O. Box 259, Tung Chung Post Office,
Lantau, NT, Hong Kong SAR, China.
Email: proverse@netvigator.com;
Web: www.proversepublishing.com

The right of Jun Fang and Lifang He to be identified
as the authors of this work
has been asserted by them in accordance with
the Copyright, Designs and Patents Act 1988.
Cover design by Artist Hong Kong.

**British Library Cataloguing in Publication Data
A catalogue record is available
from the British Library**

TABLE OF CONTENTS

NOTE ON EDITORIAL PRACTICES

The Pinyin system of Romanization is used throughout the book.

In Chinese names, the surname is given first, followed by the given name. Therefore, in the case of Dong Xiaowan, Dong is the surname and Xiaowan the given name.

In general, offices and official titles in this book follow Charles O. Hucker's *A Dictionary of Official Titles in Imperial China*.

Only the modern page numbers are cited for those modern reprints of Ming-Qing source materials which have both the new page numbers and the old ones. For those reprints which have only old page numbers, the original chapter (*juan*) and page numbers are cited. The letters *a* and *b* are used to denote the first and second halves of a double page.

Except for a few large cities, most of the place names in the English translation are the pre-modern ones used by the author Mao Xiang.

Chinese terms, except personal and place names, are italicized.

Publications in Chinese mentioned in this book are indicated by Pinyin in italics with the English translation in parenthesis.

The Chinese characters of the persons, places, publications, and other terms that appear in the book are all listed in the Glossary.

TABLE OF ILLUSTRATIONS

Chaomin Laoren Mao Xiang. Hanging scroll, ink on paper. 46 5/8 x 173/8in. Dated fifth month of *Jisi* year (1689). *Courtesy and © 2001 Christie's Image Limited.*

18. "Bird and Flowers" by Mao Xiang and Cai Han, Dong Xiaowan and Jin Yue (three of Mao's concubines). Hanging scroll, ink and colour on paper. 37 1/3 x 16in. Inscribed and signed by Mao Xiang, with three seals. Cai Han painted the bird, with two seals. Dong Xiaowan painted the narcissus and rock, with one seal. Jin Yue painted camellia and *lingzhi*, with one seal. Dated the 22nd day, twelfth month of *Jiyou* year (January 13, 1670). Two collectors' seals. (As Dong Xiaowan died in 1651, perhaps Jin and Cai painted on an unfinished old painting by Dong.) *Courtesy and © 1999 Christie's Image Limited.* 125

19. Portraits of Dong Xiaowan and Mao Xiang, at the Dequan Hall at Painted-in-Water Garden, Rugao. *Adapted from China Tour Advisor website.* 126

20. Paper-cut portraits of Dong Xiaowan and Mao Xiang, at gift shop, Painted-in-Water Garden, Rugao. *Adapted from China Tour Advisor website.* 126

ACKNOWLEDGEMENTS

We would like to thank the following friends and colleagues whose encouragement and assistance have made the publication of this annotated translation possible: Jack Blocker, Timothy Brook, James Flath, Guo Junrong, Lai Ming Chiu, Yuan-chu Lam, Geoff Read, Nicholas Van Allen, Wang Jixian, Wang Shuanghuai, and Zhu Bangwei. Our gratitude also goes to Gillian Bickley for her meticulous editing of the manuscript and thoughtful advice for improvement. Thanks are also due to the online and interlibrary loan services rendered by the libraries at the Education University of Hong Kong, Huron University, and the University of Western Ontario. We are, needless to say, solely responsible for any deficiencies and errors that may remain.

IMAGE ACKNOWLEDGEMENTS

Allen Memorial Art Museum, Oberlin College, Ohio, General Acquisitions Fund, 1970.39, for "Waiting for the Moon at Six Bridges" by Mao Xiang.

Sotheby's, New York for "Plum Blossom" by Dong Xiaowan.

Christie's Image Limited for, "Plum Blossom" by Dong Xaiowan, Poem in cursive script calligraphy, signed Chaomin Laoren Mao Xiang, "Bird and Flowers" by Mao Xiang and Cai Han, Dong Xiaowan and Jin Yue.

Images of portraits of Dong Xiaowan and Mao Xiang, at the Dequan Hall at Painted-in-Water Garden, Rugao and paper-cut portraits of Dong Xiaowan and Mao Xiang, at gift shop, Painted-in-Water Garden, Rugao, were adapted from China Tour Advisor website.

An image of a portrait painting of Dong Xiaowan at the Painted-in-Water Garden in Rugao is adapted from *Shanghai Daily*, 3 December 2017, A3, p. A16. https://archive.shine.cn/sunday/now-and-then/Dong-Xiaowans-talented-legacy/shdaily.shtml

INTRODUCTION

The Romance of a Literatus and his Concubine in Seventeenth-century China is an annotated translation of *Yingmeian yiyu* (Reminiscences of the Plum-shaded Convent) (henceforth "Reminiscences", "memoir of Dong Xiaowan", or "memoir"), a short memoir written by Mao Xiang (1611-1693), a seventeenth-century Chinese literatus dubbed as one of the reputable "Four Masters of the Late Ming" (*Mingmo sigongzi*). Merely 8,000 Chinese characters in length, the memoir narrates the courtship between Mao and the famed courtesan Dong Xiaowan (1624-1651) in 1639-1642, the eight-years of their life together until early 1651, and Mao's perception of Dong's feminine virtues and multiple talents. It has been a popular text among both men of letters and ordinary readers in China since its first publication in the 1650s and has appeared in more than two dozen editions to date. To appreciate the memoir better, a few words about the author, the heroine, and the book are in order.

1. Mao Xiang

Mao Xiang, courtesy name Pijiang, nicknames (*hao*) Chaomin and Pu'an, was born on 27 April 1611 and died on 31 December 1693 in Rugao, Nan Zhili. In the late Ming, he was a well-known poet, essayist, calligrapher, and social activist; in the early Qing he became a so-called "leftover person" (*yimin*) for his steadfast refusal to serve the Manchu Qing rulers. He was born into a prominent scholar-official family, which may have had Mongol origins.[1] One of his distinguished ancestors, Mao Zheng

(1443-1519), courtesy name, Youheng and nickname Lüzhen, obtained his provincial degree (*juren*) in 1474 and his metropolitan degree (*jinshi*) in 1475. He served successively as secretary, deputy director, and director at the Nanjing ministry of revenue and assumed the post of prefect of Wuchang in 1490. In recognition of his meritorious service, he was promoted in 1506 to the post of provincial governor of Jiangxi. In his later years he was assigned to Ningxia as grand coordinator and vice censor-in-chief. He suffered a major political setback in the Zhengde era (1506-21) when he offended the powerful chief eunuch Liu Jin (1451-1510) by refusing to offer a bribe. Mao was subsequently punished by having 3,000 piculs of his official salary rice confiscated. After Liu lost favour and was punished by death by slicing (*lingchi*),[2] Mao was allowed to retire with the benefits stemming from his former position.[3] His son Mao Luan, a *jinshi* of 1493, served as secretary at the Nanjing ministry of justice and as assistant administrative commissioner in Fujian prior to retirement.[4]

Mao Xiang's grandfather Mao Mengling (1565-1635), courtesy name, Rujiu and nickname Yuantong, was recommended by his local school as a tribute student[5] qualified to study in the capital. In 1612 he was appointed magistrate of Huichang county in Jiangxi province.[6] Later on during the early Tianqi era (1621-27) he assumed the positions of magistrate of Fengdu county in Sichuan and sub-prefect of Nanning before retiring to his hometown in 1623.[7] He was said to be an honest and upright official who did not enlarge even slightly the family's land holdings during his official career.[8]

Mao Xiang's father Mao Qizong (1590-1654, courtesy name, Zongqi, nicknames Songshao and Zongying), passed the *jinshi* degree examination in 1628, together with Shi Kefa (1601-45) who served as Nanjing minister of war in the closing years of the Ming dynasty and who would famously die resisting the invading Manchu forces. Mao Qizong held a string of posts as court messenger, secretary of the bureau of evaluation at the Nanjing ministry of personnel, director of the bureau of evaluation of the Beijing ministry of personnel, and assistant surveillance commissioner, before assuming the position of chief military inspector (*jianjun*) to the troops commanded by General Zuo Liangyu (1599-1645). The highest position he held was that of vice commissioner of surveillance in Shandong supervising the shipment of tribute grain along the Grand Canal.[9] His literary collection, *Zhuocuntang yigao* (Collected works from the Zhuocun Hall), has survived.[10]

As the eldest son of Mao Qizong, Mao Xiang began his studies of the *Great Learning*, one of the Confucian "four books," at age four and subsequently showed a great aptitude for learning the classics and literature.[11] At the age of thirteen, he sent some of his poems to Dong Qichang (1555-1636), a celebrated man of letters who was then the vice minister of rites in Beijing, requesting him to comment on them. Dong was impressed by Mao's poetic talents and praised him as the Wang Bo (649-76), a Tang poetic prodigy, of his times.[12] According to Dong, "Although the poems were composed by Pijiang at the tender age of fourteen *sui*, yet his literary talents and writing sophistication were already those of a famous master."[13] With Dong's approval, the Mao family had the poems printed the same year under the title, *Xiangliyuan oucun* (Surviving poems from the Fragrant Garden). This was the first of Mao's many books. It was first published in a single fascicle in 1625 and was reprinted many times. The edition of the *Rugao Maoshi congshu* (Collectanea of works by prominent members of the Mao family in Rugao) is still widely available.

Mao Xiang's path to success and fame was alternately smooth and bumpy. On the one hand, he passed the examinations at the county and prefectural levels and the *yuan* examination [14] with distinction, thus obtaining government student (licentiate, *shengyuan*) status at age sixteen. [15] His literary talents were widely acknowledged by his peers, and he was eventually identified as one of the legendary "Four Masters of the Late Ming", together with Chen Zhenhui (1604-56), Fang Yizhi (1611-71), and Hou Fangyu (1618-54). [16] On the other hand, his attempt to become a provincial graduate was frustratingly unsuccessful. From 1630 until the end of the Ming in 1644, he four times failed the triennial provincial examinations held in Nanjing, passing only on his fifth attempt in 1642. Even then he was placed on the waiting list (*fubang*), which meant he was eligible only to retake the provincial examination or to hold minor posts. As a result, Mao never became part of the Ming bureaucracy, even though he was recommended for a position of junior army inspector in 1642 by the Grand Coordinator of Huaiyang, Shi Kefa, and was offered the minor post of prefectural judge (*sili*) in Taizhou the following year. He turned down both offers, probably due to his confidence in his ability to pass the coveted metropolitan examination eventually and to secure a more respectable post. [17] Having never served the Ming, Mao might reasonably have accepted a position with the Qing, but although he was recommended several times by high-ranking officials, some of whom were his close friends, he resolutely declined all offers. During the half century from 1644 to his death in 1693, Mao kept his distance from Qing officialdom.

Although, then, Mao Xiang never became an official, he was nevertheless quite politically active. In the late Ming he was a devoted member of the Restoration Society (Fushe), a literary organization with some 3,000 members and overt political concerns. [18] He enthusiastically participated in Fushe activities, including the exposure of the misdeeds of the scholar-official Ruan Dacheng (1587-

1646) who was regarded as an ally of the hated eunuch chief Wei Zhongxian (1568-1627). In 1639 he was involved in the promulgation of a manifesto entitled "A Public Notice to Ward off Disturbances in the Auxiliary Capital" (*Liudu fangluan gongjie*). Three years later, while watching in Nanjing the performance of Ruan's drama, *Swallow Letter,* a play on a Tang dynasty love triangle, he participated in the uproarious condemnation of the "treacherous official". Some writers attempt to find evidence in scattered lines of poetry by Mao Xiang and his friends to suggest that Mao participated in efforts to resist the Qing and restore the Ming. Gu Qi goes further to assert that Mao secretly participated in the military campaigns staged by the various Southern Ming régimes against the Qing government, although without providing concrete textual evidence for his claims.[19] It was certainly possible that Mao Xiang was anti-Qing and pro-Ming from the bottom of his heart, but a number of considerations prevented him from taking part in anti-Manchu activities. First and foremost, Mao Xiang was a filial son, who viewed the guarantee of his parents' safety as his priority. His father Mao Qizong retired to Rugao at the end of the Ming and did not encounter any political trouble for the rest of his life. Mao took meticulous care of his parents before they died of natural causes in 1654 and 1676 respectively. Second, as a pillar of his large, three-generation family of more than 100 members and servants, Mao did not want to endanger their lives by his own actions.[20] Third, Mao's loyalty toward the Ming régime was perhaps less strong than that of many Ming loyalists, who committed suicide or staged military resistance, because he had repeatedly failed the higher level examinations and had never served the Ming government.[21]

After the Qing was established, Mao Xiang refused to participate in civil service examinations organized by the new dynasty despite the repeated urgings of its rulers. In

1673 when the Kangxi court decided to recruit "hermits hiding in the forests and mountains" to serve the new government, his close friend Gong Dingzhi (1615-73), then minister of rites, sent several letters inviting him to Beijing; Mao, however, cited his need to take care of his aging mother to avoid service in the Qing. In 1679 the Qing authorities raised the level of reward by formally holding the Erudite Scholars Examination (*boxue hongci*), an extraordinary measure which allowed even commoners to compete for the highest metropolitan degree and for significant government posts. The editor-in-chief of the Ming history project and censor-in-chief Xu Yuanwen (1634-91) pressed Mao to participate in the examination. Mao's pretext for not serving the state this time was an acute foot ailment, a fairly standard affliction assumed by those who did not want to serve in office.[22] In 1683 he was invited for the third time to serve in the modest post of compiler of the Jiangsu provincial gazetteer. Once again, he declined, citing his old age and illness as justification.[23] Mao's consistent refusal to serve the Qing despite his qualifications and repeated offers of appointment earned him plaudits from later observers.[24] Although Mao Xiang firmly declined to accept the Qing government's offers of service, he did not expect his sons to follow suit. In fact he encouraged Mao Heshu (b. 1635; courtesy names, Guliang, Jiasui) and Mao Danshu (1639-95; courtesy name, Qingruo,) to take part in the Qing civil service examinations and both became government students (*shengyuan*) at the age of fifteen.[25] Moreover, Mao continued his friendship with those who took the Qing examinations, as well as those, formerly Ming officials who accepted Qing government appointments.

Mao Xiang also carried on a family tradition by attempting to provide relief in times of famine during the late Ming and early Qing. In 1641, when Rugao was struck by a severe drought, Mao sold his family's jewelry to help raise relief funds managed by the magistrate.[26] In 1652, crop failures caused by drought in Rugao resulted in an even more devastating disaster. The county magistrate Chen Bingyi set up soup kitchens (*zhouchang*) at the four gates of the county seat, Rucheng, for one hundred days. Mao Xiang and his father promptly responded to the relief efforts. The senior Mao was assigned the duty of distributing rice at the Eastern Gate, while Mao Xiang was put in charge of the soup kitchen at the Western Gate, the most challenging among the four, as it bordered the disaster-stricken county of Taixin, where thousands of refugees came to receive their daily share of relief grain. The Mao family, as in the past, supplemented the county coffer with their own money and food and also made their servants available to assist with distributing relief grain. Due to the outbreak of infectious diseases during this famine, Mao and each of his sixteen servants who handled the redistribution of food and other relief supplies fell seriously ill.[27]

Compared with his political and social activities, Mao Xiang's literary achievements earned him even greater renown. During his lifetime, Mao published close to twenty collections of literary and miscellaneous writings.[28] Twelve of them are included in the *Rugao Maoshi congshu* and *Mao Pijiang quanji* (Complete works of Mao Xiang), published in 2014. They are of two categories.

The first, poems and prose, includes *Xiangliyuan oucun* (one *juan*), *Hanbi guyin* (Lone chantings from the Hanbi Tower, one *juan*), *Jimeiren mingshi* (Poems on beauties, one *juan*), *Fanxue xiaocao* (Snowy grass, one *juan*), *Puchao wenxuan* (Selected prose from the Puchao Treehouse, 4 *juan*), *Chaomin wenji* (Collected works of Mao Xiang, 7 *juan*), *Puchao shixuan* (Selected poems from the Puchao Treehouse, one *juan*), *Chaomin shiji* (Collected poems of Mao Xiang, 6 *juan*), and *Yingmeian yiyu* (one *juan*).

The second category contains Mao's writings on various special topics, including *Lan yan* (Notes on orchids, one *juan*), *Xuanlu gezhu* (On the incense burners from the Xuande era, one *juan*), and *Jiecha huichao* (Selected writings on the *Jie* tea, one *juan*). In addition, Mao also edited or co-edited at least seven books. Among them were collected works of Mao Xiang and his friends: *Shuihuian shixuan* (Selected poems from the Shuihui Convent, 6 *juan*), *Shuihuian erji* (Sequel to the poems from the Shuihui Convent), and *Liushi nian shiyou shiwen tongren ji* (Collected writings of kindred spirits in the past sixty years, 12 *juan*; henceforth referred to as *Tongren ji*). *Shuihuian shixuan* and *Shuihuian erji* include selected poems composed by Mao and his friends at his famous Shuihui Garden over an extended period of time, and the third is a collection of the writings of Mao and his hundreds of friends over a span of six decades.[29]

Thanks to his literary fame and some similarities between the life of the Mao family and that of the Jia family in the *Dream of the Red Chamber*, some amateur researchers in Rugao, including Mao Lianquan, argue that Mao Xiang was in fact the real author of this great Chinese classical novel.[30]

Mao Xiang had extensive social contacts and was never short of friends. He visited men of letters and made friends with them on his travels, and also enjoyed receiving guests at his family's famed Painted-in-Water Garden (Shuihuiyuan). The Mao family treated visitors generously and entertained them with dramatic performances.[31] *Collected Writings of Kindred Spirit* (*Tongren ji*), a 12-*juan* collection edited by Mao and printed in 1673, contains poems, prose, and letters of 462 authors produced over decades. The oldest author was Dong Qichang who was nearly sixty years older than Mao; the youngest was Zhang Chao (1650-1707) who was almost forty years Mao's junior.

In spite of their difference in age, as we have seen, Dong Qichang valued Mao's first writings in 1624, and the two became friends. It appears that Mao Xiang visited Dong numerous times and showed the older man some of the art works he had collected. Dong wrote calligraphic colophons on many of them, including the *Dejing* (classics of virtue)[32] and the *Rhapsody to the Goddess of Luo River* (*Luoshen fu*) which had been copied in small-character script by the Yuan painter and calligrapher, Zhao Mengfu (1254-1322) and the Ming painting master, Zhu Zhishan (1460-1526) respectively. Dong also copied some poems of the prominent Tang poet Du Fu in the calligraphic style of Yan Zhenqing (709-85) and he also transcribed Mao's distant ancestor, Mao Zheng's *Zhengde shilu xiaozhuan* (Brief record of the Zhengde reign).[33] In the memoir we learn that Dong Qichang's handwritten copy of Xie Zhuang's (421-466) masterpiece, *Rhapsody on the Moon* (*Yuefu*), specially prepared for Mao, became the model for Dong Xiaowan's calligraphic practice.[34] (There was no family relationship between Mao's concubine and the elderly master.) Admiring Dong Qichang's extraordinary skills in painting and calligraphy, in 1635 Mao hired the veteran stonemason, Gu Gongyan, to carve the balustrades and walls of the Hanbi Tower in the Shuihui Garden with all the calligraphic works Dong had sent to him, including prefaces and postscripts, remarks and annotations, letters and poems, as well as the calligraphic works of Yan Zhenqing and Mi Fu (1051-1107) which had been copied by Dong. Similarly, Dong spoke highly of Mao Xiang's calligraphy, commenting that he had mastered the essence of the penmanship of Yan Zhenqing, the Tang master then (as now) widely considered one of China's greatest calligraphers.[35]

Qian Qianyi (1582-1664) was perhaps the closest of Mao Xiang's older friends. Their relationship was strengthened by the "sisterly" bond between Qian's concubine, Liu Rushi (1618-64) and Dong Xiaowan which had developed during their time together in the pleasure quarter of Qinhuai.[36] Qian admired Mao's literary talents and physical appearance, calling him "a handsome man from the Huaihai-Yangzhou region."[37] Mao in turn proudly regarded Qian as his mentor. In 1640, he and Zheng Yuanxun (1604-45) organized a poem-composing competition at the latter's Shadowy Garden (Yingyuan) on the theme of the yellow peonies which were then blossoming. He sent all the poems without revealing the names of the authors to Qian asking him to be the adjudicator.[38]

Most of Mao Xiang's friends, however, were of an age similar to his, and are too many to list comprehensively. As an active member and possibly the Rugao convener of the Fushe, Mao had frequent contact with other major members of the society. The other three members of the four late Ming masters, Chen, Fang, and Hou, as well as Mao's sworn brothers, Zhang Mingbi (1584-1653),[39] Lü Zhaolong, Chen Liang, and Liu Lüding, were among Mao's closest friends. Noted men of letters who visited Mao and composed poems with him at the Painted-in-Water Garden included Wang Shizhen (1634-1711),[40] Li Qing (1602-83),[41] Yu Huai (1616-96),[42] Deng Hanyi (1617-89), Shao Qian (1581-1665), Song Shiying (1625-1705), Du Jun (1611-87), Wu Qi (1619-94), Ji Yinzhong (1609-1701), Qian Zeng (1629-1701), Huang Zhouxing (1611-80), Zong Yuanding (1620-98), and You Tong (1618-1704). Most of their compositions at the Shuihui Garden are collected in *Tongren ji.*

Mao Xiang also had many friends among the younger generation. He was protective of and warm toward the children and grand-children of the Donglin activists and his Fushe friends, especially the children of the "Six Early Donglin Gentlemen" and the "Seven Later Donglin Gentlemen".[43] He once held an expensive banquet in 1639 at Nanjing's Peach-Leaf Pier (Taoyedu) for the offspring of the Donglin martyrs, and he continued to be hospitable to them and other literary talents of the younger generation. His most celebrated younger friend was Chen Weisong (1625-82), son of Chen Zhenhui who was considered Mao's dearest friend. A towering figure in the Qing poetic world in his later years, the younger Chen lived in Mao's elegant Painted-in-Water Garden under his financial care and literary tutorship for much of the 1658-66 period.[44] During his residence in Rugao, Chen studied with Mao's two sons and his younger half-brother Mao Bao (b. 1645), joined Mao's meetings with his friends from across the country and took part in most, if not all the cultural events Mao organized. Mao even provided him as companion in his studies, Xu Ziyun (1644-75), an actor belonging to the Mao family troupe who was "handsome and good at singing", often addressed affectionately as "Yunlang" (literally, "Cloud Boy"). Xu's company made Chen's sojourn in Rugao both productive and enjoyable. It is speculated that a homosexual relationship existed between the two, as explicitly suggested in Chen's congratulatory poem composed on the occasion of Xu's marriage in 1664.[45]

Mao's hundreds of friends could be broadly classified into two groups in terms of their political attitudes towards the fallen Ming and the ruling Qing. The first included the literati who were anti-eunuch and anti-Ruan Dacheng in the late Ming; and anti-Manchu in the early Qing. Mao maintained a lifelong, loyal relationship with them. In the process of editing *Tongren ji*, Mao was advised not to incorporate the writings of the anti-Qing loyalists, Gu Gao (1607-1645), Wu Yingji (1594-1645), Xia Yunyi (1596-1645), Yang Youlong (1596-1646), and Huang Daozhou (1585-1646) to avoid becoming a target of literary inquisition, but he refused to take their advice, claiming, "These are talented people whom I once appreciated and befriended, and I will not forget them for the rest of my life."[46] Noticeably he also continued his friendship with those who decided to join the Qing government. Qian Qianyi, his older friend and mentor, had accepted the Qing post of vice minister of rites. Gong Dingzi had surrendered to the rebel forces of Li Zicheng (1606-45) before joining the Qing government and serving successively as the ministers of justice, of war, and of rites. Wu Weiye had stayed away from Qing officialdom for a while but eventually assumed the presidency of State University (*Guozijian*) under the new régime. Hou Fangyu reluctantly took part in the civil service examination of the Qing.[47] It appears that Mao Xiang himself was determined not to serve the Qing, but he did not demand the same from others. In other words, he cared about his own reputation for "preserving his own purity," but appeared to be understanding of those who chose and acted differently. He clearly placed great value on his relationship with mentors, peers and protégés, and his friendship was not politically based. His realistic assessment of the Qing rule,[48] shared by many others, certainly assisted the Qing in steadily strengthening and improving its governance over China.

Mao Xiang's personal life was the object of envy for many of his friends. His engagement to Su Yuanfang (1611-72), the third daughter of the secretarial drafter Su Wenhan (*jinshi* 1562) from the same county, was decided by Su's father and Mao's grandfather Mao Mengling while the latter was serving in Huichang as county magistrate in 1613, and the children were but two years of age. Mao and Su were married in 1629 at the age of eighteen, and produced three sons and one daughter, of whom the eldest son (Mao Yan, 1634-38) and the daughter both died young. Su is recorded in the *Reminiscences* and other early Qing sources as a kind, loving, and understanding spouse, who readily agreed to Mao's taking of Dong Xiaowan as his concubine in 1642. After Dong's passing in 1651, Su

Yuanfang personally chose future concubines for her husband. Mao was grateful for her magnanimity and never remarried after Su's death at the age of sixty-one.[49]

It was not unusual for rich and powerful men in imperial China to have several concubines. Many of the élite did so. Mao Xiang's most famous concubine was Dong Xiaowan, the subject of Mao's *Reminiscences* and the focus of the next section of this introduction.

During the four decades from Dong's death in 1651 until his own passing in 1693, Mao took at least four more concubines. Wu Meilan (1643-61; courtesy names, Xiangyi and Koukou), was originally a maid of Dong Xiaowan, but was recommended by her mistress to Mao as his future concubine when Wu was about ten years old. From around the age of thirteen or fourteen, Wu began to accompany Mao in his study. According to the sources available, Wu was an avid learner who enjoyed reading the *Wenxuan* (Selections of refined literature)[50] and the poems of Du Fu (712-70), and was able to compose poems by herself. She was lauded for being similar to Dong Xiaowan in possessing the qualities of understanding, unselfishness, and lack of interest in jewelry and fine clothing. In 1661, when the eighteen year old was about to become Mao's concubine formally, she fell ill and soon died.[51]

In the spring of 1665, Mao took a new concubine named Cai Han (1647-86; courtesy name, Nüluo), the daughter of Mao's butler, Cai Mengzhao (1607-86) from Wuxian (in present-day Jiangsu).[52] After entering the Mao household, Cai became a Buddhist and devoted her energy and time to studying Chinese painting, taking the noted Suzhou painter Wu Qi (b. 1644) as her tutor. She was a talented painter and was good at depicting natural scenes, especially excelling at painting pine trees. [53] From the poems contained in the *Tongren ji*, many of Mao's friends eagerly sought to obtain her paintings. For example, Wu Qi (that is, Mao's close friend from Jiangdu, not Cai's mentor – whose name was pronounced similarly) brought in person a large quantity of refined Suzhou silk to Rugao to "barter" for her painting,[54] and Dai Xun asked for one of Cai's paintings as a birthday present for his mother.[55] Cai often painted together with yet another of Mao's concubines, Jin Yue, and the charm of their paintings was enhanced by the calligraphy added by Mao and his artistic friends. The painting on which Cai and Jin collaborated in 1675 which bore Mao's calligraphic remarks and was entitled *Wurui tu* (Auspicious Double Fifth Festival), has been preserved in the Nanjing Museum. Her paintings *Maoting qiuse tu* (Roof-thatched pavilion in autumn) and *Shanshui tu* (Mountains and waterfalls), completed in 1681 and 1686 respectively, are now housed at the Suzhou and Luzhou Municipal Museums.[56]

Jin Yue (courtesy name, Xiaozhu, nickname Yuanyu), a native of Kunshan, was taken as Mao's concubine in 1667. She became a major figure in his life and assumed the responsibility of taking care of Mao's health after Cai's passing at age thirty-nine. When Mao fell ill at the age of seventy-seven, it was said that Jin Yue cut a slice of flesh from her thigh and cooked it with medicine to cure Mao's illness,[57] as some chaste women and filial men had been known to do since the beginning of the Song period. Jin Yue also excelled in painting, especially in depicting flowers and plants. In his colophon on Jin's *Autumn Sunflower*, Mao wrote, "I am no good at drinking, but have drunk fragrant wine profusely in this flower painting." [58] Her skill is also reflected in the poem composed by Wang Maolin (1640-88) in 1676 after meeting Mao Xiang and viewing the painting jointly made by Cai and Jin entitled *Two Birds Perching on a Tree Branch*. Jin and Cai were oftentimes addressed as "*Er nüshi*" (two erudite female scholars) or "*Er huashi*" (two master painters).[59] According to Ōki Yasushi, Jin Yue's painting, *Melon and Flowers*, is now held in Chokaido Art

Museum, Yokkaichi City, Japan.[60] Another of Jin's paintings, with Mao Xiang's colophon, *The Hundred Flowers*, is included in *Views from Jade Terrace: Chinese Women Artists*.[61]

In addition, in 1668 Mao Xiang took one more concubine, née Zhang (her full name is not recorded in the sources). As in the case of each of Wu, Cai, and Jin, she was also raised as a maid in Mao's house and her concubinage to him was arranged by Mao's wife Su Yuanfang. It is worth mentioning that none of the concubines except Zhang (who gave birth to a daughter in 1671) bore Mao any child even though they all became part of his household before the age of twenty.[62] It is also noteworthy that available sources do not reveal any animosity between Mao and his multiple partners, between his wife and concubines, or among the concubines. Mao's openness to people, evident in his political relations, seems to have been reflected as well in his private life.

2.   Dong Xiaowan

Dong Xaiowan, the subject of the Reminiscences, was Mao Xiang's most famous concubine and one of the famed "Eight Beauties" (*bayan*) of seventeenth-century China.[63] Dong's given name was Bai, but she is better known in Chinese history and literature by her courtesy name, "Xiaowan". Her other courtesy names were Qinglian and Qinglian nüshi, both of which reflect her parents' and later her own admiration for the great Tang poet, Li Bai (701-62), who was also known by his pen name, Qinglian jushi (literally, Householder of Green Lotus).[64] Compared to the sources on Mao Xiang, records about Dong Xiaowan are few and elusive. Most of the historical sources state that Dong Xaiowan was a Nanjing native. Mao Xiang himself in Reminiscences confirms that she was a native of Qinhuai (in Nanjing). His Jiangdu friend Wu Qi was more specific about her birth place, Peach Leaf Pier (Taoyedu) in the

Qinhuai Pleasure Quarter of Nanjing.[65] Her mother Chen Shi (possibly her foster mother), who raised her to be a high society singing girl, began to teach her singing and reading when she was about seven.[66] By the time Dong reached the age of twelve, she was already a much talked about beauty in Qinhuai and was esteemed for having a flair for singing, cooking, needlework, and brewing tea.[67]

Available sources indicate that Dong Xiaowan became a registered courtesan in Qinhuai under the music office (*jiaofangsi*) of the Nanjing ministry of rites in 1636 when she was twelve and her fame spread quickly among pleasure seekers.[68] It seems that in her first two years as courtesan Dong entertained her clients only by singing songs and playing musical instruments. Mao Xiang recalls in the Reminiscences that after joining his household in Rugao in December 1642, Dong "appreciated the quiet and serene environment…she felt as if she had jumped out of a vast expanse of burning fire into a cool refreshing atmosphere. She looked back into the past five years of her singing-girl's life as if she had woken from a dream or as if she had been released from a prison." [69] This passage implies that Dong was obliged to render full service to clients sometime in 1638 when she turned fourteen. This is consistent with an earlier line in Reminiscences regarding Fang Yizhi's remark on her in the spring of 1639 that, "among the singing girls in Qinhuai, there is recently a girl named Shuangcheng (i.e. Xiaowan) who is rather young in age and has remarkable talents and fascinating features."[70]

Although Dong Xiaowan was very popular among late Ming sensualists, she is said to have loathed her singing girl life. Instead of enjoying boisterous parties and entertaining performances, she preferred to be alone to appreciate the beauty of nature by herself. In late 1636, the very year when she became a registered entertainer and instantly acquired fame in Qinhuai,[71] she left Nanjing for Suzhou to live in Bantang, the northern end of the city's most famous street – Shantang Street – which was near the scenic spot, Tiger Hill. As an entertainer registered at the music office, she fulfilled her singing girl duties by shuttling between Suzhou and Nanjing. The noted late Ming essayist, Zhang Dai (1597-1679), records in his *Tao'an mengyi* (Reminiscences in dreams of Tao'an) a hunting trip by a group of high officials in the winter of 1638 to the Niushou Mountains in the suburb of Nanjing, when Dong was one of the courtesans hired to accompany the group throughout the journey.[72] It seems that Dong had some freedom in scheduling her time in Suzhou so long as she paid her entertainer dues. For example, she was invited by Qian Qianyi and his courtesan-turned-concubine, Liu Rushi, to be a tour companion during their trip to the Huangshan-Xin'an region in 1639-1641.[73] As a result of the friendship formed before and during the trip with Qian and Liu, Dong was able to secure generous financial assistance from Qian in late 1642 when she was in dire financial straits. Qian paid the accumulated bills of her creditors and the redemption fees (for being removed from the register of the music office) exceeding in all 3,000 taels of silver,[74] a colossal amount which theoretically approximated twenty years of Qian's official salary as a vice minister of grade 3a[75] or two-month's dining expenses of the last Ming emperor Chongzhen (1611-44).[76] After holding a banquet celebrating her freedom, Qian hired a boat to take her to join Mao Xiang in Rugao.[77] Qian apparently took this action for several reasons. First, he treasured Dong's companionship during his three-year sojourn of the Huangshan-Xin'an region.[78] Second, his favourite concubine Liu Rushi was an intimate friend of Dong at Qinghuai. – Although textual evidence is lacking, Liu may have played a role in redeeming Dong's debt and singing girl's bondage. – Third, the older man, Qian, cherished his inter-generational friendship with Mao Xiang. Regardless of the exact cause of his generosity, Qian obviously liked Dong and came to her rescue on behalf of his friend Mao.[79]

As a soul-mate of Mao Xiang, Dong Xiaowan spent a considerable amount of time of her eight-year life as his concubine, assisting him in his literary pursuits, especially his eventually unrealized project of compiling a complete compendium of Tang poems. According to Mao, the two often sat in their study reading and annotating literary works for a whole day without exchanging a single word. In the process of searching, copying, and editing relevant material for Mao, Dong also compiled her own collection of works related to women's matters from antiquity to the late Ming. The collection was highly praised by Gong Dingzi and Gu Mei, another husband-concubine couple who were dear friends of Mao and Dong.[80] At the urging of Gong and Gu during their visit to Rugao, Mao had the three-*juan* collection published after the passing of Dong, possibly in 1650s. Entitled *Lianyan* (Toiletries of past beauties), the work apparently earned Dong the semi-honorific, *nüjiaoshu* (female editor).[81] *Lianyan* was later included in the 230-*juan Ranzhi ji* (Works written by female writers in Chinese history) compiled by Wang Shilu (1626-73) in 1665.[82] Unfortunately Wang lacked the financial resources to print it for a wider circulation, and only 40 *juan* of his self-copied collection are preserved in libraries in Shanghai and Shandong. It appears that *Lianyan* is not among the surviving volumes.[83]

Some of Dong Xiaowan's calligraphic works, paintings, and poems are preserved both inside and outside China,[84] and one of her poems, "Lüchuang oucheng" (Casual composition by the green window), has been translated by Daria Berg as follows:

> I gaze at the flowers with my sick eyes, steeped in melancholy thoughts,
> Sitting alone by the secluded window I play the jade-decorated zither.

The yellow orioles also seem to understand people's minds,
From beyond the window they send out beautiful sounds time and again.[85]

Dong Xiaowan's life, especially her unwavering pursuit of love, has been a focus of several twentieth-century plays, movies, and novels. Examples include a stage play written in the 1940s by a Mao Xiang descendant Mao Shuyin (1914-99), the Hong Kong movie *Dong Xiaowan*, which was directed by Zhu Shilin (1899-1967) and starred Xia Meng (Hsia Moon, 1933-2016), in 1963, a variety of Chinese regional operas, mostly entitled *Dong Xiaowan*, as well as novels and narrative poems such as *Boming hongyan* (A beauty who died young) by Du Hong, *Dong Xiaowan* by Dong Qianli (1921-2007) and Li Bao, and *Shuihui xianlü* (A fairy couple from the Shuihui Garden) by Bai Hua.

3. Reminiscences of the Plum-shaded Convent

Among all of Mao Xiang's published works, the best known is undoubtedly Reminiscences of the Plum-shaded Convent (*Yingmeian yiyu*), named after the place where Dong was buried. Elegantly written, skillfully presented, and full of self-reproach, this memoir narrates the couple's early encounters, the twists and turns of their courtship, and details of Dong's exceptional talents and feminine virtues. In addition to recounting a notable scholar-concubine romance, the book reveals official abuses in the late Ming. For example, the memoir tells that officials from the imperial court, possibly the subordinates of the Chongzhen emperor's father-in-law, Tian Hongyu (d. 1643), forcefully kidnapped the famous courtesan Chen Yuanyuan (1623-81) from Suzhou.[86] Mao also described atrocities committed by the invading Qing forces during their conquest of the Jiangnan region, and the brutal pillaging by roaming bandits who "slaughtered their victims as if mowing grass."

Without doubt, the most fascinating feature of the memoir is its masterful portrayal of Dong Xiaowan and her daring pursuit of love and freedom. Additionally, the memoir celebrates her many talents – in needle-work, cooking delicacies, composing poems, arranging flowers, growing plants, appreciating the moon, enjoying tea, practicing calligraphy, and assisting Mao in his literary pursuits, as well as her devoted care of him and his family. The memoir was the first of the *yiyu* (reminiscence) genre in Qing China, [87] which was followed by Shen Fu's (b. 1763) *Fusheng liuji* (Six Chapters of Floating Life), Chen Peizhi's (1794-1826) *Xaingwan lou yiyu* (Reminiscences of the House of Fragrant Earth), and Jiang Tan's (b. 1823) *Qiudeng suoyi* (Fragments of Memories under the Autumn Lamp), [88] Mao's memoir is largely responsible for the enduring fame of Dong Xiaowan as one of the eight most admired beauties of the late Ming and early Qing.

Since its first publication in the 1650s, the memoir has appeared in over two dozen editions[89] and it has been translated into several foreign languages.[90] A number of factors contributed to its long-lasting popularity. First, the memoir is a work of passion, honesty, and candor. In the book Mao Xiang frankly admits his lack of "generosity" and consideration as well as his hesitancy in taking action in his early relationship with Dong Xiaowan. He constantly regrets what he did and candidly assigns fault to himself. Mao writes honestly of his repeated rejection of Dong Xiaowan's plea to marry him and of his ongoing failure to take immediate action to help solve her financial difficulties.[91] For example, when Mao departed after their second encounter in the spring of 1642, Dong sailed with him for almost four weeks, although, every day, Mao bade her to go back to Suzhou. In another example, Mao promised that he would take Dong to Nanjing for his provincial examination in the fall, but later he travelled to the Ming southern capital alone without informing her.

When she risked her life – she was almost killed in a violent robbery on her way to Nanjing – to rejoin him, Mao suddenly left the city for nearby Yizheng to meet his father who had recently resigned from government service. After Dong had followed him to Yizheng and the boat they travelled on together from there later reached the pier of Rugao,[92] Mao ordered her again to settle her debts in Suzhou before considering their marriage. He also confesses that he often flew into a rage and berated Dong, even though she had nursed him through his grave illness during the turbulent years of the Ming-Qing transition. Mao's undisguised admission and heartfelt self-reproach have been effective in generating increased sympathy and admiration for Dong from readers.

Second, in Mao Xiang's narrative, Dong Xiaowan appears as almost a perfect traditional Chinese female; beautiful, caring, thoughtful, gifted, and modest. But what truly makes her the darling of many Chinese readers, especially male readers, both in dynastic and modern times, is her boldness and courage in pursuing her own path in life. She was quick in deciding to spend the rest of her life with Mao the second time they met. After Mao promised to marry her but asked her to wait patiently in Suzhou for the time being, she wasted no time in dispatching her father to Rugao to inform Mao's wife, Su Yuanfang, about Mao's commitment to her. During the ensuring six months in Suzhou, when she was pursued by her debtors in late 1642, she sought the assistance of Qian Qianyi who unstintingly paid her massive debts and redemption fees. Understandably, many readers – especially male readers in imperial times – appreciated her resourcefulness and determination, and were delighted with the outcome of her courtship with Mao.

In addition to personal and all-too-human details, such as these, the beautiful language and good taste of the memoir have also appealed to readers.

The Chinese original has been acclaimed as a literary classic. Both Ming-Qing literati such as Du Jun, Wang Shilu, and Wu Weiye, as well as twentieth-century critics, including Zhu Jianmang (1890-1972), Zhou Shoujuan (1895-1968), Yu Pingbo (1900-90), Yao Xueyin (1910-99), and Huang Shang (1919-2012), all speak highly of the work, especially its genuine expression of emotion and its elegant language.[93]

As to good taste, the descriptions of Dong Xiaowan and other courtesans (such as Chen Yuanyuan, Sha Jiuwan, and Dong Xiaosheng) and what is said about the author's relationship with them do not display even the slightest vulgarity. Mao Xiang writes nothing unfavourable about any of his family members or friends. He writes nothing disrespectful of women and never shows a frivolous attitude towards them. By comparison, the depictions of women by other celebrated literary personalities of his time, including Zhang Dai and Li Yu (1610-80), are full of sexual innuendo – reference to willow waist (*liuyao*), cherry lips (*yingchun*), golden lotus (*jinlian*), and so on.

The first English translation of *Yingmeian yiyu* was published by Shanghai Commercial Press as long ago as 1931. We have improved on this excellent translation, and added considerably to its 21 brief notes. The current translation has additionally identified essentially all the historical figures encountered in the memoir, giving explanatory notes. Also, to help readers better to understand the context of this work, we include a number of illustrations, including photos of some of the places mentioned in the memoir which we took during our visits to Jiangnan in 2018 as well as examples of Mao Xiang's calligraphy and Dong Xiaowan's painting.

Reminiscences of the Plum-shaded Convent

by
Mao Xiang (1611-1693)

Translated and annotated

by Jun Fang and Lifang He

1

L ove arises from intimacy, and people often embellish those with whom they are intimate. If people love their lovers more because of this kind of embellishment, then truly loveable persons are really rare in this world. Moreover, the innermost recess of the inner chamber hides feminine grace, which is often portrayed and imagined by men of letters who are fond of phrase-mongering and who let their imaginations run wild, as in the illusory depiction of Magu[94] and the vain portrayal of Shennü.[95] Furthermore, mouthy scribblers nowadays use various literary forms to fabricate ornate tales of miraculous unions of lovers, with the result that numerous books about renowned beauties such as Xi Shi,[96] Yi Guang,[97] Wenjun,[98] or Hongdu,[99] are in every household. This is an extraordinary injustice to the fair sex and a pernicious practice of those who seek fame.

My late concubine Dongshi, whose given name was Bai, was also known by her courtesy names of Xiaowan and Qinglian. She was registered at Qinhuai[100] and later moved to Suzhou.[101] Although she enjoyed great fame in the entertainment world for her surpassing beauty, she herself took little interest in the life of a singing-girl. After meeting me she was determined to marry me, and since she came to my house, her talent and wisdom displayed themselves one after another. During the nine years she lived with me,[102] she strove her utmost to be on cordial terms with all the members of my household. She helped me to write books during my seclusion from public life, assisted my wife in her needlework, and carried out the more laborious part of my wife's household duties. While we were seeking refuge away from home during the dynastic change[103] and when I fell seriously ill, she not only never failed to face danger with composure but was also able to bear hardships without complaint.

Now, she has suddenly died. I do not know whether she has died or whether I have died! I only saw my wife, in an agony of grief and loneliness, staring blankly at her two hands and not knowing what to do. All those in my household, high or low, inside or outside, old or young, have been overwhelmed with deep sorrow, and think it impossible to replace her. Those who have heard of her wisdom and her hidden traits of character cannot but sigh and remark that not even a Confucian scholar or a righteous person could be her match.

Although I have expressed my mournful feelings in an eulogistic dirge of several thousand characters dedicated to her memory,[104] its rhythmic restrictions prevent my feelings from being fully expressed. Hence, I again take up my pen to try to set down my reminiscences of the years we spent together. Whenever I am in deep grief, thinking of Xiaowan's past and our nine years' close relationship, all of my mournful memories rise so vehemently in my mind that I fear I could not succeed in putting my ideas down in a readable form, even were I gifted with magnificent writing talent. Since my own dull and heavy pen, saturated with my tears and tarnished by my grief, can hardly describe my passionate love, why should I needlessly embellish a tale to deceive my readers? Moreover, from beginning to end, Xiaowan's attention to me was never tainted with lust. I am already forty and my beard and eyebrows are thick and white. Fifteen years ago Mr Meigong[105] jokingly remarked that I value beauties clad in gorgeous silk jackets or in green gauze costumes more than anything else, and I laughed it off. How can I imitate dissipated youth in fabricating amorous tales to betray my beloved? I therefore hope that those of my friends who have placed their trust in me as to my admiration for Xiaowan's rare accomplishments will favour me with their esteemed literary works and I will make use of my writing skills to do her posthumous honour, so that her soul may be consoled and I myself shall have no regret.

In the early summer of 1639, the year of Yimao, I went to Nanjing[106] to take the provincial examination.[107] I met my friend Mizhi[108] who said to me, "Among the singing-girls of the Qinhuai, there is recently a girl named Shuangcheng[109] who is rather young in age and has remarkable talents and fascinating features." I called on her and found that she, tired of the bustle of the Qinhuai Pleasure Quarter, had removed to Suzhou with all of her family.[110] Later, after my failure to pass the provincial examination, I took a pleasure-seeking trip to Suzhou. I went to call several times at her house in Bantang,[111] but found that she was staying away at Dongting.[112] There were two other girls, Sha Jiuwan and Yang Yizhao by name, whose fame was almost equal to Xiaowan's. I sought their company almost daily but did not meet Xiaowan though she seemed within my reach.

When I was about to leave for home, I went again to her house in the hope of catching a glimpse of her. Xiaowan's mother,[113] delicate and kind-hearted, comforted me by saying, "You have been here many times. Fortunately, my daughter is at home, but she is sleeping under the light influence of liquor." She went inside and later supporting Xiaowan with her hands, walked along a narrow path and paused in front of a winding balustrade to greet me. Her countenance was crimson with the warmth of springtime; her eyes glanced at me timidly; her skin was possessed of a natural fragrance and her complexion as white as purest white jade; and her graceful mien was fascinating beyond description. She stood before me quietly and languidly, and did not utter a word. I was captivated by her dazzling beauty, but sympathizing with her weariness, I soon took my leave. This marked the beginning of our auspicious encounters, when Xiaowan was sixteen *sui*.[114]

In the summer of 1640, the year of Gengchen, I stayed at the Shadowy Garden,[115] and I wanted to visit Xiaowan again. A friend of mine, who had just returned from Suzhou, told me that she had gone on a trip to the West Lake and thence to the Yellow Mountain and the White Mountain,[116] so I had to give up my attempt. Early in the spring of 1641, the year of Xinsi, I went to visit my parents in Hengyue[117] by way of Zhejiang. While passing Bantang, I asked about Xiaowan, and was told that she was still lingering at the Yellow Mountain.

Mr Xu Zhongjie[118] was going to assume an official post in Guangdong, and his boat was sailing along together with mine. One day, returning from a banquet, he said to me, "Not far from where we anchored, there is a singing-girl by the surname of Chen,[119] who excels in opera performance. We must not miss the chance to get a glimpse of her." I assisted Mr Xu in arranging a boat trip to her place and we finally came across her after rowing several times back and forth.

Lightly made-up but charming, the girl walked with a graceful gait as if wafted by the wind. Dressed in scented silk and embroidered skirt, her elegant appearance, looked upon from the back, closely resembled that of a lone phoenix fluttering behind a screen of mist. That day she entertained us with the Yiyang opera[120] entitled, *Red Plum*. When the otherwise unrefined folk play and the tone of babbling noise were performed and sung by her, we felt as if we were seeing clouds emerging from behind mountain peaks or pearls rolling on a plate. In this spellbinding atmosphere, indeed, one would feel as if one had entered fairy-land or as if one's soul had been taken out of one's body. When four strokes of the watchman's drum were beaten,[121] wind and rain set in all of a sudden, and we were forced to embark. I pulled her sleeve and asked to see her again, to which she replied, "The plum-blossom in the town of Guangfu[122] is like a sea of cold clouds at this time of the year. Do you mind taking a trip there with me tomorrow morning? The plum blossom will wither within half a month." As I wanted to hurry back to see my parents, I said to her, "I will wait for you among the cassia flowers of Huliu[123] on my return from Huguang roughly around the eighth month."

So we parted. It was the fifteenth day of the eighth month [124] when I accompanied my mother to depart for home. When we arrived at the West Lake,[125] I heard that my father had been transferred to Xiangyang, which had fallen into the hands of anti-government insurgents.[126] My heartstrings were burning with anxiety. To relieve myself from the depression caused by the news, I inquired about Miss Chen, but learned, to my chagrin, that she had been forcibly carried away by the men of a powerful imperial relative. [127] On arriving at Changmen, [128] I found the waterway unnavigable, the boat traffic being congested all the way, fifteen *li* from Huguan.[129] There I bumped into a friend, and in the course of conversation, I expressed my regret at "not being able to see the beautiful girl again." My friend replied, "You are misinformed. The girl kidnapped by force is not the girl you want to see. The singing girl's hiding place is quite near here, and I'll go with you to see her."

On arrival at Miss Chen's abode, I found her, as expected, like a fragrant orchid flower growing in a deepened, secluded valley. We looked at each other smiling, and she said to me, "You have finally come. Are you not the man who made an appointment with me on a boat one rainy night? I was rather moved by your hospitality, but was worried that I might not see you again. I have nearly gone into the mouth of a tiger and it is truly fortunate for me to meet you a second time. Living in an out-of-the-way spot and receiving no clients, I have only tea cups and incense burners by my side. May I keep you here to enjoy the beautiful scenery in the moonlight beneath the shadows cast by cassia trees? Besides, I have something to consult you about."

Since my aged mother[130] had been left on board and our escort of a hundred odd armed personnel, who had been accompanying us because of the disturbed condition of the route along the lower Yangzi River, were taking shelter by the riverside, I was rather anxious to go back to my boat. Just at dusk I heard the deafening sound of cannon shots, and as it seemed to be coming from somewhere near our vessels, I hurried back, only to find that a brawl had started between our escort and that of some imperial eunuchs in their struggle to get through the river.[131] It was through my mediation that the latter went away. I did not go ashore that night.

Next morning, Miss Chen arrived at our boat with light makeup. She asked permission to call on my mother, the Respected Lady.[132] After seeing my mother, Miss Chen earnestly asked me to come with her to her house. As our boats were still unable to proceed that night, I went to see her again under the light of the moon. On seeing me, she said unexpectedly, "My body has just been set free as if from a cage, and I want to choose a husband and serve him for the rest of my life. There is no man whom I believe I could depend on more for my entire life than you. When I saw the Respected Lady, I felt as if I were wrapped in the clouds of spring or as if I were drinking sweet dew. This is indeed a heavenly arrangement. Please do not turn down my request."

I said with a forced smile, "Nothing in this world is as easy as you seem to think. My father has recently been transferred to a war-ravaged area, and I want to get back to bid farewell to my wife and children so that I may accompany him and die for him whenever it might become necessary. I have come to see you twice, but it was because I was bored owing to the delays in my journeys. Your unexpected requests have quite surprised me. Even though what you said makes sense, I still cannot help covering my ears and repeating my firm refusal, for I do not want to mislead you." She replied in a tactful and mild tone, "If you do not abandon me, I swear I will wait to serve you in your house after your safe return." I replied, "If that is the case, I should make an appointment with you." Thrilled and surprised, she kept urging me with a flood of pleasing words not to change my mind, which I cannot remember well enough. Before parting with her, I composed eight stanzas for her.[133]

In the autumn and winter, I was quite busy travelling from one place to another. It was in the mid-spring of 1642, the year of Renwu, that the government censors at the capital, sympathizing with the ill-fated man's privations and pitying his only son's distress, conveyed the information about my father's promotion to me by the express relay system when I was at Changzhou.[134] I received the news with a sigh of relief, feeling as if a stone had been removed from my chest. While passing Suzhou, I sought to console Miss Chen, for I had not replied to the many inquiries she had sent at the end of last winter.

I went to her house, only to find that ten days before she had again been forcibly carried away by the man-servants of the imperial relative. Previously, a certain Suzhou native who was fond of her had assembled a thousand persons to kidnap her, but the imperial relative had threatened him and at the same time bribed the local authorities with several thousand taels of silver.[135] The local officials, apprehensive that they might get into trouble for offending the imperial relative, had forced the locals to release Miss Chen and sent her back to the imperial relative. Although greatly disconsolate (upon hearing this news), I had no regret at having let a girl down simply because I had been earnestly trying to relieve my father from danger. I was rather depressed that evening, so with a friend I hired a boat on a night excursion to Huliu. My plan was to dispatch a messenger to Xiangyang next morning and then set out homeward.

As our boat passed under a bridge, I saw a small storied building standing by the waterside. I chanced to ask some passers-by, "What is this place? Who is living there?" My friend told me that it was Shuangcheng's home. I was ecstatic, as I had been thinking about her all the past three years. I made our boat stop and wanted to call on Xiaowan at once. My friend, however, stopped me, saying, "She was frightened by a powerful man and has been seriously ill for eighteen days. Since her mother's death, she has been locking her door and refraining from receiving any guests." Nevertheless I compelled him to go ashore. Only after I had knocked many times was the door opened. Finding no light in the house, I groped my way upstairs and saw herbs and drugs profusely littering the table and bed.

Upon seeing me Xiaowan inquired quietly why I had come. I told her that I was the person who once saw her in a tipsy mood beside a winding balustrade. Recalling the happening with tears falling down her cheeks, Xiaowan sobbed, "You called at my house several times in the past, although we only met once. My mother spoke highly of you in your absence for your good looks and fine manners, and pitied me for being unable to spend time with you. Three years have passed, and my mother died recently. On seeing you now, I recall her remarks as if they are still ringing in my ears. Now, where have you come from this time?"

With an effort, she rose to draw aside the bed curtains and gazed at me closely. She moved the lamp and asked me to sit on her bed. After talking for a while, I, in consideration of her illness, prepared to depart. She held my hands asking me to remain, saying, "During the past eighteen days I have had no appetite for food, and I have been unable to sleep well. I have lost my spirits, dreaming all the time. But on seeing you, I feel as if my spirits have returned and my energy has been restored." She then bade her servant to serve wine and food, which I took by her bedside. Xiaowan filled my cup with wine and again and again made me stay after I expressed my intention to leave. Finally I said, "Early tomorrow morning, I intend to send a servant to Xiangyang to inform my father of the good news of his promotion. If I stay here overnight, the messenger will not be able to leave at daybreak. When the messenger departs, I am willing to stop over here for a few moments." Xiaowan replied, "You are very sincere, and I dare not press you to stay any longer." Thereupon, I rose to depart.

The next morning at daybreak my messenger left for Huguang.[136] I was eager to set out for home without delay, but my friends and servants all said, "Xiaowan treated you like an old friend last night, you should not let her down by breaking your promise to see her again." Hearing this, I went to bid her farewell. I found her, freshly made-up, leaning against an upstairs window and staring out attentively. Upon seeing my boat draw alongside the bank, she came out and hurriedly came aboard to greet me. I wanted to leave after finishing my farewell words, but Xiaowan said, "I have packed up my belongings and will accompany you on your journey home." I could not stop her, nor bear to reject her request.

We went from Huguan to Wuxi,[137] Changzhou, Yixing,[138] Jiangyin,[139] and finally arrived at the Beigu Hill.[140] All this took twenty-seven days, and I bade her to go back twenty-seven times, but Xiaowan was firm in her desire to follow me. On mounting the Golden Hill,[141] she pointed to the river below and swore, "My body is like the waters of the Yangzi running eastward, and I am determined not to go back to Suzhou again!"

On hearing this, I changed my countenance and told her that the provincial examination was drawing near. And because of my father's appointment to a dangerous place in recent years, I had failed to attend to my home affairs, and had also been unable to look after my aged mother in person. Only now had I begun to find it possible to get back to straighten everything out. Moreover, Xiaowan had many creditors in Suzhou, and it would require much effort to redeem her singing-girl bondage at Nanjing. I suggested that she go back to Suzhou for the time being. After I had taken the annual examination[142] in late summer, I would take her to Nanjing. I would only have time to consider our affairs after the autumn provincial examination regardless of the result. Being over-sentimental at the present moment would do neither of us any good.

Xiaowan still hesitated and was reluctant to leave. There was a set of dice on the table, and one of my friends said to her jokingly, "Should your desire be gratified at last, the dice would fall down on the same side after being tossed." Xiaowan then solemnly knelt down in the boat cabin, and cast the dice after praying to Heaven. Miraculously, all of them fell down on the side of six. All on board expressed their surprise. I then told her that if we were destined to be a couple, we might bungle the whole thing if we proceeded too hurriedly. It would be better for her to leave me temporarily, and let both of us plan our future carefully and thoroughly. Thus, against her wish, she bade farewell to me, burying her face in her hands and breaking into tears which choked her further utterance. Though pitying Xiaowan's lot, I felt I had thrown off a burden and could now return home with a light heart.

Upon arriving at Taizhou,[143] I sat for the annual examination immediately. It was in the sixth month (of 1642) that I arrived home. My wife said to me, "Xiaowan bade her father cross the river and bring word to you that since her return to Suzhou, she has stopped receiving clients and confined herself at home, on tiptoe to expect you to go to Nanjing with her as you promised. Feeling quite surprised, I gave her father ten taels of silver, and said to him, 'I am in sympathy with her and agree to her request, but she should wait till the provincial examination is over.'" I was grateful to my wife for her kindness in allowing me to take Xiaowan as my concubine. I proceeded to Nanjing directly without keeping my promise to travel with Xiaowan, for I intended to inform her after I had finished the examination.

On the fifteenth day of the eighth month (in 1642),[144] right after I had come out of the examination hall, Xiaowan hurriedly arrived at my lodging-house in the Peach Leaf Pier area.[145] It turned out that she had waited in vain to hear from me and therefore hired a boat, set out from Suzhou, and proceeded along the river with an old woman as her companion. They met with robbers on the way, and her boat had to hide in reeds. With the rudder broken, the boat could not proceed, and they had practically nothing to cook for three days. When she arrived at Nanjing, she stayed outside the Sanshan Gate[146] for fear that she might disturb my literary thoughts for the first part of my examination. She did not enter the city until two days later.

Although Xiaowan was overjoyed at seeing me, she appeared rather miserable both in her voice and appearance while she gave a detailed description of what had happened during the hundred days of our separation, such as her confinement at home and refusal to receive clients, her encounter with robbers on the river, and her terrifying voyage fraught with danger. She was more insistent than ever in trying to marry me. Of the members of our literary society from Jiashan[147] and Songjiang,[148] as well as Fujian and Henan, there were none who did not admire Xiaowan's far-sightedness and sympathize with her sincerity. They all encouraged her with their poems and paintings.

When the examination was over, I flattered myself that I would pass it, and I thought that thereafter I should be able to settle my affairs with Xiaowan to fulfill her desire. Unexpectedly, on the seventeenth day (of the eighth month), [149] I was suddenly informed that my father had arrived by boat at the bank of the Yangzi River. He had turned down the government appointment to transfer him to Baoqing, [150] and he was returning from Huguang after retirement from official life. As I had not waited on him for more than two years, I could not find adequate words to express my joy at his return alive from the scene of internecine war. I could find no time to plan the future arrangement for Xiaowan, and immediately went to Longtan [151] to follow my father's boat until we reached Luanjiang. [152] My father asked about my examination essays and, on hearing my answers, was of the opinion that I certainly would succeed. He asked me to stay at Luanjinag to await the result.

In the meantime, Xiaowan set out by boat from the lodging-house at Peach Leaf Pier in pursuit of me. She was beset by a storm at the Swallow's Ledge, [153] which almost cost her her life. She came to stay on board with me again at Yizheng. When the result of the examination was announced on the seventh day of the ninth month, [154] I found my name standing on the waiting list of successful candidates. [155] I then proceeded on my way home, by day and by night, while Xiaowan followed me, weeping and crying, unwilling to return to her home. I was, however, well aware that it would be very difficult for me to settle her affairs at Suzhou single-handedly. Her creditors would, on finding her absent, increase their demands and make a din. Moreover, my father's unexpected return home and my disappointment at my failure to pass the provincial examination had made it impossible to gratify her desire at once. On arrival at my Pucao Treehouse [156] on the outskirts of my hometown, I assumed an icy countenance and became iron-hearted in an effort to part from Xiaowan, bidding her to return to Suzhou to set her creditors at ease so as to pave the way for our future plans.

In the tenth month (of 1642), while passing Zhenjiang,[157] I called on my examination supervisor Mr Zheng. At that time, Liu Daxing[158] of Fujian province had arrived from the capital, and while he was holding a drinking party in his boat with General Chen, my literary society friend Prefect Liu, and me, my servant returned from his visit to Xiaowan at home. He told us that, on arrival at Suzhou, Xiaowan had not put off her autumn clothing and was still wearing a very thin gauze garment, saying that if I did not go to Suzhou to settle her affairs promptly, she would rather die of cold.

Liu Daxing pointed to me and said, "Pijiang, you are well known for your caring and virtuous conduct; how could you let down a woman like this?" I replied, "The gallant deeds of chivalrous persons such as Junping[159] and Xianke[160] could not be done without help from others." Raising his goblet with a gesture of excitement, Prefect Liu declared, "If I can have a thousand taels of silver at my disposal, I'll start right away today for Suzhou to settle Xiaowan's affairs." General Chen at once lent me hundreds of taels of silver, and Liu Daxing also assisted me with a present of several catties of ginseng. Unfortunately, when the prefect arrived at Suzhou, he acted poorly as an intermediary, and the creditors kicked up a row, so the prefect fled to Wujiang.[161] I returned home shortly afterwards, and made no further inquiries.

Xiaowan was left in a precarious position. She could hardly find a way out of her difficulty. On hearing of her trouble, Minister Qian of Changshu[162] went to Bantang himself and brought Xiaowan to his boat. He approached her creditors, from the gentry to commoners, and within three days managed to clear her every debt, irrespective of whether the amount involved was large or small, the bills redeemed piling up more than one foot[163] high. This done, he held a farewell banquet in a gaily-painted pleasure boat and entertained Xiaowan at Huliu. He then hired a boat and sent his servants to see her safely through to my hometown, Rugao.

On the early evening of the fifteenth day of the eleventh month (of 1642),[164] when I was drinking with my father at his Zuocun Hall,[165] I was suddenly informed that Xiaowan had arrived at the pier. Upon reading the long and detailed letter I was brought from Minister Qian, I began to understand the whole story. I also learned that Minister Qian had written to his protégé surnamed Zhang at the Nanjing Ministry of Rites, asking him to redeem Xiaowan's singing-girl bondage. Her minor affairs at Suzhou were later settled by Director Zhou[166] of the same ministry, while Censor-in-chief Li of the Nanjing Censorate[167] also rendered her great assistance in Nanjing. Ten months later, Xiaowan's desire was finally gratified. It was achieved through countless painstaking efforts and assistance rendered by my mentors and friends.

On the last day of the fourth month in 1642, the year of Renwu,[168] Xiaowan accompanied me to the foot of the Beigu Hill, insisting on crossing the Yangzi River and following me to my home. Upon my rejection of her proposal, she was moved to greater grief and became more determined than ever in her reluctance to depart. Our boat was moored by the bank. A piece of occidental cloth sent to me by my Western friend Bi Jinliang,[169] which was as thin as a cicada's wing and as white as snow, had been made into a light robe with a pink lining for Xiaowan, and might be compared favourably with the feathery skirt of the famed consort Zhang Lihua of Cassia Palace.[170] When we mounted the Golden Hill together, four to five dragon boats fought their way ahead in the surging billows, while crowds of sightseers loitering about the hill followed on our heels, calling us a pair of immortals. We sauntered around the hill, and wherever we paused, the dragon boats struggled toward us, and they did not retreat after circling us several times. I called out to inquire, and realized that those at the rudders were the pilots of the barge on which I had embarked last autumn on my return from Zhejiang. I therefore gave them a few presents, and we spent a whole day on the hill. There was a large white porcelain jar from the Xuande era[171] in our boat which was filled with a few catties of cherries. Together we munched them in such a manner as to make our lips and the fruit look alike. On this occasion, the splendid landscape amid the hustle and bustle of sightseers was resplendent and people have talked about it repeatedly ever since.

2

On the day of the Mid-Autumn Festival (in 1642), the friends of our literary society[172] from across the country, who had felt a warm admiration for Xiaowan's having risked her life for my sake by perservering in the face of robbers and storm, invited us to a banquet which was spread in a waterside pavilion at Peach Leaf Pier. Among those present were Xiaowan's close friends Madame Gu of Meilou[173] and Madame Li of Hanxiuzhai.[174] Overjoyed by Xiaowan's wedlock with me, they came to offer their congratulations upon her success in uniting with me. On that day, the play, *Swallow's Letter*,[175] was performed for the first time, full of sweet and loving scenes. When it came to the most touching point, describing the separation and reunion of the hero Huo Duliang and the heroine Hua Xingyun,[176] Xiaowan wept, and so did Madames Gu and Li. The meeting of a crowd of scholars and beauties amongst towers and pavilions, amid misty rain, and in the bright moonlight, with melodious dramatic songs cheering up one's senses, was something to be remembered forever. Recalling the night now, it appears like a dream on a fairy pillow.

The gardens and pavilions belonging to Wang Ruwei of Yizheng[177] were all laid out in a most magnificent fashion, and his little garden standing on the bank of the Yangzi River was in the best possible position to command a magnificent view of the river and its surrounding hills. On the first day of the ninth month in 1642, the year of Renwu,[178] Ruwei invited Xiaowan and me to dinner at his Plum-blossom Pavilion overlooking the river. The silvery waves of the Yangzi rolled in enormous clouds of foam beneath our wine-cups. Xiaowan drank ferociously out of a big goblet, and we had strict rules for our drinking bout. The singing-girls attending the feast were very much the worse for liquor and almost passed out, while Xiaowan, who was the most temperate and gentle, was moved to such high exhilaration that day as I had never seen before or since.

In 1645, the year of Yiyou, I accompanied my mother and the rest of my family in flight to Yanguan[179] for safety. In the spring, while passing Bantang, we found Xiaowan's old house standing there just as it did before. Her younger sister Xiaosheng [180] turned out with Sha Jiuwan to greet us on our boat. On finding that Xiaowan was treasured as if she were my "Wish-gratifying Pearl", that my wife was amiable and virtuous, and that a perfect harmony existed between her and Xiaowan like a mixture of water and milk, both of them entertained a feeling of commingled admiration and jealousy. As we moved to the summit of Tiger Hill together, they reminded me of the old familiar scenes we had visited, and we indulged in chatting about our past affairs. Those at Suzhou who knew Xiaowan were unanimous in their praise of her far-sightedness in having chosen me as her life partner.

On Mandarin Duck Lake stands aloft the Tower of Smoke-and-Rain.[181] To the east of the tower, the gardens with pavilions and bamboo groves lie partially on the surface of the lake. Although famous gardens and monasteries encircle the city in every direction, the truly beautiful sights are the ripples on the lake surrounding the low-lying islets. Still, sightseers, on reaching the Tower of Smoke-and-Rain, tend to think that they have had a full view of the beautiful scenery of the lake. The truth is that they do not know that both the grand and secluded aspects of the lake are not to be seen at that spot. I once enjoyed myself all day long on the lake with Xiaowan. When we recalled the enchanting scenery of green waves and rugged cliffs along the Yanling Rapids of the Tong River,[182] Xiaowan told me that the serene landscape of Xin'an[183] is all the more enjoyable because it is of such easy access for its inhabitants, almost as if it is right in the midst of their kitchens and bedchambers.

When Xiaowan, accompanied by the men dispatched by Minister Qian, arrived at Rugao, I was drinking with my father in his private hall. I dared not report the matter to him at once, nor could I leave him immediately, so we dragged on till the fourth watch. Without waiting for my return, my wife had prepared a separate house for Xiaowan's use, and all of the household necessities such as curtains and lamps, furniture and utensils, beverage and food were at once made ready. After finishing drinking wine with my father, I went to see Xiaowan, who said to me, "Upon my arrival, I could not understand why I did not see you, and as I saw only a crowd of maid-servants assisting me to disembark, I felt suspicious and also quite frightened. On entering my house and finding everything prepared for my comfort, I made inquiries and was moved by the graciousness of the mistress, which made me feel all the more gratified by my unfaltering decision to follow you for almost a year."

From that time on, Xiaowan confined herself to her house. She desisted from playing musical instruments, and dispensed with powder and rouge. Instead she applied herself diligently to needlework. It frequently happened that she did not go out of her door for over a month. Appreciating the quiet and serene environment, she told me that she felt as if she had jumped out of a vast expanse of burning fire into a cool refreshing atmosphere. She looked back into the past five years of her singing-girl's life[184] as if she had woken from a dream or as if she had been released from prison. After a few months, there was no branch of needlework in which she was not proficient. In embroidery she was especially skillful; every day she could embroider six handkerchiefs or skirts with designs so deftly interwoven as to leave no fabric visible among the tiny stitches. Additionally, she mastered several associated abilities such as cutting paper flowers, interweaving characters, carving gold-leaves into ornamental designs, and making palindromes. Her skill in needlework overshadowed that of the ancients.

After living in her separate house for four months, Xiaowan was invited by my wife to my house. My mother and my wife, on seeing her, took a great liking to her at once, both treating her with special favour. My youngest aunt and elder sister, all on cordial terms with her, considered that both her virtuous nature and her elegant manners were extraordinary. Nevertheless, she was always willing to wait on them and carry out their wishes with greater obedience than the maid-servants did. She would attend to such menial household duties as preparing tea or peeling fruit and serving it with her own hands. She would always smile to please us and massage and scratch my back. In the coldest period of winter or in the hottest time of summer, she would stand waiting beside the dinner table, and on being told to sit down and take her food, she would, after sitting down and finishing her meal quickly, rise to her feet once more to do the work as usual.

Whenever I was dissatisfied with the compositions written by my two sons[185] on the topics of the lectures I had given them, I punished them with blows. Xiaowan always instructed them to improve their work and to submit it to me in neat handwriting. She never relaxed her effort in supervising them till nightfall. During the period of nine years she was with me, she and my wife never had any heated exchange of words. In dealing with servants, Xiaowan was always mild and humble, and so everybody was grateful for her kind attitude. My personal and social expenses and my wife's daily household outlay were all managed by Xiaowan, and yet she did not store any amount for her own use, nor care about her private savings, nor purchase a single article of jewelry. When she was dying on the second day of the New Year (of 1651), [186] she insisted on seeing my mother, and then breathed her last. She had willed that none of her jewelry and clothes should be entombed with her remains. She was indeed an exceptional human being!

During the past few years, I had been devoting my time to the collection of poetical works from the four periods of the Tang dynasty. [187] I had bought all the available complete works of the poets of the dynasty, gleaned all available details about their lives, and gathered together the comments of all literary critics on their works. It was my intention to arrange the poets and poems in chronological order – the former in accordance with their birthdates and the latter in their order of composition, to add detailed commentaries on the works of each poet, and to search extensively for every missing link of the chain, in the hope that my work might be one of the most comprehensive about the epoch in question. The poetical works of the early and high Tang periods were more or less complete, but in writings about the middle and late Tang periods the poets' names appear either without their complete works or with no works at all, and it is not infrequent for both the poets' names and their works to be missing. In *Pinghui* (The Graded Compendium of Tang Poetry)[188] there is a collection of six hundred poets of the Tang dynasty. In *Jishi benmo* (The Record of the Poetical Works from Beginning to End of the Tang Dynasty)[189] the names of a thousand odd poets are listed without their complete works. *Quan Tang shihu* (The Poetical Analysis of the Tang Dynasty) [190] leaves even more to be desired.

In his preface to *Shi'er Tangren* (The Poems of Twelve Tang Poets), [191] Mr Zhiyu [192] pointed out that a certain distinguished family in Nanchang had kept in manuscript form over seven hundred unpublished works of poetical compositions belonging to the middle and late Tang periods. My mentor Mr Wang of Mengjin[193] told me that he had bought of a certain Xu of Lingbao[194] several full cartloads of the poetical writings of the whole Tang dynasty; and that Director Hu Xiaoyuan[195] of the ministry of war, who once sought refuge at Haiyan, had spent thousands of taels of silver to print the Tang poems which he had perused.

Now in this out-of-the-way place no books could be borrowed and I was staying at home without a chance to go out to buy them. It was hard to search for materials to carry out my research work. But whenever I came across a volume, I reviewed it carefully, added my own remarks, based on what I had read in other books relating to the volume in question, and finally passed it to Xiaowan for safekeeping. The chronological order of poets in which my work was arranged was set in accordance with *Tangshu* (The History of the Tang Dynasty)[196] Xiaowan assisted me all day long in examining and copying the manuscripts and carefully collating the text. We often sat face to face without speaking a word for a whole day and night.

Xiaowan understood every poem she read and was in the habit of interpreting them in her clever way. She was especially fond of learning by heart *Chuci* (The Verses of Chu),[197] the poems of Shaolin,[198] Yishan,[199] and those describing court life by the three prominent poets Wang Jian,[200] Madame Hua Rui,[201] and Wang Gui.[202] Voluminous books in piles as high as her height surrounded her desk on every side. She often slept with the works of scores of Tang poets huddled beside her pillow or under her bedclothes at midnight. Her bedchamber is now locked up and covered with thick dust; I cannot bear to open it again. From now on who will help me complete my unfinished work? I cannot do anything but dismiss my thought with a sigh of regret.

I remember, last year while reading the History of the Eastern Han Dynasty up to the biographies of Chen Zhongju, [203] Fan Pang, [204] and Guo Liang, [205] I sighed in anger at their sufferings. Xiaowan asked me to explain every detail about these. On hearing my explanations, she voiced her indignation, expressing her own impartial views, which indeed could be regarded as the insightful commentary of a competent historian.

During my sojourn at Yanguan in 1645, the year of Yiyou, I borrowed some books from my friends and asked Xiaowan to copy all unusual and curious passages for me. She also made for her own reference an additional copy of those concerning women's matters. After returning home, Xiaowan and I delved deep into other books, and I helped her complete her work entitled *Lianyan* (The Toiletries of Past Beauties). [206] It deals with all the unusual and abstruse aspects of female life. It contains a complete description of the women of ancient times, their clothes and food, their furniture and utensils, their pavilions and towers, their singing and dancing activities, their attainments in needlework and in the literary realm, including their writings on birds, fish, and animals, even grass or wood which, when related to something sensitive, she also included in the collection.

This collection, written on red paper in small script and methodically classified, is now lying in her bedchamber. Last spring, Madame Gu asked Xiaowan to let her have a look at it, and she and Minister Gong [207] expressed their hearty admiration. Both urged me to have it printed. I will, therefore, restrain my grief and attempt to collate Xiaowan's work for publication to fulfill her desire.

Shortly after coming to my house, Xiaowan, who had seen the Rhapsody on the Moon, [208] which had been copied for me by Dong Wenmin [209] in the style of the calligrapher Zhong Yao, [210] became very fond of practicing her handwriting after this model, and searched far and wide for Grand Mentor Zhong's calligraphic works. However, after finding that one of them, entitled Memorial from My Chariot,[211] brands Lord Guan[212] as a bandit general, she immediately cast aside Zhong's works and committed herself instead to the copybook *Cao E Stele*.[213] It was her practice to write thousands of characters every day without a single mistake or omission. Whenever I had occasion to glean data or take extracts from a book, she at once copied them down for me. When researching historical and poetical works or scrutinizing anecdotes and interesting passages, I always depended on Xiaowan to commit them to writing. On my behalf, she once inscribed a fan, which was kept by one of my close friends, in small regular script. Besides all this, she made a complete record of my wife's household receipts and payments relating to items such as rice, salt, and similar without omitting a single entry. Her carefulness and her ability to concentrate were hardly to be equaled by diligent scholars such as myself and my friends.

While at Suzhou, Xiaowan studied the art of painting, but without mastering it. She could paint wintery shrubs and trees fairly well, and often scribbled on the ink-slab or desk. She took a great fancy to paintings, ancient and modern, and every long or short scroll she came across as well as those antique productions which she and I kept in bamboo containers, she would unfold and review now and then. Even at the time of our taking shelter away from home, she preferred to abandon the articles of her dowry in favour of taking along her works of calligraphy and paintings. She later was forced to get rid of all the mountings and retain only the art works themselves on paper and silk, but even these she could not keep in her possession forever. Xiaowan put her body and soul into her hobby; but even so her collection of calligraphy and paintings was ill-fated.

3

Xiaowan was able to drink, but after entering my home and noticing my inability to take even a cupful of wine, she broke her habit and only drank a few cups every night to keep my wife company. She was fond of tea and shared this habit with me. We took a particular fancy to the *jie* tea, [214] and Gu Zijian [215] of Bantang used to select the best quality of that brand and to send it to us every year. Its leaves are in the shape of fish scales, and each leaf has the quaint appearance of a cicada's wing. In preparing tea with spring water, boiled in a tiny kettle over a slow-burning stove amid fine wreaths of smoke, Xiaowan always blew the fire and washed everything herself. Whenever I recited the line of Zuo Si's poem, "Dainty Girls", [216] describing how his two lively daughters "huff and puff at the kettle," she would respond with a smile. The following poetical lines accurately reflect Xiaowan's enjoyment in brewing tea. "The boiling water bubbles like a cluster of crabs' eyes or fish scales, and the porcelain teapot shines like the moon's splendour and the iridescence of the clouds."

While sipping tea together in a serene atmosphere while looking at flowers or in the moonlight, we experienced the ecstasy described by the tea connoisseurs Lu Tong [217] and Lu Yu, [218] watching the green leaves sinking down and the fragrant smell diffusing like fairy grass growing on the brink of waves.

Su Dongpo[219] once lamented, "I have not had the good fortune to have a beauty hand me a jade cup from which to drink." For my part, I tasted such bliss in the nine years I spent with Xiaowan. After that my happiness was brought to an end!

Xiaowan often seated herself quietly with me in her bedchamber to examine carefully the quality of some famous perfumes. Those used by court ladies are seductive in quality, while the agalloch (*chenshuixiang*) is average. The ordinary people are in the habit of setting the agalloch alight, and the smoke, on touching an oily or greasy substance, disappears instantly. Apart from the fact that the essence of the perfume still lies latent, the smoke usually fills one's sleeve with a slightly rancid and scorching smell. The garro-wood of hard quality with sidewise grain is called *henggechen*, one of the four kinds of plant-bearing horizontal fibres, and possesses an excellent fragrant smell. There is another species known as *Penglaixiang*, which has the shape of a little conical rain hat or a big mushroom, and is buoyant in water. I kept many of this species. When burned slowly over fire and covered with a thin layer of sand to prevent the smoke from spreading, the perfume fills the chamber with a balmy atmosphere like aromatic aloeswood wafted by winds, or like the smell of a cluster of roses saturated with genial dew, or like a piece of amber rubbed till it turns hot, or like the taste of wine poured into a goblet made of rhinoceros horn. This sweet odour, if allowed to diffuse for some time among the pillows and quilts and to mingle with the natural fragrance of the fair one's skin, is exceptionally pleasing to the senses and has a soothing effect on one's dreams. In addition to this, I had obtained from the imperial palace treasury a genuine western formula for making perfume, which was quite different from that procurable on the market.

In 1646, the year of Bingshu, while staying at Taizhou, Xiaowan and I made a hundred pills of this perfume with our own hands. This is, indeed, a rare article for the inner chamber. While this perfume is burning, it is better to keep out the smoke. Had the burning not been handled by Xiaowan's sensitive and refined hand, I would not have been able to appreciate the perfume so fully.

The *huangshu* plant is indigenous to various foreign countries, and the one produced in Cambodia is of the best quality. The one with hard bark is called *huangshutong*; another – which emits a fine aroma and is pitch-black in colour – *gejian huangshu*. The natives of Chayuan village in Dongguan,[220] south Guangdong, are said to grow this plant in the same way as the people of Jiangnan grow their tea bushes. Its trunk is low, its branches are luxuriant, and its aroma lies in the root. After the root has been severed and the trunk cut into sections by the sawyers of Suzhou, all the essence of the aroma becomes perceptible, with all the loose and decayed portions discarded. During our stay at Bantang (in 1645), when we learned that Jin Pingshu was an expert in this work, on several occasions we paid a high price for his manufactures. The products in bulk form are pure and unadulterated; while those parts which are long and crooked like curling twigs are engraved, to suggest yellow clouds or purple embroidery or somewhat in the form of partridges (following the natural fibres of the knotty parts of the root), so that one may hold them in one's hand to toy with them.

On winter nights in Xiaowan's tiny chamber with jade-coloured curtains falling down on four sides, blankets spread one over the other, two or three red candles a little over two feet long alight, furniture and ornamental articles arranged out of their usual order, we would gather together a few incense-burners of the Xuande period,[221] large and small, with ashes glowing like melted gold or brown jade, and – after gently raking over an inch of the smoldering embers in each burner – we would place some of the perfume on a layer of sand over the embers. The perfume would keep burning till midnight without getting scorched or exhausted, the sweet smell diffusing profusely after the crystallizing of its resinous substance, sending forth a hot pleasing aroma somewhat like the flavour of half-open plum-blossoms or of goose-pears stimulating one's spleen. We would keep quiet, inhaling the fragrant air to our hearts' content. I remember that during recent years we used to enjoy our time together in this spellbinding atmosphere, not going to bed till daybreak. As Xiaowan and I meditated over women's expressions of dissatisfaction,[222] she leaned on the frame over a brazier and raked the fire repeatedly, pretending she was a solitary wife waiting in vain for her husband's return. I felt as if we were sitting among the pistils of fragrant flowers. Alas! Both the fragrant smell and Xiaowan have disappeared. Where can I get a resuscitating pill to bring back her soul into her quiet locked-up chamber?

There is a sort of raw yellow perfume – a tender undeveloped resinous substance – that can be obtained from the withered and decayed part of the plant. While passing through Suzhou and Nanjing, I secured a quantity of massive pieces (including those carried by merchants from Guangdong), which were being stored in incense shops in boxes and baskets, and I spared no effort to obtain even huge roots or long branches caked with dust. After bringing my purchases home, I made it a rule that every morning and night Xiaowan and I would supervise the serving maids in peeling the bark. Only a few candareens were cut away from a catty of the wood – a mere fragment was pared off a piece the size of a palm – the material being so cut and hewn as to lose no part of the essence. Whether burned directly over fire or on a layer of sand, this substance is fragrant with the perfume of orchids, and when placed in layers on a tiny tray, it has a peculiar colour and a strange smell most attractive to one's senses. Some time ago, I showed one or two pieces of this species to my friend Li Meizhou[223] of Guangdong, and he was so surprised at its fine quality that he immediately asked me what it was and where I had obtained it. He believed that it was probably not to be found even in the biography of Weizong.[224]

In the county of Dongguan, *nüerxiang* (girl's perfume) is regarded as unrivalled in quality, for the natives of the area always employ young girls to collect the perfume and often the girls stealthily take away the best and largest pieces and exchange them for toilet lubricant and powder, and the wily seekers, in turn, obtain these pieces from those dealing in such toilet articles. I received a few pieces from my friend surnamed Wang, and Xiaowan valued them greatly.

Plum trees were planted in nearly every available space of my residence and gardens,[225] so in spring we strolled among brilliant plum-blossoms, morning and night. Xiaowan was in the habit of keeping an eye out for those twigs which would fit the vases on the table when the flowers were budding, so that when the flowers were in full bloom, she might pluck the twigs and put them into the vases. She would also trim the previous year's sprigs according to her fancy. Additionally, there was no bamboo, grass or flower blossoming during any of the four seasons of the year which she did not manage to cultivate in her own witty way. She appreciated the most graceful species, so a cold serene fragrant air usually diffused itself throughout the labyrinth of her rooms and tiny chambers. Those gaudy in colour and odour were, however, not to her liking.

In autumn, she was especially fond of late-flowering chrysanthemums. During her illness last autumn, my friend presented me with a kind of chrysanthemum called *jiantaohong*, which had dense thick petals, green leaves, and graceful stems of a charming style. Every stem had a quaint appearance as if shaded by the clouds or bent over in the wind. Xiaowan had been ill for three months, her hair partially combed and face only perfunctorily washed, but on seeing the chrysanthemum, she liked it tremendously and moved it to her bedside. Every night she lit green candles and threw a white screen of six folds round the flowers on three sides, placing a seat among the flowers and adjusting the position of the chrysanthemum in such a way as to make it cast its shadow on the screen in the most graceful manner imaginable. She would then draw herself into the enclosure, and when she was among the flowers, both her shadow and that of the flowers were thrown on the screen. Turning around to look at the screen, she said to me, "The fascinating appearance of the chrysanthemum has been fully displayed; but how about my slender figure?" On recalling it today, the whole captivating scene rises vividly before my eyes as in a picture.

Xiaowan once kept nine stalks of the vernal orchid and also some of the Fujian species, so that from spring till autumn a most pleasing odour filled her chambers as if one were carried to the orchid-producing centres in Hunan. The flowers touched by Xiaowan's hands seemed to increase in fragrance. "The Song on the Cultivating of Orchids during the Twelve Months,"[226] transcribed by her on green paper, was pasted on the wall. Last winter during the time when Xiaowan was ill, a greater part of the flowers she kept withered. Even the yellow plum tree in our courtyard, which usually burst into full bloom in the depth of every winter and whose flowers would have been sufficient for the female members of the family to use for three months, did not produce a single bud over its hundreds of branches last winter after she had gone to stay in Xiangli Garden[227] to recuperate; only the sound of the howling wind was audible from among the pine trees, which added further grief to a melancholy scene.

Xiaowan was fondest of the moon; she used to bask in its beams from the time it rose till it sank below the horizon. In summer when seeking coolness in the garden and reciting to my children verses by the Tang poets describing the moon, the firefly, and the silk fan, she would often move her couch and tea table to enjoy every ray of moonlight. After retiring to her bedchamber at midnight, she would open her windows to let the moonbeams fall full upon her bed. Finally after the moon was out of her sight, she would roll up the curtains again and lean against the window-sill to gaze into the sky with longing eyes. She said to me, "When copying the 'Rhapsody on the Moon' by Xie Xiyi,[228] I began to realize that the ancients preferred nocturnal entertainment to daytime pleasure, because at night when everything is still and the moon is quiet, the blue sky and cold frost set against the glowing sun and bustling atmosphere are as different as fairyland is from the mortal world. Human beings hustle about from morning till night, and some even fall into snoring sleep before the moon makes her appearance; so they do not have the good fortune to enjoy her dazzling beauty and the shadow of the dew. Only you and I, perhaps, can appreciate her beautiful soul all the year round, and I am inclined to think that the transcendental beauty of fairyland and of Buddha's Paradise is in this quietness within our reach."

In a poem composed by Li Changji,[229] there appears this line, "The bright moon is made up of ripples, smoke and jade." Whenever reading the three words "ripples", "smoke", and "jade", Xiaowan always thought about them over and over, saying that both the spiritual and material aspects of the moon had been fully described. Living in the world of ripples, smoke, and jade, the eyes of a human being are a horizontal ripple, his or her breath is fragrant smoke, and his or her body white jade. Or to put it another way, the moon is like a human being, and there seems to be no difference between the two. For this reason, the idea conveyed by Jia Changjiang's[230] words, "With man and shadow in the moonbeams there are three beings," appears to me rather superfluous, but the line, "While enjoying moonlight, one can find no means of satiating one's ambition to become the toad in the moon's palace," indicates a full appreciation of the moon's elegance.

Not interested in fame and wealth, Xiaowan had little appetite for oily and sweet delicacies. At every meal she filled her rice bowl with a little pot of lukewarm infusion of *jie* tea[231] and took only a mouthful of vegetables and peas, all of which were enough to satisfy her modest appetite. I too eat little, but I relish immensely sweet dishes, seafood delicacies, and dry smoked eatables. I, however, do not take much when alone, for I like to enjoy these together with my guests. Knowing this, Xiaowan always entertained myself and my guests with the choicest and daintiest meals she could prepare. The delicacies are too numerous to remember. Below, I pick out at random a few items as examples.

There is a beverage made from an infusion of salt and plum by a process of fermentation. Sweet coloured flower-buds plucked at the beginning of their blossoming are dipped, entire, into the solution. After the lapse of a year, the petals remain unchanged in colour and flavour, appearing as fresh and beautiful as they did when the flower-buds had just been plucked from the tree. On touching one's lips, the juice of the flower, dissolved in the sweet liquor, sends a fragrant scent into the nostrils. Its fascinating hue and sweet smell are incomparable. Among the flowers so prepared, the most charming is the begonia, which – though in itself odourless – diffuses a sweet odour after being dipped into the liquid. The graceful jasmine (*duanchangcao*), which people think is not edible, ranks first in flavour, and the plum-blossom, the sweetbrier, the rose, the cassia, and the chrysanthemum come next; while, with their threadlike fibres removed, yellow and red oranges, Buddha's-hand fruit,[232] and the ordinary citron also excel in colour and flavour. After drinking wine, we used to make a display of scores of varieties of the beverage with flowers and fruits of various colours floating within white porcelain bowls. This beverage has the property of quenching thirst and making those who are drunk sober; not even the genial dew of the "Bronze Tray"[233] could have surpassed it. We would remove the pulp and fibre from peaches of the fifth month and from water melons and simmer the juice over a fire, and when about seven- or eight-tenths of it was left, we would begin to pour sugar into the kettle, so that the mixture became condensed. The jam of the peach looks like red amber, and that of the water melon is comparable to gold-thread sweetmeat.

Every hot summer, Xiaowan would produce the juice with her own hands to keep it clean, and then sit beside the stove watching it boil and condense without becoming dried up or scorched. Further, she could distinguish the thick jam from the thin and separate it into several categories, each of which had a colour and taste peculiar to itself.

In preparing black soy beans, their delicacy lies not so much in taste as in colour and odour. The beans should be washed and sun-dried nine times, and, after being stripped of peel and membrane, mixed with a variety of delicate articles such as melon and almond, ginger and cassia, in addition to fermented bean juice all of which should be kept as clean as possible. At the end of the process, the beans are taken out of the mixture still in their original shape, but their sweet odour, charming colour, and excellent taste are quite different from those of ordinary beans.

Red bean-curd, after being baked and stewed five or six times, having become crisp, should be stripped of its outer coat and mixed with seasoning. It will be edible in a few days, and its taste excels by far Jianning bean-curd[234] which is stored for three years before eating. Xiaowan could also prepare winter and spring vegetables, as yellow as wax or as green as moss, which she dipped into a mixture of water and salt. The lotus-root and rush-shoot, the bamboo-shoot and the bracken, the fresh flower and the wild vegetable, the wolfberry and the crown daisy, the hibiscus and the chrysanthemum were all collected by her as eatables and deliciously spread out on our table as a feast.

Aged ham is not greasy but has the flavour of pine or cypress; stale dried fish, like the ham, possesses the taste of venison; clams dipped in wine look like the peach-flower; the bone of sturgeon steeped in wine is as delicate as white jade; the butterfish fried in oil is similar to sturgeon in relish; dried minced shrimps look like a dragon's antennae; roast rabbit and crisp pheasant, like cakes, can be cooked in bamboo steamers; dried mushroom resembles chicken; bean-curd soup is like milk – all these delicacies are part and parcel of the recipes invented by Xiaowan. She always sought after novelty in the line of cuisine, and after familiarizing herself with a new delicacy, she would proceed to make it in her own clever way – and the result was always marvelous.

4

The distressing news of the incident of the nineteenth day of the third month in 1644, the year of Jiashen,[235] was not brought to my county until after the middle of the fourth month. Owing to cowardice on the part of the local authorities, rapacious elements were active in the county seat and there was a threat of looting and arson. Added to this, people were alarmed by the possibility of pillage by the fleeing troops of the Earl of Xingping. [236] Gentry and rich families living in our neighborhood had fled like a flock of frightened birds, seeking refuge on the south side of the Yangzi River. My father inclined to take the view that simply not stepping outside the house was adequate as a means of self-protection, as our family in the Jixian Lane was known for generations for being honest and amiable towards people.

A few days afterwards, among the thirty-odd families in the neighborhood, only ours had smoke rising from the chimney. Nevertheless my mother and my wife were so frightened that they left for the suburb outside the county wall. Xiaowan was asked to stay behind with me, to help with locking up our inner apartments, gathering together clothes and other things, including paintings and calligraphic works, documents, and bonds, discriminating between the valuable and the valueless, and entrusting them to servants and maids sealed with labels written by herself. Looting was the order of the day, and bandits slaughtered their victims as if mowing grass. People in our neighborhood were as few and far between as the morning stars. We could not afford to linger any longer, and so I had to hire a small boat for my parents and family to flee[237] this dangerous place by way of Nanjiang and Jiangyin. Our boat proceeded sixty *li* one dark night, and we reached (our friend) Mr Zhu's residence at the village of Fanhuzhou.[238]

Since bandits were already active along the river, I had first to escort my father to Jingjiang[239] by a side path and in plain dress. At midnight, my father said to me, "We cannot do anything without some small pieces of silver." I asked Xiaowan for some, and she produced a cloth bag containing silver fragments weighing from slightly more than a candareen to a little over a mace apiece– hundreds of pieces to every ten taels – with the weight written nicely on each so as to facilitate handling when needed urgently. My father was amazed by this convenient arrangement, wondering with a sigh of satisfaction how Xiaowan could find time to be so meticulous about such a trifle.

At that time, the cost of every service had soared ten times as high as in normal times, yet some boatmen were still unwilling to accept offers. We had to wait a day and then chartered ten boats for a hundred taels of silver and engaged an escort of two hundred men for a little over the same amount.

We had travelled but a few *li* on our way before the tide ebbed, and our vessels could proceed no further. I noticed at a distance hundreds of bandits occupying six boats and lying in wait at strategic points, but thanks to the ebbing tide, they could not reach our boats. Meanwhile, a sturdy man was sent from the Zhu residence to wade through the river to reach us and he reported as follows. "The bandits are blocking your way to the rear and you must not retreat. Even worse, there are many outlaws in your 200-man escort." Pandemonium broke out in all our ten boats; our servants began shouting and crying. I pointed at those on the river, and smilingly said, "A hundred members of our family of three generations are all on board. For the past sixty or seventy years, my late great-grandfather, my grandfather, my father, and myself, whether holding government appointments or living at home, have never done anybody wrong nor sinned against our own conscience. Therefore, should all of us today meet our death at the hands of the brigands and feed the fishes, there would be neither Heaven above nor Earth below. But as the tide has suddenly ebbed earlier than usual, preventing the vessels on both sides from coming together, I do believe that Heaven has come to our rescue. You should not be afraid; not even the enemy positioned in our own boats can do us any harm."

The previous night when we were packing up our belongings and about to go aboard, it flashed across my mind that since the Yangzi flowing into the sea is so extensive and my aged mother and my small sons had never before experienced a voyage so fraught with danger, if we should be beset by adverse winds on the river and need to go ashore wherever possible, we might be at a loss as to where to secure sedan-chairs and wheel-barrows. Consequently, at the third watch of the night, I paid twenty taels of silver to a boatman surnamed Shen, asking him to hire two sedan-chairs and one wheel-barrow with six labourers. Both Shen and the others expressed their surprise and laughed at me, saying, "Since your boats are setting out in the morning, they can reach the other side of the river before noon, why do you want to waste your money in the dead of night?" All those nearby laughed at me for wanting to hire boatmen and sedan-chair bearers.

I nevertheless insisted on getting both before I went aboard. Although at this critical moment I was able to retain my presence of mind, we were in a difficult dilemma. As we had not gone very far out of the tributary of the Yangzi, I asked the boatman if we might disembark somewhere and then find our way back to Fanhuzhou by land. He told me that half a li^{240} away in an oblique line there was a small path, six or seven *li* in length, leading directly to our destination. Thereupon, I lost no time in making our boats pull up to the shore, and we presently took to the two sedan-chairs and one wheel-barrow which were available for the seven members of our family only, leaving on board all our belongings and maid-servants. It was not long before we arrived at Zhu's residence. Upon our arrival, all expressed surprise at my having anticipated difficulties unseen by others and thus prepared all means of communication both by land and by water the previous midnight.

On hearing that we had retreated and that the Zhu family had arranged several hundred people to escort our luggage and retinue, the bandits, though dispersing, felt very dissatisfied. Taking advantage of the fact that the law could not reach those on the river or rather perhaps that no law was enforced at that time, they instantly mustered up hundreds of their men and sent one to inform me that unless I could pay them a thousand taels of silver, they would proceed to besiege the Zhu residence and set fire to it on all sides. I replied with a smile, "What stupid fellows you bandits are! You failed to beseige us midstream, how do you expect to attack us with fire in the midst of hundreds of houses on land?"

Among the villagers of Fanhuzhou who were presumably acting as our guard, there were plenty of rascals. I gave all of them whatever money I had, to allow them to buy wine and meat to enjoy at night, asking them to be on guard to protect the village against any mishap that might happen. But the consequence was that hundreds of them went to share the money and have a drink. The same night, supporting my mother with one hand and pulling my wife with the other, and putting my two small sons and my ten-day old step-brother Jifu[241] and his mother[242] under the care of a trusted maid-servant who came along behind us, we went staggering out of the thick bamboo grove in the rear of the residence. I could not render Xiaowan any assistance, but turning round to look at her, I said, "Please quicken your steps to follow us, or you will be left behind." She therefore ran stumbling along for over a *li*, and then we availed ourselves of the sedan-chairs and wheel-barrow we had hired the night before. Finally we found ourselves beside the city wall by the time five strokes of the watchman's drum had been beaten. Meanwhile, neither the bandits nor the rascals in the Zhu residence had had an inkling of our unexpected departure.

Though escaping with our lives, we had lost the greater part of our belongings. Almost all of Xiaowan's treasures were gone as well. On reaching home, Xiaowan said to me, "At that most critical moment it was right for you to look after your aged mother first and then the mistress, your children, and your younger brother. Had I been unable to follow you, I would have died in the thick bamboo grove without regret."

It was on the day of the Dragon-Boat Festival (of 1644) [243] that we returned home. During the next one hundred days, the Northern Amy [244] and local rascals ran wild. At the Mid-autumn Festival I crossed the river to travel to Nanjing, leaving Xiaowan behind. I was away for nearly five months, not returning until the end of the year. Then taking my family with me, I again travelled to the south side of the river to accompany my father on his assumption of office as Superintendent of the Chief Transport Office. [245] Later, we went to stay at Yanguan. I cannot but admire Xiaowan for her noble sensibility and understanding. Could a profoundly educated scholar have acquitted himself so well?

In 1645, the year of Yiyou, we were staying at Yanguan, [246] but in the fifth month that city also fell into the hands of the advancing Northern troops. At this time, our family consisted only of eight members. [247] The trouble we faced on the river the previous summer was due to the fact that we had some one hundred servants, male and female, accompanying us in disorderly haste. Also, our cumbersome luggage filled several boats and carts to their capacity, on the one hand keeping us from moving freely and on the other hand tempting outsiders to look at us with covetous eyes. On this occasion, we decided to stay indoors and accept whatever fate might be in store for us. Internecine war, however, broke out inside the city. My parents were so horrified that they sought shelter outside the city at Dabaiju.[248] I instructed Xiaowan to take care of the house by herself, with the help of the maid-servants, giving the order that no-one and nothing should leave the city lest they involve us in trouble. I was determined to go empty-handed even if I had to seek safety in flight with my parents, my wife, and my children. Nevertheless, contrary to my expectations, both our attendants and belongings came pouring out of the house in defiance of my instructions.

Meanwhile, the Great (Northern) Army was marching toward Zuili,[249] and the edict instructing male subjects to shave their foreheads had just been promulgated.[250] The masses were agitated. My father had left for Re Hill[251] and we were at our wits' end. I accordingly decided to part with Xiaowan, telling her, "Our present plight is different from what we faced in our county, where we still had many to help us. Since I have to look after many kinsfolk, it would be far better for me to find a safe place for you rather than possibly having to abandon you at the last moment. I have a same-year friend,[252] a trustworthy and talented man, and I would like to entrust you to his care. If we meet again in the future, I assure you I will renew our blissful life together; if not, you may do as you please and you do not need to worry about me anymore."

Xiaowan replied, "What you have said is sensible. The whole family looks to you for guidance. Even though you did not ask me to do so, I do think that your parents and your children are a hundred times more important than I, so if my remaining with you will make you worry, I will only do you harm instead of good. If I stay with your friend and eventually escape unharmed, I swear I will fall on my knees to await your return; but if worse should come to worst, the surging billows of the mighty deep which you and I have witnessed will be my burial place."

When I was about to bid her farewell, my parents, who did not want me to give up Xiaowan, made her follow us again. From that time, we passed almost one hundred days trudging either among dense forests or along out-of-the-way paths, taking shelter in thatched dwellings or on fishing-boats, and changing our abode once a month, or once a day, or even several times a day. During all this time we, hungry and cold, were exposed to wind and rain and laboured under indescribable privations. Finally we came upon the Great Army at Ma'anshan,[253] and they relentlessly robbed us and killed many people. Fortunately, we obtained a sampan, and the eight of us got away safely. However, Xiaowan had been strained to the utmost by fright, fatigue, and illness.

5

Emerging from disastrous encounters with the Northern Army at Qinxi,[254] only the eight of us had escaped unscathed, while close to twenty of our servants and maids had been killed, and nearly all of our long-treasured articles and clothes had been lost. When the situation had settled down to some extent, I went secretly into the (Yanguan) city to seek relief from my friends, but not even bedclothes could be obtained from them.

At night I put up at the house of Fang Tan'an,[255] my father's same-year friend. Fang had just returned from refuge as well and was sleeping under one blanket with his three brothers in a side-chamber. It was toward the end of autumn; a cold wind came shooting through the windows in every direction. Next day, each of us went to borrow a peck of rice and a few bundles of firewood from our friends. Then I went to fetch my parents and the other members of our family to go to stay temporarily at our old residence (in Yanguan). I began to suffer from a cold followed by diarrhea and fever. A wooden door-plank lying about a foot above the ground served as my bed, and some cotton refuse as my mattress. In the place of medicine, some mulberry branches were kept burning in a stove to expel the bad humours from my body. Furthermore, while weltering in the thick of turmoil at Suzhou, I received the news that my family had also experienced trouble in my hometown. From the ninth day of the ninth month (in 1645)[256] my mind was disordered and I fainted frequently, coming to myself only on the eve of the Winter Solstice. Finally I sailed homeward with a few old boats through an appalling scene of corpses and skeletons. Crossing the river at the risk of our lives, we dared not return home directly but stayed for a while at Taizhou. It was one hundred and fifty days, from the winter (of 1645) till the spring (of 1646), before I recovered.

During these one hundred and fifty days, Xiaowan lay by my bedside, having only a torn mat to lie on, embracing me when I was cold, fanning me when I was hot, and rubbing me when I felt pain. Making a pillow of her body or leaning on her feet while stretching myself or tossing and turning on my bed, I would make use of her body and limbs to soothe my sick body. Vigilant all night long, she always strained her ears to listen and her eyes to see, though there was nothing to hear or see. She would taste every dose of my medicine and then give it to me with her own hands. She would even examine my stool, expressing her joy if it was normal or her sorrow if it was not. Every day she took but a coarse meal, and if not engaged in offering her prayers to the heavens, she would invariably stand by my side or kneel down before me, resorting to sweet words to make me smile.

My sickness had made me lose my temper, and I was often in violent anger and scolded Xiaowan repeatedly; but she never for a moment was irritated. Her behaviour remained unchanged during the five long months. On finding Xiaowan's dimpled cheeks turning pale like wax and her body growing as thin as a stick, my mother the Respected Lady and my wife not only felt sorry for her but felt exceedingly grateful to her, and proposed to relieve her for a while. Xiaowan, however, said to them, "I am only too glad to do all I can for my man. If he is living and I am dead, I'll still find solace in the nether world; but, on the other hand, should he come to a tragic end and I survive him, who else might I expect to depend on for existence in these times of war and crisis?"

I also remember that when my sickness was growing serious, I could not sleep throughout the night, hearing the howling wind moaning among the roof tiles. In the city of Yanguan hundreds of people were killed every day, [257] and at midnight the murmuring of ghosts was audible at the broken windows sounding like the chirping of insects or the shooting of arrows. When all others in the house, hungry and cold, were tired and fell into a sound sleep, I was in a sitting posture with my back close to Xiaowan's breast, her hands holding mine firmly, and we were straining our ears to hear the pathetic, wailing sound which made us sob and burst into tears. Xiaowan said to me emotionally, "During the past four years since I came to your house I have found your conduct always noble and generous, and even in trivial matters you have never been mean or wicked. Only I realize and excuse your action for which you have been blamed. [258] In fact, I respect your heart more than I love your body. I think the spirits would admire and respect you with awe. Therefore, if Heaven has knowledge, I am sure it will silently bless you without end! We mortals are not made of metal or stone; who could escape death after enduring such hardships and tribulations? Some day if we can get back alive, I hope we will abandon all our worldly possessions and live the remainder of our lives, free and unfettered from mundane cares. Please do not forget my words." Alas! How can I seek to return Xiaowan's generosity and love in this life of mine? Without any doubt, Xiaowan was no ordinary woman of this world!

In 1647, the year of Dinghai, I was accused by vicious slanderers, who had changed their attitude towards me as unexpectedly as if the ever-winding paths of Mount Taihang [259] were written large on their faces. I was so indignant that I felt as if my breast was swelling up like the five sacred mountains. [260] In an agony of grief that long summer, I found no relief other than to appeal to Lord

Guan by burning prayers on two slips of paper morning and night. Suffering from a strange chronic disease, I had discharged plenty of blood and had numerous stone-like accretions deposited in my bowels and stomach. Seized with fits of intermittent fever, I was in delirium, letting out at one moment a thousand words, broken and incoherent, or remaining in a trance for days and nights at a time. The doctor had wrongly prescribed tonics for me, which had so aggravated my disease that I could not drink even a ladleful of water for more than twenty days. At that time, everybody predicted my death. I was, however, rather clear in mind, for my sickness was not caused by my adverse circumstances.

During the sweltering summer days, Xiaowan did not even wipe away her sweat nor did she drive away the mosquitoes. She sat all day and all night long beside the stove over which my medicinal herbs were boiling. For sixty days and nights, she was constantly at my pillow or close to my feet, carrying out my intentions or anticipating my wishes.

In the autumn of 1649, the year of Yichou, I again suffered from an ulcer on the back, and Xiaowan waited on me for another hundred days in a similar manner. During a period of five years, I was seriously ill three times, and every time my illness could have proved incurable, but I entertained no evil forebodings at heart. Without Xiaowan's meticulous care, I could not have been confident that I would not succumb to the fatal disease. Now she has died before me, and in her dying hours she still worried that her death might aggravate my sickness and expressed her regret that she could no longer care for me during my illness. Alas, how sad it is that the matter of her life and death has entangled my heartstrings to such an extent!

Every year on New Year's Day, it was my habit to draw a lot before the temple of Lord Guan to divine my affairs during the coming year. In 1642 when I was rather eager in pursuit of civil service examination honours,[261] I observed after praying that the first character on the lot I drew was "*yi*" meaning "recall" which headed the sentence, "Recalling to mind the dividing of hairpins into halves in the orchid chambers in the past, she wonders why her lover has all of a sudden kept her in the dark, but deep in her veins she hopes to unite with him like intertwined branches. Who knows whether her expectations might not be fulfilled at last?" I read over the lines, but could not make them out, and the oracle, taken as a whole, did not seem to have anything to do with my examination ambitions.

Some time afterwards, I met Xiaowan, and on the last day of the fourth month (of 1642),[262] she bade farewell to me on Golden Hill. After she had returned home and stopped receiving clients, Xiaowan went to the temple of Lord Guan at Huliu to seek advice by divination about her wish to serve me for the rest of her life and she received the same oracular message. On seeing me at Nanjing in the autumn, she told me of this incident, dreading that our affairs might not end in success. Surprised to hear of this coincidence I told her that I had received the same oracular message on New Year's Day. One of my friends sitting beside us at the time said to us, "I will draw a lot on your behalf at the temple at Xihuamen."[263] Curiously, the same oracle turned up once more. Thereupon, Xiaowan grew even more suspicious, and fearing that I might be inspired by the oracle to change my mind, she turned pale with grief. Her cherished hope was, however, finally fulfilled. The words on the lot in question such as "orchid chamber", "hairpins into halves", "vain hopes", and "intertwined branches" are certainly words belonging to the inner chamber; while the clause, "at last her expectations might not be fulfilled," has now come true. Alas! I will devote myself to "recalling" her past during the remaining years of my life. The preternatural word "recall" has proved so prophetic!

Xiaowan's clothes and ornamental articles had all been lost in times of trouble, but after returning home, she was content and did not buy any new ones. On the night of the seventh day of the seventh month[264] in 1648, the year of Wuzi,[265] on seeing red clouds moving in the sky, she hit upon the idea of having them inscribed on her gold bracelet and asked me to write upon it two characters "*qiqiao*" meaning "begging for feminine skill". As I could not get the antithetical counterparts of these characters, she told me that in former years, while travelling on the Yellow Mountain, at the house of a rich man, she came across an incense-burner of the Xuande period on which were engraved the characters "*fuxiang yunzhen*" with excellent inscriptions, and suggested that the characters "*fuxiang*" meaning "covered with auspiciousness" would be a fitting antithesis to "*qiqiao*". Her bracelet was inscribed quite dexterously, but one year afterwards, it suddenly broke. It happened that exactly in the seventh month it was repaired. This time I wrote the characters "*biyi lianli*" instead, meaning "birds flying side by side" and "intertwined branches".[266]

At the time of her death, Xiaowan was, from head to toe, not adorned by a single gold article or a single pearl nor was she clad in silken clothes, but she retained her bracelet because I had inscribed my words on it. The secret vow made at the Hall of Immortality[267] was conveyed to the emperor Minghuang[268] by the honoured guest of Hongdu[269] after the death of his beloved Consort, Yang Taizhen.[270] How was I to understand that the inscription I had had made on her bracelet had inadvertently given rise to a recurrence of the scene described in the 'Song of Everlasting Sorrow'?[271]

Xiaowan's calligraphic handwriting was neat and elegant. She had imitated the style of the Grand Mentor

Zhong, but her calligraphy appeared a little slenderer than this model. Later, she modeled her calligraphy after the *Cao E Stele*. Whenever I had thoughts or comments while reading books, she sat opposite me, either practicing her calligraphy, or copying my comments with minute care. Of the poetical and historical works now lying in her bedchamber in book form, all bear traces of her handwriting. Occasionally she composed verses but did not keep most of her manuscripts. Last year, on the second day of the New Year, she selected and copied for me into two volumes the quatrain verses[272] (with either five or seven characters to the line), of the whole Tang dynasty. On that day, she happened to read the passage of a six-year-old girl's lamentation that, "Unlike wild geese, human beings do not come back pair by pair". Feeling sad and bursting into tears, she composed eight stanzas in response at night. Her stanzas were filled with so much dismal pathos that one could not read them without feeling depressed. On taking hold of a lamp and glancing them over, I was greatly displeased, carrying the poem sheet away from her and throwing it into the flames. The manuscript was thus lost. Alas! How could one know that she would pass away on the very same day of the following year?

In the third month of last year, I wanted to go to Yanguan again to visit my friends who had assisted me in one way or another while we were taking refuge there, but on arriving at Yangzhou, I was surrounded by the members of our literary society.[273] I was then forty *sui* of age, so many distinguished scholars honoured me with their complimentary poems. Among them Minister Gong had written a long poem of several thousand words narrating the story of Xiaowan's courtship with me from beginning to end – a work which could not be equaled even by the two masterpieces of the Tang dynasty, *The Imperial Capital* and *The Lianchang Palace*.[274] Minister Gong said to me, "If this poem is not to be annotated by yourself, my considerable effort will be wasted. For instance, the line, 'The peace-flower is withering, while the spring is stupefied with drink,' alludes to the circumstances in which you twice met Xiaowan; the first time in 1639 when she was tipsy; the second time in 1642 when she was ill. Who else knows this so well?" I agreed to comply with his request, but did not take up the work at once.

Among the other complimentary verses are Yuanci's,[275] "The man of letters has since olden time been called a filial son, while the distinguished scholar naturally falls in love with the astounding beauty;" Yuhuang's,[276] "The wife strolls along with her husband, while the concubine follows behind;" Xiaowei's,[277] "The gentleman among the trees is lost in musings, while the lady among the flowers writes capably;" Xinfu's,[278] "Beside the coral pen-rack shuffle the elegant lady's shoes, while the author of voluminous works has a beauty in his chambers;" Xianqi's,[279] "The husband and wife are destined to live a long life together while the hibiscus garden has flowers in full bloom;" Zhongmou's,[280] "You can live in retirement at the age of forty, while I admire you for having a virtuous wife helping you pound with a pestle;" my townsman Culai's,[281] "The scholar from the treehouse has eminent talents in statecraft, his wife and concubine are in harmony, while frolicking among the splendid scenery of springtime;" Yuandan's,[282] "The beauty's attempt at questioning the scholar helps him in his literary efforts." – All these verses congratulated me on having taken Xiaowan as my concubine. Who could have known that these verses, complimenting me on my birthday, would have now become her elegies. On reaching this point of my narrative, the reader is surely in a position to appreciate the beauty of these scholars' verses. Since I failed to annotate Minister Gong's work last spring, I shall have to do it now, my tears and blood mingling with the ink.

At the end of the third month (in 1650), I went again to lodge in my friend Zhao Youyi's [283] house, "Friendly Cloud Residence". Having left home for a long time and hearing, while lying on my bed, the pattering of raindrops, I was overwhelmed with feelings of homesickness. The rain stopped one evening, when Minister Gong dropped by with my friends Yuhuang and Yuanci. I entertained them with wine. While my servants played musical instruments and sang songs to entertain them, I yearned for home even more eagerly. Each of us then set to compose four stanzas which were made to rhyme with the characters we had given. Surprising to relate, the symbol of sorrow permeated every stanza without our knowing it. My friends took their leave after three strokes of the watchman's drum had been beaten. On touching the pillow, I dreamed that I had arrived home and seen everyone in my family except Xiaowan; that after asking my wife hastily where Xiaowan was, receiving no answer from her, I proceeded to search everywhere and found my wife weeping with her back toward me. I shouted aloud, still in my dream, "Can it really be that she is dead?" After this, I awoke with a loud cry. Since Xiaowan was sick almost every spring, I was quite ill at ease.

Shortly afterwards, I returned home and was relieved to find Xiaowan well. When I told her of my dream, Xiaowan said, "What a strange coincidence! That very night I also dreamed that several people were attempting to drag me away by force, but luckily I escaped by hiding; and they kept shouting for some time." It is impossible to understand how what we dream becomes true and how the stanzas I had composed proved prophetic, bringing unfortunate news to me beforehand!

影梅庵憶語

一

愛生於暱，暱則無所不飾。緣飾著愛，天下鮮有真可愛者矣。矧內屋深屏，貯光閟彩，止憑雕心鏤質之文人描摹想像，麻姑幻譜，神女浪傳。近好事家，復假箋聲詩，侈談奇合，遂使西施、夷光、文君、洪度，人人閣中有之，此亦閨秀之奇冤，而嗷名之惡習已。

亡妾董氏，原名白，字小宛，復字青蓮。籍秦淮，徙吳門。在風塵雖有艷名，非其本色。傾蓋矢從余，入吾門，智慧才識，種種始露。凡九年，上下內外大小，無忤無間。其佐余著書肥遯，佐余婦精女紅，親操井臼，以及蒙難遘疾，莫不履險如夷，茹苦若飴，合為一人。

今忽死，余不知姬死而余死也！但見余婦煢煢粥粥，視左右手罔措也。上下內外大小之人，咸悲酸痛楚，以為不可復得也。傳其慧心隱行，聞者歎者，莫不謂文人儀士難與爭儔也。

余業為哀辭數千言哭之，格於聲韻不盡悉，復約略紀其概。每冥痛沉思姬之一生，與偕姬九年光景，一齊湧心塞眼，雖有吞鳥夢花之心手，莫能追述。區區淚筆，枯澀黮削，不能自傳其愛，何有於飾？矧姬之事余，始終本末，不緣狎昵。余年已四十，鬚眉如戟。十五年前，眉公先生謂余視錦半臂碧紗籠，一笑瞠若，豈至今復效輕薄子漫譜情豔，以欺地下？儻信余之深者，因余以知姬之果異，賜之鴻文麗藻，余得藉手報姬，姬死無恨，余生無恨。

己卯初夏，應試白門，晤密之云："秦淮佳麗，近有雙成，年甚綺，才色為一時之冠。"余訪之，則以厭薄紛華，挈家去金閶矣！嗣下第，浪遊吳門，屢訪之半塘，時逗遛洞庭不返。名與姬頡頏者，有沙九畹、楊漪炤。予日遊兩生間，獨咫尺不見姬。

將歸棹，重往冀一見。姬母秀且賢，勞余曰："君數來矣，予女幸在舍，薄醉未醒。"然稍停復他出，從兔徑扶姬於曲欄與余晤。面暈淺春，纈眼流視，香姿玉色，神韻天然，嬾慢不交一語。余驚愛之，惜其倦，遂別歸，此良晤之始也。時姬年十六。

庚辰夏，留滯影園，欲過訪姬。客從吳門來，知姬去西子湖，兼往遊黃山白嶽，遂不果行。

辛巳早春，余省觀去衡嶽，縣浙路往，過半塘訊姬，則仍滯黃山。

許忠節公赴粵任，與余聯舟行。偶一日，赴飲歸，謂與曰："此中有陳姬某，擅梨園之勝，不可不見。"余佐忠節治舟數往返，始得之。

其人淡而韻，盈盈冉冉，衣椒繭，時背顧湘裙，真如孤鸞之在煙霧。是日演弋腔《紅梅》，以燕俗之劇，咿呀啁哳之調，乃出之陳姬身口，如雲出岫，如珠在盤，令人欲仙欲死。漏下四鼓，風雨忽作，必欲駕小舟去。余牽衣訂再晤，答云："光福梅花如冷雲萬頃，子越旦偕我遊否？則有半月淹也。"余迫省觀，告以不敢遲留故，復云："南嶽歸棹，當遲子於虎嘷叢桂間。"蓋計其期，八月返也。

余別去，恰以觀濤日奉母回。至西湖，因家君調已破之襄陽，心緒如焚，便訊陳姬，則已為竇霍豪家掠去，聞之慘然！及抵閶門，水澀舟膠，去滸關十五里，皆充斥不可行。偶晤一友，語次有"佳人難再得"之歟。友云："子誤矣！前以勢劫去者，贗某也。某之匿處，去此甚邇，與子偕往。"

至果得見，又如芳蘭之在幽谷也。相視而笑曰："子至矣！子非雨夜舟中訂芳約者耶？曩感子殷勤，以淩遽不獲訂再晤。今幾入虎口，得脫，重晤子，真天幸也！我居甚僻，復長齋，茗椀爐香，留子傾倒於明月桂影之下，且有所商。"

余以老母在舟，緣江楚多梗，率健兒百餘護行，皆住河干，矍矍欲返。甫黃昏而礮械震耳，擊礮聲如在余舟旁，亟星馳回，則中貴爭持河道，與我兵鬭。解之始去。自此余不復登岸。

越旦，則姬淡粧至，求謁吾母太恭人，見後仍堅訂過其家。乃是晚，舟仍中梗，乘月一往，相見，卒然曰："余此身脫樊籠，欲擇人事之。終身可託者，無出君右。適見太恭人，如覆春雲，如飲甘露，真得所天。子毋辭！"

余笑曰："天下無此易易事。且嚴親在兵火，我歸，當棄妻子以殉。兩過子，皆路梗中無聊閒步耳。子言突至，余甚訝。即果爾，亦塞耳堅謝，無徒誤子。"復宛轉云："君倘不終棄，誓待君堂上畫錦旋。"余答曰："若爾，當與子約。"驚喜申囑，語絮絮不悉記，即席作八絕句付之。

歸歷秋冬，奔馳萬狀。至壬午仲春，都門政府言路諸公，恤勞人之勞，憐獨子之苦，馳量移之耗，先報余。時正在毘陵，聞音如石去心，因便過吳門慰陳姬。蓋殘冬屢趣余，皆未及答。

至則十日前復為竇霍門下客，以勢逼去。先，吳門有暱之者，集千人譁劫之。勢家復為大言挾詐，又不惜數千金為賄。地方恐貽伊戚，劫出復納入。余至，悵惘無極，然以急嚴親患難，負一女子無憾也。

是晚壹鬱，因與友覓舟去虎𨛦夜遊。明日，遣人之襄陽，便解維歸里。舟過一橋，見小樓立水邊。偶詢遊人："此何處？何人之居？"友以雙成館對。余三年積念，不禁狂喜，即停舟相訪。友阻云："彼前亦為勢家所驚，危病十有八日，母死，鐍戶不見客。"余強之上，叩門至再三，始啟戶，燈火闃如。宛轉登樓，則藥餌滿几榻。

姬沉吟詢何來，余告以昔年曲欄醉晤人。姬憶，淚下曰："曩君屢過余，雖僅一見，余母恒背稱君奇秀，為余惜不共君盤桓。今三年矣，余母新死，見君憶母，言猶在耳。今從何處來？"

便強起，揭帷帳審視余，且移燈留坐榻上。譚有頃，余憐姬病，願辭去。牽留之曰："我十有八日寢食俱廢，沉沉若夢，驚魂不安。今一見君，便覺神怡氣王。"旋命其家具酒食，飲榻前。姬輒進酒，屢別屢留，不使去。余告之曰："明朝遣人去襄陽，告家君量移喜耗。若宿卿處，詰旦不能報平安。俟發使行，寧少停半刻也。"姬曰："子誠殊異，不敢留。"遂別。

越旦，楚使行，余亟欲還，友人及僕從咸云："姬昨僅一傾蓋，拳切不可負。"仍往言別，至則姬已妝成，憑樓凝睇，見余舟傍岸，便疾趨登舟。余具述即欲行，姬曰："我裝已戒，隨路袓送。"余卻不得卻，阻不忍阻。

由滸關至梁溪、毘陵、陽羨、澄江，抵北固，越二十七日，凡二十七辭，姬惟堅以身從。登金山，誓江流曰："妾此身如江水東下，斷不復返吳門！"

余變色拒絕，告以期迫科試，年來以大人滯危疆，家事委棄，老母定省俱違，今始歸經理一切。且姬吳門責逋甚眾，金陵落籍，亦費商量，仍歸吳門，俟季夏應試，相約同赴金陵。秋試畢，第與否，始暇及此，此時纏綿，兩妨無益。

姬仍躊躇不肯行。時五木在几，一友戲云："卿果終如願，當一擲得巧。"姬肅拜於船窗，祝畢，一擲得全六，時同舟稱異。余謂果屬天成，倉卒不臧，反償乃事，不如暫去，徐圖之。不得已，始掩面痛哭失聲而別。余雖憐姬，然得輕身歸，如釋重負。

才抵海陵，旋就試。至六月抵家。荊人對余曰："姬令其父先已過江來云，'姬返吳門，茹素不出，惟翹首聽金陵偕行之約。'聞言心異，以十金遣其父去，曰：'我已憐其意而許之，但令靜俟畢場事後無不可耳。'"余感荊人相成相許之雅，遂不踐走使迎姬之約。競赴金陵，俟場後報姬。

金桂月三五之辰，余方出闈，姬猝到桃葉寓館。蓋望余耗不至，孤身挈一嫗，買舟自吳門江行。遇盜，舟匿蘆葦中，柁損不可行，炊煙遂斷三日。初入抵三山門，只恐擾余首場文思，復遲二日始入。

姬見余雖甚喜，細述別後百日，茹素杜門，與江行風波盜賊驚魂狀，則聲色俱淒，求歸愈固。時魏塘、雲間、閩、豫諸同社，無不高姬之識，憫姬之誠，咸為賦詩作畫以堅之。

場事既竣，余妄意必第，自謂此後當料理姬事，以報其志。詎十七日，忽傳家君舟抵江干，蓋不赴寶慶之調，自楚休致矣！時已二載違養，冒兵火生還，喜出望外，遂不及為姬謀去留，竟從龍潭尾家君舟抵鑾江。家君問余文，謂余必第，復留之鑾江候榜。

姬從桃葉寓館仍發舟追余，燕子磯阻風，幾復罹不測，重盤桓鑾江舟中。七日乃榜發，余中副車，窮日夜力歸里門，而姬痛哭相隨，不肯返，且細悉姬吳門諸事，非一手足力所能了。責逋者見其遠來，益多奢望，眾口猖猖。且嚴親速歸，余復下第意阻，萬難即詣。舟抵郭外樸巢，遂冷面鐵心，與姬決別，仍令姬返吳門，以厭責逋者之意，而後事可為也。

陽月過潤州，謁房師鄭公，時閩中劉大行自都門來，陳大將軍及同盟劉刺史飲舟中。適奴子自姬處來，云："姬歸不脫去時衣，此時尚方空在體。謂余不速往圖之，彼甘凍死。"

劉大行指余曰："辟疆夙稱風義，固如負一女子耶？"余云："黃衫押衙，非君平、仙客所能自為。"刺史舉杯奮袂曰："若以千金恣我出入，即於今日往！"陳大將軍立貸數百金，大行以葭數斤佐之。詎謂刺史至吳門，不善調停，眾嘩決裂，逸去吳江。余復還里，不及訊。

姬孤身維谷，難以收拾。虞山宗伯聞之，親至半塘，納姬舟中。上至薦紳，下及市井，纖悉大小，三日為之區畫立盡，索券盈尺。樓船張宴，與姬餞於虎邱，旋買舟送至吾皋。

至月之望，薄暮侍家君飲於拙存堂，忽傳姬抵河干。接宗伯書，娓娓灑灑，始悉其狀，且即馳書貴門生張祠部立為落籍。吳門後有細瑣，則周儀部終之，而南中則李總憲舊為禮垣者與力焉。越十月，願始畢，然往返葛藤，則萬斛心血所灌注而成也。

壬午清和晦日，姬送余至北固山下，堅欲從渡江歸里。余辭之，益哀切，不肯行。舟泊江邊，時西先生畢今梁寄余夏西洋布一端，薄如蟬紗，潔比雪豔。以退紅為裏，為姬製輕衫，不減張麗華桂宮霓裳也！偕登金山，時四五龍舟衝波激盪而上，山中遊人數千，尾余兩人，指為神仙。繞山而行，凡我兩人所止則龍舟爭赴，迴環數匝不去。呼詢之，則駕舟者皆余去秋溯回官舫長年也。勞以鵝酒，竟日返舟，舟中宣瓷大白盂，盛櫻珠數升，共啖之，不辨其為櫻為唇也。江山人物之盛，照映一時，至今譚者侈美。

二

秦淮中秋日，四方同社諸友，感姬為余不辭盜賊風波之
險，間關相從，因置酒桃葉水閣。時在座為眉樓顧夫
人、寒秀齋李夫人，皆與姬為至戚，美其屬余，咸來相
慶。是日新演《燕子箋》，曲盡情豔。至霍華離合處，
姬泣下，顧、李亦泣下。一時才子佳人，樓臺煙水，新
聲明月，俱足千古，至今思之，不啻遊仙枕上夢幻也。

　　鑾江汪汝為園亭極盛，而江上小園，尤收拾江山
勝概。壬午鞠月之朔，汝為曾延予及姬於江口梅花亭子
上。長江白浪擁象，犇赴杯底，姬轟飲巨叵羅，觴政明
肅，一時在座諸姬，皆頹唐潰逸。姬最溫謹，是日豪情
逸致，則余僅見。

　　乙酉，余奉母及家眷，流寓鹽官，春過半塘，則
姬之舊寓，固宛然在也。姬有妹曉生，同沙九畹登舟過
訪，見姬為余如意珠，而荊人賢淑，相視復如水乳，群
美之，群妒之。同上虎邱，與予指點舊遊，重理前事，
吳門知姬者，咸稱其俊識，得所歸云。

　　鴛鴦湖上，煙雨樓高。逶迤而東，則竹亭園半在
湖內，然環城四面，名園勝寺，夾淺渚層溪而激灩者，
皆湖也。遊人一登煙雨樓，遂謂已盡其勝，不知浩瀚幽
渺之致，正不在此。與姬曾為竟日遊，又共追憶錢塘江
下桐君嚴瀨、碧浪蒼巖之勝，姬更云："新安山水之
逸，在人枕簞間，尤足樂也。"

　　虞山宗伯送姬抵吾皋，時侍家君飲於家園，倉卒
不敢告嚴君。又侍飲至四鼓，不得散。荊人不待余歸，
先為潔治別室，帷帳燈火器具飲食，無一不頃刻具。酒

闌見姬，姬云：「始至，正不知何故不見君，但見婢婦簇我登岸，心竊懷疑，且深恫駭。抵斯室，見無所不備。旁詢之，始感歎主母之賢，而益快經歲之矢相從不誤也。」

自此姬局別室，卻管弦，洗鉛華，精學女紅，恒月餘不啟戶。耽寂享恬，謂驟出萬頃火雲，得憩清涼界，回視五載風塵，如夢如獄。居數月，於女紅無所不妍巧，錦繡工鮮。刺巾裾，如蠶無痕，日可六幅。剪綵織字，縷金迴文，各厭其技，鍼神鍼絕，前無古人已！

姬在別室四月，荊人攜之歸。入門，吾母太恭人與荊人見而愛異之，加以殊眷。幼姑長姊，尤珍重相親，謂其德性舉止，均非常人。而姬之侍左右，服勞承旨，較婢婦有加無已。烹茗剝果，必手進；開眉解意，爬背喻癢。當大寒暑，折膠鑠金時，必拱立座隅，強之坐飲食，旋坐旋飲食，旋起執役，拱立如初。

余每課兩兒文，不稱意，加夏楚，姬必督之改削成章，莊書以進，至夜不懈。越九年，與荊人無一言枘鑿。至於視眾御下，慈讓不遑，咸感其惠。余出入應酬之費與荊人日用金錯泉布，皆出姬手。姬不私銖兩，不愛積蓄，不製一寶粟釵鈿。死能彌留，元旦次日，必欲求見老母，始瞑目，而一身之外，金珠紅紫盡卻之，不以殉，洵稱異人。

余數年來，欲裒集四唐詩，購全集、類逸事、集眾評，列人與年為次第，每集細加評選。廣搜遺失，成一代大觀。初盛稍有次第，中晚有名無集、有集不全，並名集俱未見行甚夥，《品彙》六百家，大略耳，即《紀事本末》，千餘家名姓稍存，而詩不具。《全唐詩話》更覺寥寥。

芝隰先生序《十二唐人》，稱豫章大家，藏中晚未刻集七百餘種。孟津王師向余言：買靈寶許氏《全唐詩》數車滿載，即囊流寓鹽官胡孝轅職方批閱唐人詩，剖劂工費，需數千金。

僻地無書可借，近復裹足牖下，不能出遊購之，以此經營搜索，殊費工力，然每得一帙，必細加丹黃。他書有涉此集者，皆錄首簡，付姬收貯。至編年論人，準之《唐書》。姬終日佐余稽查抄寫，細心商訂，永日終使，相對忘言。

閱詩無所不解，而又出慧解以解之。尤好熟讀《楚辭》、少陵、義山、王建、花蕊夫人、王珪三家宮詞，等身之書，周迴座右，午夜衾枕間，猶擁數十家唐詩而臥。今秘閣塵封，余不忍啟，將來此志，誰克與終？付之一歎而已！

猶憶前歲，余讀《東漢》，至陳仲舉、范、郭諸傳，為之撫几，姬一一求解其始末，發不平之色，而妙出持平之議，堪作一則史論。

乙酉客鹽官，嘗向諸友借書讀之，凡有奇僻，命姬手抄。姬於事涉閨閣者，則另錄一帙。歸來與姬遍搜諸書，續成之，名曰《奩豔》。其書之魂異精秘，凡古人女子，自頂至踵，以及服食器具、亭臺歌舞、鍼神才藻，下及禽魚鳥獸，即草木之無情者，稍涉有情，皆歸香麗。

今細字紅箋，類分條析，俱在奩中。客春顧夫人遠向姬借閱此書，與龔奉常極讚其妙，促繡梓之。余即當忍痛為之校讎鳩工，以終姬志。

姬初入吾家，見董文敏為余書《月賦》，仿鍾繇筆意者，酷愛臨摹，嗣遍覓鍾太傅諸帖學之。閱《戎輅表》稱關帝君為賊將。遂廢鍾學《曹娥碑》，日寫數千字，不訛不落。余凡有選摘，立抄成帙，或史或詩，或遺事妙句，皆以姬為紺珠。又嘗代余書小楷扇，存戚友處，而荊人米鹽瑣細，以及內外出入，無不各登手記；毫髮無遺。其細心專力，即吾輩好學人鮮及也。

姬於吳門曾學畫未成，能作小叢寒樹，筆墨楚楚，時於几硯上輒自圖寫，故於古今繪事，別有殊好。偶得長卷小軸與笥中舊珍，時時展玩不置。流離時，寧委奩具，而以書畫捆載自隨。末後盡裁裝潢，獨存紙絹，猶不得免焉，則書畫之厄，而姬之嗜好，真且至矣！

三

姬能飲，自入吾門，見余量不勝蕉葉，遂罷飲，每晚侍
荊人數杯而已。而嗜茶與余同性，又同嗜岕片。每歲半
塘顧子兼擇最精者緘寄，具有片甲蟬翼之異。文火細
煙，小鼎長泉，必手自吹滌。余每誦左思《嬌女詩》
"吹噓對鼎䥶"之句，姬為解頤。至"沸乳看蟹目魚
鱗，傳瓷選月魂雲魄"，尤為精絕。

　　每花前月下，靜試對嘗，碧沈香泛，真如木蘭沾
露，瑤草臨波，備極盧陸之致。東坡云："分無玉椀捧
峨眉。"余一生清福，九年占盡，九年折盡矣。

　　姬每與余靜坐香閣，細品名香。宮香諸品淫，沉
水香俗。俗人以沉香著火上，煙撲油膩，頃刻而滅。無
論香之性情未出，即著懷袖，皆帶焦腥。沉香堅緻而紋
橫者，謂之"橫隔沉"，即四種沉香內革沉橫紋者是
也，其香特妙。又有沉水結而未成，如小笠大菌，名
"蓬萊香"，余多蓄之。每慢火隔砂，使不見煙，則閣
中皆如風過伽楠、露沃薔薇、熱磨琥珀、酒傾犀斝之
味，久蒸衾枕間，和以肌香，甜艷非常，夢魂俱適。外
此則有真西洋香方，得之內府，迥非肆料。

　　丙戌客海陵，曾與姬手製百丸，誠閨中異品，然
爇時亦以不見煙為佳，非姬細心秀致，不能領略到此。

　　黃熟出諸番，而真臘為上，皮堅者為"黃熟
桶"，氣佳而通黑者為"隔棧黃熟"。近南粵東莞茶園
村，土人種黃熟，如江南之藝茶，樹矮枝繁，其香在
根。自吳門解人剔根切白，而香之鬆朽盡削，油尖鐵面
盡出。余與姬客半塘時，知金平叔最精於此。重價數購

之，塊者淨潤，長曲者如枝如虯，皆就其根之有結處，隨紋縷出。黃雲紫繡，半雜鷓鴣斑，可拭可玩。

寒夜小室，玉幃四垂，獸炭重疊，燒二尺許絳蠟二三枝，陳設參差，堂几錯列，大小數宣爐，宿火常熱，色如液金粟玉。細撥活灰一寸，灰上隔砂選香蒸之，歷半夜，一香凝然，不焦不竭，鬱勃氤氳，純是糖結。熱香間有梅英半舒，荷鵝梨蜜脾之氣，靜參鼻觀。憶年來共戀此味此境，恒打曉鐘，尚未著枕，與姬細想閨怨，有斜倚薰籃，撥盡寒爐之苦，我兩人如在藥珠眾香深處，今人與香氣俱散矣！安得返魂一粒，起於幽房扃室中也？

一種生黃香，亦從枯腫朽癭中取其脂凝脈結、嫩而未成者。余嘗過三吳白下，遍收筐箱中，蓋面大塊，與粵客自攜者，甚有大根株塵封如土，皆留意覓得，攜歸與姬為晨夕清課，督婢子手自剝落，或斤許僅得數錢，盈掌者僅削一片，嵌空鏤剔，纖悉不遺，無論焚蒸，即嗅之味如芳蘭，盛之小盤，層撞中色珠香別，可弄可餐。曩曾以一二示粵友黎美周，訝為何物，何從得如此精妙？即《蔚宗傳》中恐未見耳！

又東莞以女兒香為絕品，蓋土人揀香，皆用少女。女子先藏最佳大塊，暗易油粉，好事者復從油粉擔中易出。余曾得數塊於汪友處，姬最珍之。

余家及園亭，凡有隙地皆植梅，春來早夜出入，皆爛漫香雪中。姬於含蓄時，先相枝之橫斜與几上軍持相受，或隔歲便芟剪得宜，至花放恰採入供。即四時草花竹葉，無不經營絕慧，領略殊清，使冷韻幽香，恒霏微於曲房斗室。至穠豔肥紅，則非其所賞也。

秋來猶耽晚菊，即去秋病中，客貽我"剪桃紅"，花繁而厚，葉碧如染，濃條婀娜，枝枝具雲罨風斜之態。姬扶病三月，猶半梳洗，見之甚愛，遂留榻右。每晚高燒翠蠟，以白團迴六曲，圍三面，設小座於花間，位置菊影，極其參橫妙麗。始以身入，人在菊中，菊與人俱在影中。迴視屏上，顧余曰：“菊之意態盡矣！其如人瘦何？”至今思之，澹秀如畫。

閨中蓄春蘭九節，及建蘭。自春徂秋，皆有三湘七澤之韻，沐浴姬手，尤增芳香。《藝蘭十二月歌》，皆以碧箋手錄黏壁。去冬姬病，枯萎過半。樓下黃梅一株，每臘萬花，可供三月插戴。去冬姬移居香儷園靜攝，數百枚不生一蘗，惟聽五靄濤聲，增其淒響而已。

姬最愛月，每以身隨升沉為去住。夏納涼小苑，與幼兒誦唐人詠月及流螢紈扇詩，半榻小几，恒屢移以領月之四面。午夜歸閣，仍推窗延月於枕簟間，月去復捲幔倚窗而望。語余曰：“吾書謝希逸《月賦》，‘古人厭晨歡，樂宵宴’，蓋夜之時逸，月之氣靜，碧海青天，霜縞冰淨，較赤日紅塵，迥隔仙凡。人生攘攘，至夜不休，或有月未出已齁睡者，桂華露影，無福消受。與子長歷四序，娟秀浣潔，領略幽香，仙路禪關，於此靜得矣！”

李長吉詩云：“月漉漉，波煙玉”。姬每誦此三字，則反復迴環，日月之精神氣韻光景，盡於斯矣。人以身入波煙玉世界之下，眼如橫波，氣如湘煙，體如白玉，人如月矣！月復似人，是一是二，覺賈長江“倚影為三”之語尚贅，至“淫耽無厭化蟾”之句，則得酖月三昧矣。

姬性澹泊，於肥甘一無嗜好，每飯，以岕茶一小壺溫淘，佐以水菜、香豉數莖粒，便足一餐。余飲食最少，而嗜香甜及海錯風熏之味，又不甚自食，每喜與賓客共賞之。姬知余意，竭其美潔，出佐盤盂，種種不可悉記，隨手數則，可覘一斑也。

釀飴為露，和以鹽梅，凡有色香花藥，皆於初放時採漬之。經年香味顏色不變，紅鮮如摘，而花汁融液露中，入口噴鼻，奇香異豔，非復恒有。最嬌者為秋海棠露。海棠無香，此獨露凝香發。又俗名斷腸草，以為不食，而味美獨冠諸花。次則梅英、野薔薇、玫瑰、丹桂、甘菊之屬。至橙黃、橘紅、佛手、香櫞，去白縷絲，色味更勝。酒後出數十種，五色浮動白瓷中，解酲消渴，金莖仙掌，難與爭衡也。取五月桃汁、西瓜汁，一攘一絲漉盡，以文火煎至七八分，始攪糖細煉。桃膏，如大紅琥珀；瓜膏，可比金絲內糖。

每酷暑，姬必手取示潔，坐爐邊，靜看火候成膏，不使焦枯，分濃淡為數種，此尤異色異味也。

製豉，取色取氣，先於取味。豆黃九曬九洗為度，顆瓣皆剝去衣膜，種種細料，瓜杏薑桂，以及釀豉之汁，極精潔以和之。豉熟擎出，粒粒可數，而香氣醋色殊味，迥與常別。

紅乳腐烘蒸各五六次，內肉既酥，然後剝其膚，益之以味，數日成者，絕勝建寧三年之蓄。他如冬春水鹽諸菜，能使黃者如蠟，碧者如菭。蒲藕筍蕨、鮮花野菜、枸蒿蓉菊之類，無不采入食品，芳旨盈席。

火肉久者無油，有松柏之味。風魚久者如火肉，有麂鹿之味。醉蛤如桃花，醉鱘骨如白玉，油鯧如鱘魚，蝦鬆如龍鬚，烘兔酥雉如餅餌，可以籠而食之。菌脯如雞塅，腐湯牛乳。細攷之食譜，四方郇廚中一種偶異，即加訪求，而又以慧巧變化為之，莫不異妙。

四

甲申三月十九日之變，余邑清和望後，始聞的耗。邑之司命者甚懦，豺虎猙獰踞城內，聲言焚劫。郡中又有興平兵四潰之警。同里紳衿大戶，一時鳥獸駭散，咸去江南。余家集賢里，世恂讓，家君以不出門自固。

閱數日，上下三十餘家，僅我竈有炊煙耳。老母、荊人懼，暫避郭外，留姬侍余。姬扃內室，經紀衣物、書畫、文券，各分精粗，散付諸僕婢，皆手書封識。群橫日劫，殺人如草，而鄰右人影落落如晨星，勢難獨立，只得覓小舟，奉兩親，挈家累，欲衝險從南江渡澄江北。一黑夜六十里，抵泛湖州朱宅。

江上已盜賊蜂起，先從間道微服送家君從靖江行，夜半，家君向余曰：「途行需碎金，無從辦。」余向姬索之，姬出一布囊，自分許至錢許，每十兩，可數百小塊，皆小書輕重於其上，以便倉卒隨手取用。家君見之，訝且歎，謂姬何暇精細及此！

維時諸費較平日溢十倍，尚不肯行，又遲一日，以百金雇十舟，百餘金募二百人護舟。

甫行數里，潮落舟膠，不得上。遙望江口，大盜數百人，踞六舟為犄角。守隘以俟，幸潮落不能下逼我舟。朱宅遣有力人，負浪踏水馳報曰：「後岸盜截歸路，不可返，護舟二百人中且多盜黨。」時十舟哄動，僕從呼號垂涕。余笑指江上眾人曰：「余三世百口咸在舟。自先祖及余祖孫父子，六七十年來，居官居里，從無負心負人之事，若今日盡死盜手，葬魚腹，是上無蒼蒼，下無茫茫矣！潮忽早落，彼此舟停不相值，便是天相。爾輩無恐，即舟中敵國，不能為我害也。”

先夜拾行李登舟時，思大江連海，老母幼子，從未履此奇險，萬一阻石尤，欲隨路登岸，何從覓輿輛？三鼓時以二十金付沈姓人，求雇二輿一車、夫六人。沈與眾咸詫異笑之，謂“明早一帆，未午便登彼岸，何故黑夜多此難尋無益之資？”倩榜人募輿夫，觀者絕倒。

余必欲此二者，登舟始行，至斯時雖神氣自若，然進退維谷，無從飛脫，因詢出江未遠，果有別口登岸通泛湖洲者？舟子曰：“橫去半里，有小路六七里，竟通彼。”余急命鼓枻至岸，所募輿車三事，恰受俯仰七人。余行李婢婦，盡棄舟中。頃刻抵朱宅，眾始歎余之夜半必欲水陸兼備之為奇中也！

大盜知余中遁，又朱宅聯絡數百人，為余護發行李人口，盜雖散去，而未厭其志，恃江上法網不到，且值無法之時，明集數百人，遣人諭余以千金相致，否則竟圍朱宅，四面舉火。余復笑答曰：“盜愚甚，爾不能截我於中流，乃欲從平陸數百家中火攻之，安可得哉？”

然泛湖洲人，名雖相衛，亦多不軌。余傾囊召閭莊人付之，令其夜設牲酒，齊心於莊外備不虞。數百人飲酒分金，咸去他所，余即於是夜，一手扶老母，一手曳荊人，兩兒又小，季甫生旬日，同其母付一信僕偕行，從莊後竹園深箐中蹣跚出，維時更無能手援姬。余回顧姬曰：“汝速蹴步，則尾余後，遲不及矣！”姬一人顛連趨蹶，仆行里許，始仍得昨所僱輿輛，星馳至五鼓，達城下，盜與朱宅之不軌者，未知余全家已去其地也。

然身脫而行囊大半散矣，姬之珍愛盡失焉！姬返舍謂余：當大難時，首急老母，次急荊人、兒子、幼弟為是。彼即顛連不及，死深箐中無憾也。

午節返吾廬，衽金革與城內梟獍為伍者十旬，至中秋，始渡江入南都。別姬五閱月，殘臘乃回，挈家隨家君之督漕任。去江南，嗣寄居鹽官。因歎姬明大義，達權變如此，讀破萬卷者有是哉？

　　乙酉流寓鹽官，五月復值崩陷，余骨肉不過八口，去夏江上之累，緣僕婦雜沓犇赴，動至百口，又以笨重行李，四塞舟車，故不能輕身去。且來窺矙，此番決計置生死於度外，局戶不他之。乃鹽官城中，自相殘殺，甚鬨。兩親又不能安，復移郭外大白居。余獨令姬率婢婦守寓，不發一人一物出城，以貽身累。即侍兩親、挈妻子流離，亦以子身往。乃事不如意，家人行李紛沓，違命而出。

　　大兵迫檇李，薙髮之令初下，人心益皇皇。家君復先去惹山，內外莫知所措。余因與姬決：“此番潰散，不似家園，尚有左右之者，而孤身累重，與其臨難捨子，不若先為之地。我有年友，信義多才，以子託之，此後如復相見，當結平生歡，否則聽子自裁，毋以我為念。”

　　姬曰：“君言善。舉室皆倚君為命，復命不自君出，君堂上膝下，有百倍重於我者，乃以我牽君之臆，非徒無益而又害之。我隨君友去，苟可自全，誓當匍匐以俟君回；脫有不測，前與君縱觀大海，狂瀾萬頃，是吾葬身處也！”

　　方命之行，而兩親以余獨割姬為憾，復攜之去。自此百日，皆輾轉深林僻路、茅屋漁艇。或一月徙，或一日徙，或一日數徙，饑寒風雨，苦不具述，卒於馬鞍山遇大兵，殺掠奇慘，天幸得一小舟，八口飛渡，骨肉得全，而姬之驚悸瘁瘏，至矣盡矣！

五

秦谿蒙難之後，僅以俯仰八口免，維時僕婢殺掠者幾二十口，生平所蓄玩物及衣貝，靡子遺矣。亂稍定，匍匐入城，告急於諸友，即襆被不辦。

夜假蔭於方坦庵年伯。方亦竄跡初回，僅得一氈，與三兄共裹臥耳房。時當殘秋，窗風四射。翌日，各乞斗米束薪於諸家，始暫迎二親及家累返舊寓，余則感寒，痢瘧沓作矣。橫白板扉為榻，去地尺許，積數破絮為衛，爐煨桑節，藥缺攻補。且亂阻吳門，又傳聞家難劇起，自重九後潰亂沈迷，迄冬至前僵死，一夜復甦，始得間關破舟，從骨林肉莽中，冒險渡江。猶不敢竟歸家園，暫棲海陵。閱冬春百五十日，病方稍瘥。

此百五十日，姬僅捲一破席，橫陳榻邊，寒則擁抱，熱則披佛，痛則撫摩。或枕其身，或衛其足，或欠伸起伏，為之左右翼。凡病骨之所適，皆以身就之。鹿鹿永夜，無形無聲，皆存視聽。湯藥手口交進，下至糞穢，皆接以目鼻，細察色味，以為憂喜。日食粗糲一餐，與籲天稽首外，惟跪立我前，溫慰曲說，以求我之破顏。

余病失常性，時發暴怒，詬誶三至，色不少忤，越五月如一日。每見姬星靨如蠟，弱骨如柴，吾母太恭人及荊妻憐之感之，願代假一息。姬曰：“竭我心力，以殉夫子。夫子生而余死猶生也；脫夫子不測，余留此身於兵燹間，將安寄託？”

更憶病劇時，長夜不寐，莽風飄瓦，鹽官城中，日殺數十百人。夜半鬼聲啾嘯，來我破窗前，如蛩如箭。舉室饑寒之人,皆辛苦齁睡,余背貼姬心而坐,姬以手固握余手,傾耳靜聽,淒激荒慘,欷歔流涕。姬謂余曰:"我入君門整四歲,早夜見君所為,慷慨多風義,毫髮幾微,不鄰薄惡,凡君受過之處,惟余知之亮之,敬君之心,實踰於愛君之身,鬼神讚歎畏避之身也!冥漠有知,定加默祐。但人生身當此境,奇慘異險,動靜備歷,苟非金石,鮮不銷亡!異日幸生還,當與君敝屣萬有,逍遙物外,慎毋忘此際此語!"噫吁嘻!余何以報姬於此生哉!姬斷斷非人世凡女子也。

丁亥,讒口鑠金,太行千盤,橫起人面,余胸填五嶽,長夏鬱蟠,惟早夜焚二紙告關帝君。久抱奇疾,血下數斗,腸胃中積如石之塊,以千計。驟寒驟熱,片時數千語,皆首尾無端,或數晝夜不知醒。醫者妄投以補,病益篤,勺水不入口者二十餘日,此番莫不謂其必死,余心則炯炯然,蓋於之病不從境入也。

姬當大火鑠金時,不揮汗,不驅蚊,晝夜坐藥爐旁,密伺余於枕邊足畔六十晝夜,凡我意之所及,與意之所未及,咸先後之。

己丑秋,疽發於背,復如是百日。余五年危疾者三,而所逢者皆死疾,惟余以不死待之。微姬力,恐未必能堅以不死也。今姬先我死,而永訣時惟慮以伊死,增余病,又慮余病無伊以相待也,姬之生死為余纏綿如此,痛哉痛哉!

余每歲元旦,必以一歲事卜一籤於關帝君前。壬午名心甚劇,禱看籤首第一字,得"憶"字,蓋"憶昔蘭房半分釵,如今忽把音信乖。癡心指望成連理,到底誰知事不諧"。余時占玩不解,即占全詞,亦非功名語。

比遇姬,清和晦日,金山別去,姬茹素歸,虔卜於虎嘷關帝君前,願以終身事余,正得此籤。秋過秦淮,述以相告,恐有不諧之歎,余聞而訝之,謂與元旦籤合。時友人在座,曰:"我當為爾二人,合卜於西華門。"則仍此籤也。姬愈疑懼，且慮余見此籤中解，憂形於面，乃後卒滿其願。"蘭房"、"半釵"、"癡心"、"連理"，皆天然閨閣中語，"到底"、"不諧"，則今日驗矣。嗟乎！余有生之年，皆長相憶之年也。"憶"字之奇，呈驗若此！

姬之衣飾，盡失於患難，歸來澹足，不置一物。戊子七夕，看天上流霞，忽欲以黃跳脫摹之，命余書"乞巧"二字，無以屬對，姬云："曩於黃山巨室，見覆祥雲真宣爐，款式佳絕，請以'覆祥'對'乞巧'。"鐫摹頗妙。越一歲，釧忽中斷，復為之，恰七月也，余易書"比翼"、"連理"。

姬臨終前，自頂至踵，不用一金珠紈綺，獨跳脫不去手，以余勒書故。長生私語，乃太真死後，憑洪都客寄明皇者，當日何以率書，竟令《長恨》再譜也！

姬書法秀媚，學鐘太傅稍瘦，後又學《曹娥》。余每有丹黃，必對泓穎，或靜夜焚香，細細手錄。閨中詩史成帙，皆遺跡也。小有吟詠，多不自存。客歲新春二日，即為余鈔寫《全唐五七言絕句》，上下二卷，是日偶讀七歲女子"所嗟人異雁，不作一行歸"之句，為之淒然下淚，至夜和成八絕，哀聲怨響，不堪卒讀。余挑燈一見，大為不懌，即奪之焚去，遂失其稿。傷哉異哉！今歲恰以是日長逝也。

客春三月，欲重去鹽官，訪患難相恤諸友。至邗上，為同社所淹。時余正四十，諸名流咸為賦詩，龔奉常獨譜姬始末，成數千言，《帝京篇》、《連昌篇》不足比擬。奉常云："子不自註，則余苦心不見。如'桃花瘦盡春醒面'七字，綰合已卯醉晤、壬午病晤兩番光景，誰則知者？"余時應之，未即下筆。

他如園次之"自昔文人稱孝子，果然名士悅傾城"、于皇之"大婦同行小婦隨"、孝威之"人在樹間殊有意，婦來花下卻能文"、心甫之"珊瑚架筆香印屑，著富名山金屋尊"、仙期之"錦瑟峨眉隨分老，芙蓉園上萬花紅"、仲謀之"君今四十能高舉，羨爾鴻妻佐春杵"、吾邑徂徠先生"韜藏經濟一巢樸，游戲鶯花兩閣和"、元旦之"峨眉問難佐書幃"，皆為余慶得姬。詎謂我侑卮之辭，乃姬誓墓之狀耶？讀余此雜述，當知諸公之詩之妙，而去春不註奉常詩，蓋至遲之今日，當以血淚和隃糜也。

三月之杪，余復移寓友沂"友雲軒"。久客臥雨，懷家正劇。晚霽，龔奉常偕于皇、園次過慰留飲，聽小奚管弦度曲。時余歸思更切，因限韻各作詩四首。不知何故，詩中咸有商音。三鼓別去，余甫著枕，便夢還家，舉室皆見，獨不見姬。急詢荊人，不答。復遍覓之，但見荊人背余淚下。余夢中大呼曰："豈死耶？"一慟而醒。姬每春必報病，余深疑慮。

旋歸，則姬則固無恙，因間述此相告。姬曰："甚異！前亦於是夜夢數人強余去，匿之幸脫，其人尚猖猖不休也。"詎知夢真而詩讖咸來先告哉？

1. Statue of Mao Xiang in the "Painted-in-Water Garden".
Formerly, the Mao family's private garden, this is now the largest
public garden in the county-level city of Rugao.

冒巢民先生

Romance of a Literatus and his Concubine   113

2. The "Painted-in-Water Garden", Rugao.

3. Jixian Lane (Mao Family Lane).
Location of the Mao family's principal residence.

Romance of a Literatus and his Concubine   114

4. Jiangnan Gongyuan in the Qinhuai area of Nanjing,
the largest examination hall in late imperial China.
Here Mao Xiang five times sat the triennial provincial examinations.

5. Taizhou Examination Hall.
Here Mao Xiang sat the annual post-*Xiucai* examination.

Romance of a Literatus and his Concubine   115

6. The Peach-leaf Pier on the Qinhuai River in Nanjing.
Here visitors travelling by water to the Qinhuai Pleasure Quarters
in Ming-Qing times disembarked from their boats.

7. Bantang in Suzhou.
Dong Xiaowan lived in one of the waterfront houses here
from 1636-42.

8. Beigu Hill in Zhenjiang.
Here Dong Xiaowan in 1642 declared her determination
to join Mao Xiang on her way to see him off to Rugao.

9. Golden Hill in Zhenjiang.
Here Mao Xiang and Dong Xiaowan were followed
by crowds of sightseers, who called the couple a pair of immortals.

Romance of a Literatus and his Concubine   118

10. Qinhuai in Nanjing. Before moving to Suzhou in 1636,
Dong Xiaowan served in this area as a singing-girl.

11. Tiger Hill in Suzhou. Here, Qian Qianyi,
in late 1642, after holding a farewell party for Dong Xiaowan,
hired a boat to transport her to Rugao to join Mao Xiang.

12. Portrait of Dong Xiaowan
at the "Painted-in-Water Garden", Rugao.
Adapted from *Shanghai Daily*.

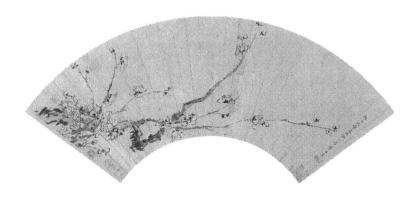

13. "Plum Blossom" by Dong Xiaowan.
Fan leaf, mounted and framed ink on paper.
15 x 46.2 cm. 5 7/8 x 18 1/8 in.
Inscribed and signed.
With two seals of Dong Xiaowan and two collector's seals.
Courtesy and © 2014 Christie's Image Limited.

14. "Plum Blossom" by Dong Xiaowan.
Ink on paper, hanging scroll.
39.3 by 78.7 cm. 15 1/2 by 31 in.
With one seal of Dong Xiaowan and one collector's seal.
Courtesy, Sotheby's, New York.

Romance of a Literatus and his Concubine   121

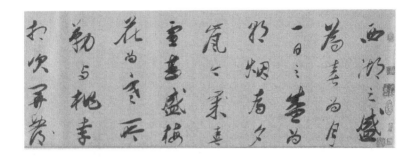

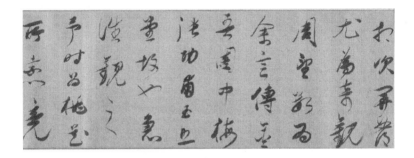

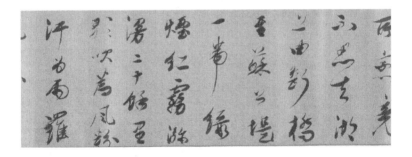

15. "Waiting for the Moon at Six Bridges" by Mao Xiang.
Handscroll, ink on satin.
36 x 555 cm. 14 1/4 x 218 1/2 in.
The seven seals at the beginning of the scroll are unidentified.
Photographed in six sections.
Above, reading from right to left, sections 1-3.
Courtesy, Allen Memorial Art Museum, Oberlin College, Ohio,
General Acquisitions Fund.

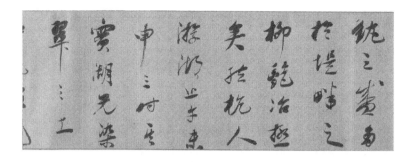

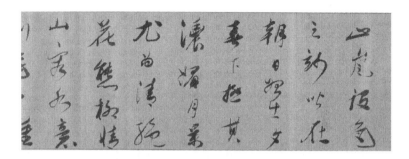

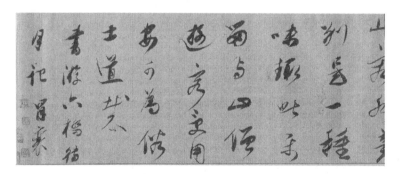

16. "Waiting for the Moon at Six Bridges" by Mao Xiang.
Handscroll, ink on satin.
36 x 555 cm. 14 1/4 x 218 1/2 in.
Of the five seals at the end of the scroll, one is of Mao Xiang
("Pijiang"), one of Wang Luben (1897-1930), and three, unidentified.
Photographed in six sections.
Above, reading from right to left, sections 4-6.
*Courtesy, Allen Memorial Art Museum, Oberlin College, Ohio,
General Acquisitions Fund.*

Romance of a Literatus and his Concubine   123

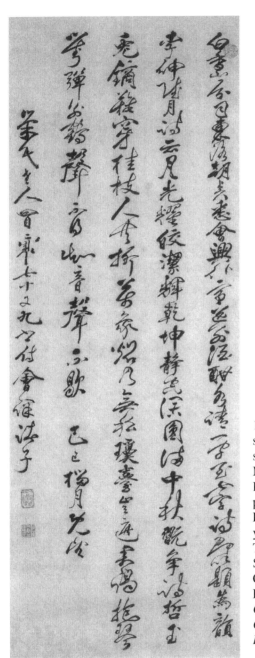

17. Poem in cursive
script calligraphy,
signed Chaomin Laoren
Mao Xiang.
Hanging scroll, ink on
paper. 46 5/8 x 173/8in.
Dated fifth month of *Jisi*
year (1689).
Three seals of the artist:
Susunfuzi Sanxiulinxia,
Chaomin Mao Xiang
Pijiang, Shuihuian.
Courtesy and © 2001
Christie's Image
Limited.

Romance of a Literatus and his Concubine

18. "Bird and Flowers" by Mao Xiang and Cai Han, Dong Xiaowan and Jin Yue (three of Mao Xiang's concubines). Hanging scroll, ink and colour on paper. 37 1/3 x 16in. Inscribed and signed by Mao Xiang, with three seals. Cai Han painted the bird, with two seals. Dong Xiaowan painted the narcissus and rock, with one seal. Jin Yue painted camellia and *lingzhi*, with one seal. Dated the 22nd day, twelfth month of *Jiyou* year (13 January 1670). Two collectors' seals. (As Dong Xiaowan died in 1651, perhaps Jin and Cai painted on an unfinished old painting by Dong.) *Courtesy and © 1999 Christie's Image Limited.*

19. Portraits of Dong Xiaowan and Mao Xiang,
at the Dequan Hall Painted-in-Water Garden, Rugao
Adapted from China Tour Advisor website.

20. Paper-cut portraits of Dong Xiaowan and Mao Xiang,
at gift shop, Painted-in-Water Garden, Rugao
Adapted from China Tour Advisor website.

Notes on illustrations with translations

13. The colophon reads, "This painting is modelled on the similar paintings of Wang Yuanzhang. I am not sure if it succeeds in imitating Master Wang's?" (The reference is to the famous late Yuan-early Ming painter Wang Mian, 1287-1359.)

14. Translation and note by Lifang He of Dong's plum blossom poem.

"My home disappeared when I looked down at it from the top of the Solitary Hill,
I am determined to cease to be an understanding belle.
The hermit scholar and the beauty cry for the same reason,
I regret that my singing-girl's career has wasted my life."

The poem was composed by Dong during the 1639-41 period when she was accompanying Qian Qianyi and Liu Rushi on a tour to the Yellow Mountain and West Lake. The Solitary Hill is the highest place in the West Lake region in Hangzhou. "I am determined to cease to be an understanding belle" means that Dong had made up her mind to end her courtesan career. The hermit scholar refers to Mao Xiang who made a good impression on her after their first encounter in 1639.

15 and 16.
The following note is based on the description found on the Oberlin College, Ohio, website,
http://www2.oberlin.edu/amam/Maoxiang.htm
Allen Memorial Art Museum.

The text of the calligraphy, inscribed, "Waiting for the Moon at Six Bridges" by Mao Xiang, is a well-known vignette from a travelogue by the late Ming poet and essayist, Yuan Hongdao (1568-1610). The essay recounts one of Yuan's visits to West Lake near the city of Hangzhou.

The Chinese text of this essay is reprinted in *Lidai xiaoshuo bijixuan, Ming ce diyi* (Taipei, 1965), p. 133.

It has been translated in Richard E. Strassberg, *Inscribed Landscapes: Travel Writing from Imperial China* (Berkeley, 1994), pp. 310-312. Another translation is included in Chou Ju-hsi, "From Mao Hsiang's Oberlin Scroll to his Relationship with Tung Ch'i-ch'ang," *Allen Memorial Art Museum Bulletin* 36, no. 2 (1978-79), pp. 141.

The following translation, also from the Oberlin College, Ohio, website, is by C. Mason, with reference to Strassberg and Chou.

"West Lake is best in springtime under moonlight; within a single day, it is best in the morning mists and evening vapors. This year the spring snow was abundant indeed, and the plum blossoms, retarded by the cold, were followed closely by the peach and pear blossoms. When one went out it was really a marvelous sight. Zhouwang [Tao Wangling] told me several times: 'The plum trees in the Jinwu Garden once belonged to Zhang Gongfu's concubine, Glistening Jade. You should hurry there to view them.' But at the time I was besotted by the peach blossoms and could not bear to take myself away. Out around the lake, from the Severed Bridge to the Su Dike, it was like a band of green mists and pink haze spread out for more than twenty li. Songs and shouts carried on the wind, and rouged perspiration fell like rain. So abundant were the gauze and silk [robed people] that they were more numerous than the willows on the shores. What an utterly beautiful scene! The people of Hangzhou only visit the lake during the midday hours. But in fact, the delicacy of the lake's light when it is tinted with azure, and its loveliness when the mountain mists are infused with colors, are both at their most bewitching when the morning sun is just rising and when dusk is just falling. Moonlight scenes are even more ethereal. The appearance of the flowers, the aura of the willows, the visage of the mountains, the sentiment of the water--each of these has a separate charm. These joys will remain to mountain priests and experienced wanderers – how could they be communicated to vulgar people?"

C. Mason

17: Note by Jun Fang. In this calligraphy, Mao Xiang copied a famous moon-themed poem composed by the Tang poet Li Shen (772-846) in 829 at a drinking party bidding adieu to the renowned poet Bai Juyi (772-846) who was leaving Chang'an for Luoyang to assume the post of Advisor to the Heir Apparent. The 78-year old Mao reproduced Li's verse on the fifteenth day of the fifth month of the year of *Yisi* (1 July, 1689) for a group of young scholars who were about to take the provincial examination.

18. Note by Jun Fang and translation of the colophon reads:

"On the twenty-second day of the twelfth month of the year of *Jiyou*, my concubines and I went drinking at the Painted-in-Water Garden. After enjoying ourselves we decided to draw a painting together, and I was asked to inscribe a few words to complete the work. Chaomin Mao Xiang."

Note: The twenty-second day of the twelfth month of the *Jiyou* year in this painting was 13 January, 1670.

APPENDIX 1. MAJOR EPOCHS OF CHINESE HISTORY

c. 2070-1600 BCE	Xia
c. 1600-1500 BCE	Shang
c. 1050-256 BCE	Zhou
	Western Zhou (1050-771 BCE)
	Eastern Zhou (c. 771-256 BCE)
221-206 BCE	Qin
206 BCE-220 CE	Han
	Western Han (206 BCE-9 CE)
	Xin (9-25 CE)
	Eastern Han (25-220 CE)
220-265	Three Kingdoms
	Wei (220-265)
	Shu (221-263)
	Wu (222-280)
265-420	Jin
	Western Jin (265-316)
	Eastern Jin (317-420)
420-589	North-South Dynasties
581-618	Sui
618-907	Tang
907-960	Five Dynasties and Ten Kingdoms
960-1279	Song
	Northern Song (960-1127)
	Southern Song (1127-1279)
	Laio (907-1125)
	Western Xia (1038-1227)
	Jin (1115-1234)
1279-1368	Yuan
1368-1644	Ming
1644-1912	Qing
1912-1949	Republican Period
1949-Present	People's Republic Period

APPENDIX 2. TABLE OF MING EMPERORS AND THEIR REIGNS

Reign Name	Duration	Personal Name	Temple Name
Hongwu	1368-1398	Zhu Yuanzhang	Taizu
Jianwen	1399-1402	Zhu Yunwen	Huizong
Yongle	1403-1424	Zhu Di	Taizong
Hongxi	1425	Zhu Gaozhi	Renzong
Xuande	1426-1435	Zhu Zhanji	Xuanzong
Zhengtong	1436-1449	Zhu Qizhen	Yingzon
Jingtai	1450-1456	Zhu Qiyu	Daizong
Tianshun	1457-1464	Zhu Qizhen (again)	Yingzong
Chenghua	1465-1487	Zhu Jianshen	Xianzong
Hongzhi	1488-1505	Zhu Youtang	Xiaozong
Zhengde	1506-1521	Zhu Houzhao	Wuzong
Jiajing	1522-1566	Zhu Houcong	Shizong
Longqing	1567-1572	Zhu Zaihou	Muzong
Wanli	1573-1620	Zhu Yijun	Shenzong
Taichang	1620	Zhu Changluo	Guangzong
Tianqi	1621-1627	Zhu Youjiao	Xizong
Chongzhen	1628-1644	Zhu Youjian	Sizong

APPENDIX 3. MING WEIGHTS AND MEASURES

	Chinese Unit	English Unit	Metric Unit
Area	1 *mu*	0.14 acre	5.803 acre
	1 *qing*	100 *mu*	5.803 hectares
Capacity	1 *sheng*	0.99 quart	1.0737 liters
	1 *dou* = 10 *sheng*	9.9 quart	10.737 liters
	1 *dan* = 10 *dou*	99 quarts	107.37 liters
Length	1 *chi* = 10 *cun*	12.3 inches	31.1 cm
	1 *bu* = 5 *chi*	61.5 inches	1.555 meters
	1 *zhang* = 10 *chi*	123 inches	3.11 meters
	1 *li*	1/3 mile	559.8 meters
Weight	1 *liang*	1.3 ounces	37.3 grams
	1 *jin* (catty) = 16 *liang*	1.3 pounds	0.5968 kg

Money

  1 *liang* (tael) = 1/16 *jin* (of silver)
  1 *qian* (copper cash) = 0.1 *liang*
  1 *guan* (string of cash) = 1,000 cash

GLOSSARY

An Lushan 安祿山

Bai 白
Bo Hua 柏樺
Bai Juyi 白居易
Baimen 白門
Baiyue 白岳
Bantang 半塘
Baoqing 寶慶
Bayan 八艷
Bei Zhili 北直隸
Beigu 北固
Beijing 北京
Bi Fangji 畢方濟
Bi Jinliang 畢今梁
Bian Yujing 卞玉京
Bianyatang shiji 變雅堂詩集
Bianyatang wenji 變雅堂文集
Bingshu 丙戌
Bingxian yuji 兵燹餘集
Biyi lianli 比翼連理
Boming hongyan 薄命紅顏
Boxue hongci 博學鴻詞
Bu 步

Cai Han 蔡含
Cai Mengzhao 蔡孟昭
Cao E 曹娥
Cao Xu 曹旴
Cen Shen 岑參
Chang'an 長安
Changhen ge 長恨歌
Changji 長吉
Changjiang 長江
Changmen 閶門

Changshu 常熟
Changxing 長興
Changzhou 常州
Chaomin 巢民
Chaomin laoren 巢民老人
Chaomin shiji 巢民詩集
Chaomin wenji 巢民文集
Chayuan 茶園
Chen Bingyi 陳秉彝
Chen Fan 陳藩
Chen Jiru 陳繼儒
Chen Liang 陳梁
Chen Peizhi 陳裴之
Chen Shi 陳氏
Chen Shubao 陳叔寶
Chen Weisong 陳維崧
Chen Xi 陳喜
Chen Yuanyuan 陳圓圓
Chen Zhenhui 陳貞慧
Chen Zi'ang 陳子昂
Chengdu 成都
Chenghua 成化
Chengjiang 澄江
Chenji 陳姬
Chenshuixiang 沉水香
Chi 尺
Chicheng sahnren gao 赤城山人稿
Chongzhen 崇禎
Chuci 楚辭
Ci 詞
Congying 琮應

Dabai xiansheng 大白先生
Dabaiju 大白居

Dai Xun 戴洵
Dan 石
Daoguang 道光
Dasheng 大生
Dejing 德經
Dequantang gao 得全堂稿
Deng Hanyi 鄧漢儀
Dijing pian 帝京篇
Dinghai 丁亥
Dong Bai 董白
Dong Qianli 董千里
Dong Qichang 董其昌
Dong Shi 董氏
Dong Xiaowan 董小宛
Dongguan 東莞
Donglin qian liujunzi 東林前
六君子
Dongpo 東坡
Dongting 洞庭
Dou 斗
Du Fu 杜甫
Du Hong 杜紅
Du Jun 杜濬
Du Mu 杜牧
Du Shaoling Kuizhou shixuan
杜少陵夔州詩選
Du Shengyan 杜審言
Duanchangcao 斷腸草

Er huashi 二畫史
Er nüshi 二女史

Fan Pang 范滂
Fan Ye 范曄
Fang Gongqian 方拱乾
Fang Tan'an 方坦庵
Fang Yizhi 方以智
Fanhuzhou 泛湖洲
Fanxue xiaocao 泛雪小草

Fengdu 豐都
Fengchang 奉常
Fubang 副榜
Fuche 副車
Fujian 福建
Fulun guangji 扶輪廣集
Fulun xinji 扶輪新集
Fushe 復社
Fusheng liuji 浮生六記
Fuxiang yunzhen 覆祥雲真
Fuzimiao 夫子廟

Ganpu 澉浦
Gao Bing 高棅
Gao Jie 高傑
Gao Panlong 高攀龍
Gao Shi 高適
Gaozu Li Yuan 高祖李淵
Gezhan huangshu 隔棧黃熟
Gengchen 庚辰
Gong Dingzhi 龔鼎孳
Gongren 恭人
Gu 古
Gu Dazhang 顧大章
Gu Gao 顧杲
Gu Gongyan 顧公彥
Gu Mei 顧眉
Gu Qi 顧啟
Guan 貫
Guan Yu 關羽
Guandi 關帝
Guangfu 光福
Guangzong 光宗
Gucheng 固城
Guifei 貴妃
Guliang 穀梁
Guningta 古寧塔
Guo Liang 郭亮

Guoling ji 過嶺集
Guozijian 國子監

Hailing 海陵
Haiyan 海鹽
Han (dynasty) 漢（朝）
Han Hong 韓翃
Hanbi guyin 寒碧孤吟
Hanbilou 寒碧樓
Hangzhou 杭州
Hanxiuzhai 寒秀齋
Hao 號
Heng 衡（山）
Heng 恆（山）
Hengbo 橫波
Henggechen 橫隔沉
Hengyong 衡永
Hengyue 衡嶽
Hongdu 洪度
Hongdu ke 鴻都客
Hongmei 紅梅
Hongwu 洪武
Hongxi 洪熙
Hongzhi 弘治
Hou Fangyu 侯方域
Hou qijunzi 後七君子
Hou Xiyi 侯希逸
Hu Zhenheng 胡震亨
Hua 華（山）
Hua Xingyun 華行雲
Huaihai Weiyang yi junren 淮海維揚一俊人
Huaiyang 淮陽
Huaiyin ji 淮陰集
Huan 桓
Huang Chuanzu 黃傳祖
Huang Daozhou 黃道周
Huang Shang 黃裳

Huang Zhouxing 黃周興
Huang Zunsu 黃尊素
Huangcheng 皇城
Huanggang 黃岡
Huangshan 黃山
Huangshu 黃熟
Huarui 花蕊
Hubei 湖北
Huguan 滸關
Huguang 湖廣
Huichang 會昌
Huizong 惠宗
Huliu 虎瞭
Hunan 湖南
Huo Duliang 霍都梁
Huqiu 虎丘
Hushu 滸墅

Ji 姬
Ji Yinzhong 紀映鍾
Ji Yougong 計有功
Jia 賈
Jia Changjiang 賈長江
Jia Dao 賈島
Jiajing 嘉靖
Jiande 建德
Jiang Tan 蔣坦
Jiangbei 江北
Jiangdu 江都
Jiangnan 江南
Jiangsu 江蘇
Jiangxi 江西
Jiangyin 江陰
Jianning 建寧
Jianjun 監軍
Jiantaohong 剪桃紅
Jianwen 建文
Jiao 焦

Jiaofangsi 教坊司
Jiashan 嘉善
Jiashen 甲申
Jiasui 佳穗
Jiaxing 嘉興
Jichou 己丑
Jie 岕
Jiecha huichao 岕茶匯鈔
Jifu 季甫
Jimeiren mingshi 集美人名詩
Jin 斤
Jin (dynasty) 金（朝）
Jin (dynasty) 晉（朝）
Jin Pingshu 金平叔
Jin Yue 金玥
Jinchang 金閶
Jingjiang 靖江
Jingkang zaijan lu 靖康雜見錄
Jingtai 景泰
Jinlian 金蓮
Jinling 金陵
Jinshan 金山
Jinshi 進士
Jishi benmo 紀事本末
Jisi 己巳
Jixian 集賢
Jiyou 己酉
Juan 卷
Jueju 絕句
Junping 君平
Juren 舉人
Jushi 居士

Kai 楷
Kong Shangren 孔尚任
Kou Baimen 寇白門
Koukou 扣扣

Kunshan 崑山

Lan yan 蘭言
Lang Ying 郎瑛
Laozi 老子
Li 里
Li 隸
Li Bai 李白
Li Banghua 李邦華
Li Bao 利寶
Li Changji 李長吉
Li Dan 李旦
Li Gu 李固
Li He 李賀
Li Meizhou 黎美周
Li Qing 李清
Li Shangyin 李商隱
Li Shimin 李世民
Li Suiqiu 黎遂球
Li Xian 李顯
Li Xiangjun 李香君
Li Xianglan 李湘蘭
Li Yingsheng 李應升
Li Yu 李漁
Li Yuan 李淵
Li Yuandan 李元旦
Li Yunfei 利雲飛
Li Zhichun 李之椿
Li Zicheng 李自成
Li Zongkong 李宗孔
Liang Ji 梁冀
Lianchang gong 連昌宮
Liang 兩
Liangxi 梁溪
Lianyan 奩艷
Liao (dynasty) 遼（朝）
Ling 靈
Lingbao 靈寶

Lingchi 凌遲
Lingzhi 靈芝
Liu 劉
Liu 柳
Liu Bei 劉備
Liu Daxing 劉大行
Liu Jin 劉瑾
Liu Liuzhou shanshui wenping
柳柳州山水文評
Liu Lüding 劉履丁
Liu Rushi 柳如是
Liu Song 劉宋
Liu Wushuang 柳無雙
Liu Xu 劉昫
Liu Zongmin 劉宗敏
Liu Zongyuan 柳宗元
Liudu fangluan gongjie 留都
防亂公揭
*Liushi nian shiyou shiwen
tongren ji* 六十年師友詩文同
人集
Liuyao 柳腰
Longqing 隆慶
Longtan 龍潭
Lu Tong 盧仝
Lu Yu 陸羽
Lu Zhaolin 盧照鄰
Lü Zhaolong 呂兆龍
Luanjiang 鑾江
Lüchuang oucheng 綠窗偶成
Luo Binwang 駱賓王
Luoshen fu 洛神賦
Lüzhen 履貞
Luzhou 瀘州

Ma 馬
Magu 麻姑
Ma Shouzhen 馬守真
Ma'anshan 馬鞍山

Mao Bao 冒褒
Mao Danshu 冒丹書
Mao Guangsheng 冒廣生
Mao Heshu 冒禾書
Mao Lianquan 冒廉泉
Mao Luan 冒鸞
Mao Mengling 冒夢齡
Mao Pijiang quanji 冒辟疆全
集
Mao Shuyin 冒舒諲
Mao Qizong 冒起宗
Mao Xiang 冒襄
Mao Yan 冒兗
Mao Zheng 冒政
Maoting qiuse tu 茅亭秋色圖
Meigong 眉公
Meilou 眉樓
Meishan 煤山
Meng Chang 孟昶
Meng Haoran 孟浩然
Meng Sen 孟森
Mengjin 孟津
Mi Fu 米芾
Miao Changqi 繆昌期
Migong 糜公
Min 閩
Ming (dynasty) 明（朝）
Minghuang 明皇
Mingmo sigongzi 明末四公子
Mingzhai 明齋
Mizhi 密之
Mu 畝
Muzhai 牧齋
Muzong 穆宗

Nan Zhili 南直隸
Nanjiang 南江
Nanjing 南京

Nanning 南寧
Neicheng 內城
Ning'an 寧安
Ningxia 寧夏
Niulang 牛郎
Niushou 牛首
Nüerxiang 女兒香
Nüjiaoshu 女校書
Nüluo 女蘿

Ouyang Xiu 歐陽修

Peng Sunyi 彭孫怡
Penglaixiang 蓬萊香
Pinghui 品匯
Pijiang 辟疆
Piling 毘陵
Pu'an 朴庵
Puchao 樸巢
Puchao shixuan 樸巢詩選
Puchao shixuan xu 樸巢詩選序
Puchao wenxuan 樸巢文選

Qian 錢
Qian Qianyi 錢謙益
Qian Zeng 錢曾
Qiantang 錢塘
Qing (dynasty) 清（朝）
Qing 頃
Qinglian 青蓮
Qinglian ji 青蓮集
Qinhuai 秦淮
Qingruo 青若
Qinxi 秦溪
Qiqiao 乞巧
Qisheng dian 七聖殿
Qiudeng suoji 秋燈瑣記
Qixiu leigao 七修類稿

Qu Yuan 屈原
Quan Tang shihua 全唐詩話

Ranzhi ji 燃脂集
Re 惹
Renwu 壬午
Renzong 仁宗
Ronglu biao 戎輅表
Ruan Dacheng 阮大鋮
Rucheng 如城
Rugao 如皋
Rugao Moashi congshu 如皋冒氏叢書
Ruizong Li Dan 睿宗李旦
Rujiu 汝久
Runzhou 潤州

Sanshan 三山
Sha Jiuwan 沙九畹
Shandong anchasi fushi 山東按察司副使
Shang (dynasty) 商（朝）
Shang 上
Shanshui tu 山水圖
Shantang 山塘
Shao Qian 邵潛
Shaoling 少陵
Shaoyang 邵陽
Shazhali 沙吒利
Shen 沈
Shen Fu 沈復
Shen Nü 神女
Shen Quanqi 沈佺期
Sheng 升
Shengyuan 生員
Shenzong 神宗
Shi Kefa 史可法
Shi Siming 史思明

Shier Tangren 十二唐人
Shiyuan chuji 詩源初集
Shizong 世宗
Shoupi Tan Youxia Zhong Xing shiwenji 手批譚友夏鍾惺詩文集
Shu 蜀
Shuangcheng 雙成
Shuihui xiannü 水繪仙侶
Shuihui yuan 水繪園
Shuihuian shiji 水繪庵詩集
Shun 舜
Shunzhi 順治
Sichuan 四川
Sili 司李
Sima Xiangru 司馬相如
Sizong 思宗
Song 嵩（山）
Song (dynasty) 宋（朝）
Song Shiying 宋實穎
Song Yu 宋玉
Song Ziwen 宋之問
Songjiang 松江
Songshao 嵩少
Songshu 宋書
Su Dongpo 蘇東坡
Su Shi 蘇軾
Su Wenhan 蘇文韓
Su Yuanfang 蘇元芳
Sui (dynasty) 隋（朝）
Suzhou 蘇州

Tai 泰（山）
Taihang 太行
Taixing 泰興
Taizhou 台州
Taizhou 泰州
Taizu 太祖

Taizong 太宗
Tan Yuanchun 譚元春
Tan'an 坦庵
Tang (dynasty) 唐（朝）
Tangshi jishi benmo 唐詩紀事本末
Tangshi pinhui 唐詩品匯
Tangshu 唐書
Taoan mengyi 陶庵夢憶
Taoyedu 桃葉渡
Tian Hongyu 田弘遇
Tian Xiuying 田秀英
Tianfei 田妃
Tianqi 天啟
Tianshun 天順
Tong 桐
Tongcheng 桐城
Tonglu 桐盧
Tongren ji 同人集

Wang Bo 王勃
Wang Duo 王鐸
Wang Gui 王珪
Wang Jian 王建
Wang Maolin 汪懋麟
Wang Ruwei 汪汝為
Wang Shilu 王士祿
Wang Shizhen 王士禛
Wang Wei 王維
Wang Xianke 王仙客
Wang Xizhi 王羲之
Wangqie Dong Xiaowan aici 亡妾董小宛哀辭
Wanli 萬曆
Wei 魏
Wei Dazhong 魏大中
Wei Zhongxian 魏忠賢
Weitang 魏塘

Weizong 蔚宗
Wenjun 文君
Wenmin 文敏
Wu 吳
Wu Meilan 吳湄蘭
Wu Qi 吳綺 (Mao Xiang's friend)
Wu Qi 吳琪 (Cai Han's painting tutor)
Wu Sangui 吳三桂
Wu Yingji 吳應箕
Wu Zetian 武則天
Wu Zixu 伍子胥
Wuchang 武昌
Wujiang 吳江
Wumen 吳門
Wurui tu 午瑞圖
Wuxi 無錫
Wuxian 吳縣
Wuye 烏夜
Wuzhong 吳中
Wuzi 戊子
Wuzong 武宗

Xi Shi 西施
Xia (dynasty) 夏（朝）
Xia Meng 夏夢
Xia Yunyi 夏允彝
Xiangli 香酈
Xiangliyuan oucun 香酈園偶存
Xiangwanlou yiyu 香畹樓憶語
Xiangyang 襄陽
Xiangyi 湘逸
Xianke 仙客
Xianqi 仙期
Xianshi qianzheng lu 先世前徵錄
Xianzong 憲宗

Xiaokai 小楷
Xiaosheng 曉生
Xiaowan 小宛
Xiaowei 孝威
Xiaoyuan 孝轅
Xiaozhu 曉珠
Xiaozong 孝宗
Xie Kangle youshan shiping 謝康樂遊山詩評
Xie Lingyun 謝靈運
Xie Xiyi 謝希逸
Xie Zhuang 謝莊
Xihu 西湖
Xihuamen 西華門
Xin (dynasty) 新（朝）
Xin'an 新安
Xinfu 心甫
Xingping 興平
Xinsi 辛巳
Xishan 西山
Xiuning 休寧
Xiushui 秀水
Xiwangmu 西王母
Xiyi 希夷
Xizihu 西子湖
Xizong 熹宗
Xu Dingguo 許定國
Xu Jun 許俊
Xu Wenxuan 續文選
Xu Yuanwen 徐元文
Xu Zhi 許直
Xu Ziyun 徐紫雲
Xu Zhongjie 許忠傑
Xuande 宣德
Xuanlu gezhu 宣爐歌註
Xuanzong (Ming) 宣宗（明）
Xuanzong (Tang) 玄宗（唐）
Xue Tao 薛濤

Yamen 衙門
Yan Guang 嚴光
Yan Zhenqing 顏真卿
Yan Ziling 嚴子陵
Yandi 炎帝
Yang Guifei 楊貴妃
Yang Jiong 楊炯
Yang Lian 楊漣
Yang Taizhen 楊太真
Yang Yizhao 楊漪炤
Yang Youlong 楊友龍
Yang Yuhuan 楊玉環
Yanguan 鹽官
Yangxian 陽羨
Yangzhou 揚州
Yangzi 揚子
Yanling 嚴陵
Yanzi jian 燕子箋
Yanziji 燕子磯
Yao Quan 姚佺
Yao Xueyin 姚雪垠
Yi (opera) 弋
Yi 憶
Yiguang 夷光
Yimao 已卯
Yimin 遺民
Yingchun 櫻唇
Yingmeian yiyu 影梅庵憶語
Yingyuan 影園
Yingzong 英宗
Yishan 義山
Yiwu 義烏
Yixing 宜興
Yiyang 弋陽
Yiyou 已酉
Yiyu 憶語
Yiyuan yin 逸園吟
Yizheng 儀徵

Yokkaichi 四日市
Yongle 永樂
You Mao 尤袤
You Tong 尤侗
Youheng 有恆
Youyi 友沂
Yu 豫
Yu Huai 余懷
Yu Pingbo 俞平伯
Yuan (dynasty) 元（朝）
Yuan Huazhong 袁化中
Yuan Zhen 元稹
Yuanci 薗次
Yuanshi 院試
Yuantong 元同
Yuanyu 圓玉
Yue 粵
Yue 越
Yuefu 月賦
Yuhuang 俞皇
Yunjian 雲間
Yushan 虞山
Yuzhong 漁仲

Zhen Wanfen ba jueju 贈畹芬
八绝句
Zhang 張
Zhang 丈
Zhang Chao 張潮
Zhang Dai 張岱
Zhang Lihua 張麗華
Zhang Mingbi 張明弼
Zhang Qiling 張奇齡
Zhang Xianzhong 張獻忠
Zhangzhou 漳州
Zhao Kaixin 趙開心
Zhao Mengfu 趙孟頫
Zhao Youyi 趙友沂

Zheng Yuanxun 鄭元勳
Zhengde 正德
Zhengde shilu xiaozhuan 正德
實錄小傳
Zhengtong 正統
Zhenjiang 鎮江
Zhinü 織女
Zhiyu 芝隅
Zhong Yao 鍾繇
Zhongchun 仲醇
Zhongju 仲舉
Zhongmou 仲謀
Zhongshu sheren 中書舍人
Zhongzong Li Xian 中宗李顯
Zhou (dynasty) 周（朝）
Zhou Chaorui 周朝瑞
Zhou Qiyuan 周起元
Zhou Shizhang 周士章
Zhou Shoujuan 周瘦鵑
Zhou Shunchang 周順昌
Zhou Zongjian 周宗建
Zhouchang 粥廠
Zhu Changluo 朱常洛
Zhu Di 朱棣
Zhu Gaozhi 朱高熾
Zhu Houcong 朱厚熜
Zhu Houzhao 朱厚照
Zhu Jianmang 朱劍芒
Zhu Jianshen 朱見深

Zhu Qiyu 朱祁鈺
Zhu Qizhen 朱祁鎮
Zhu Shilin 朱石麟
Zhu Yijun 朱翊鈞
Zhu Youjian 朱由檢
Zhu Youjiao 朱由校
Zhu Youtang 朱祐樘
Zhu Yuanzhang 朱元璋
Zhu Yunwen 朱允炆
Zhu Zaihou 朱載垕
Zhu Zhanji 朱瞻基
Zhu Zhifan 朱之藩
Zhu Zhishan 祝枝山
Zhuangyuan 狀元
Zhuji 諸暨
Zhuo Wenjun 卓文君
Zhuocun 拙存
Zhuocuntang yigao 拙存堂逸
稿
Zong Yuanding 宗元鼎
Zongqi 宗起
Zuili 檇李
Zuo Guangdou 左光斗
Zuo Liangyu 左良玉
Zuo Si 左思
Zusunfuzi Sanxiulinxia 祖孫
父子三休林下

NOTES

Introduction

[1] Wang Limin, Ding Fusheng, and Gu Qi, *Mao Pijiang yu Dong Xiaowan*, pp. 1-3. For doubts about the Mao family's Mongolian origin, see Shao Zhiyu and Yang Lili, "Rugao Maoshi de laiyuan," pp. 92-95.

[2] Timothy Brook, Jerome Bourgon, and Gregory Blue, *Death by a Thousand Cuts*, p. 11.

[3] Zhang Tingyu, *Mingshi*, p. 4943; Mao Guangsheng, *Mao Chaomin xiansheng nianpu*, p. 3a.

[4] Mao Guangsheng, *Mao Chaomin xiansheng nianpu*, pp. 3a-4a.

[55] A tribute student in Ming times was a government student who had been admitted to either the Nanjing National University or Beijing National University for advanced study and subsequent admission to the civil service.

[6] Tributary students could hold minor office in the Ming.

[7] Mao Xiang, *Chaomin wenji*, p. 7.25a; Chen Weisong, *Huhailou wenji*, p. 6.18b.

[8] Mao Xiang, *Chaomin wenji*, pp. 3.12b-13a; Chen Weisong, *Jialing wenji*, p. 5.24b. A man with a keen interest in literary pursuits, Mengling is said to have published three works, i.e. *Bingxian yuji* (War-surviving works), *Dequantang gao* (Collected works from the Dequan Hall), and *Yiyuan yin* (Chantings from Yiyuan Garden). Apparently the books were no longer extant by the early twentieth century as they were not included in the *Rugao Maoshi congshu* (Collectanea of works by prominent members of the Mao family of Rugao) printed during the 1903-23 period.

[9] Chen Weisong, *Jialing wenji*, pp. 5.24a-30a; Chen Weisong, *Huhailou wenji*, pp. 6.18a-24b.

[10] The work was published in the Shunzhi era and was reprinted by Shanghai guji chubanshe in 2010.

[11] Mao Xiang, *Chaomin wenji*, p. 6.9b.

[12] Wang Bo was considered one of the "Four Eminences of the Early Tang." The other three were Luo Bingwang (ca. 619-684), Lu Zhaolin (ca. 634-684) and Yang Jiong (b. 650).

[13] Dong Qichang's preface to *Xiangliyuan oucun*, in Mao Xiang, ed., *Tongren ji*, p. 1.1b.

[14] For more on the county, prefectural and *yuan* examinations, see Ichisada Miyazaki, *China's Examination Hell*, pp. 18-32.

[15] Mao Guangsheng, *Mao Chaomin xiansheng nianpu*, 9b.

[16] For more on Chen Zhenhui, Fang Yizhi, and Hou Fangyu, see Peterson, *Bitter Gourd*; Des Forges, *Cultural Centrality and Political Change in Chinese History: Northeast Henan in the Fall of the Ming*, pp. 129-37; Luo Wanwei, *Hou Fangyu yanjiu*; Gao Yang, *Mingmo sigongzi*, pp. 11-62, 81-122; Wang Zhonghe, *Mingmo sigongzi*, pp. 45-74, 121-190.

[17] Mao Guangsheng, *Mao Chaomin xiansheng nianpu*, pp. 30a-31a.

[18] Jiang Yixue, *Zhang Pu nianpu*, pp. 62-129; William Atwell, "From Education to Politics: The Fu She," pp. 333-67; Harry Miller, *State versus Gentry in Late Ming Dynasty China*, pp. 139-63. Mao was not a major leader of the *Fushe*, *pace* Ding Fusheng, Wang LImin, and Gu Qi, "Fushe lingxiu Mao Xiang," pp. 65-70, although he may have provided liaison with the society's Jiangbei members.

[19] Gu Qi, *Mao Xiang yanjiu*, pp. 7, 45-46.

[20] Mao Xiang, *Yingmeian yiyu*, p. 108; Pan Tzy-yen, *The Reminiscences of Tung Hsiao-wan*, p. 120.

[21] A link between anti-Qing loyalist actions and earlier Ming recognition of those loyalists in examinations and government services can be seen clearly in the Ming-Qing transition. Jun Fang, "Literati Statecraft and Military Resistance: The Case of the Possibility Society (Jishe)," p. 102.

[22] Mao Xiang, *Tongren ji*, p. 10.58b; Han Tan, *Youhuaitang wengao*, p. 16.4b.

[23] Mao Guangsheng, *Mao Chaomin xiansheng nianpu*, p. 62b.

[24] Dong Bian, Tan Deshan, and Zeng Zi, *Mao Zedong he tade mishu Tian Jiaying*, p. 319; Wang Limin, Ding Fusheng, and Gu Qi, *Mao Pijiang yu Dong Xiaowan*, pp. 224-230.

[25] Mao Guangsheng, *Mao Chaomin xiansheng nianpu*, pp. 39a, 42a. Mao Danshu's *Hanbitang shiji* and *Furen ji bu* as well as Mao Heshu's *Zhenyantang shiji* were included in *Rugao Maoshi congshu*. *Furen ji bu* was reprinted in 1996 by Hebei jiaoyu chubanshe together with Chen Weisong's *Furen ji*.

[26] Han Tan, *Youhuaitang wengao*, p. 16.3a; Ruan Yuan, *Guangling shishi*, p. 31.

[27] Han Tan, *Youhuaitang wengao*, p. 16.3a.

[28] Mao Guangsheng, *"Puchao shixuan"* (Preface to *Puchao shixuan*).

[29] Additionally Mao compiled and edited poems and prose written by other eminent literary figures, such as *Xianshi qianzheng lu* (Selected writings from the past), *Du Shaoling Kuizhou shixuan* (Selected poems of Du Fu's Kuizhou poems), *Xie Kangle youshan shiping* (Xie Lingyun's mountain tour poems with critical remarks), *Liu Liuzhou shanshui wenping* (Liu Zongyuan's mountain and water prose with remarks), *Shoupi Tan Youxia Zhong Xing shiwenji* (Collection of poems and prose of Tan Yuanchun and Zhong Xing with handwritten comments). Han Tan, *Youhuaitang wengao*, p. 16.3b; Gu Qi, *Mao Xiang yanjiu*, p. 11.

[30] See Mao Lianquan, *Xuanan buxuan: Mao Pijiang zhu Hongloumeng qishisan zheng*; Shen Xinlin, "Hongloumeng yu Rugao," pp. 118-126.

[31] For the scale and performance of Mao's family troupe, see Wang Ranye, "Mao Xiang kunban yanju kao ji qita," pp. 89-91.

[32] *Dejing* is the last 44 chapters of Lao Zi's (d. 531) 81-chapter *Dao de jing*.

[33] Wang Limin, Ding Fusheng, and Gu Qi, *Mao Pijiang yu Dong Xiaowan*, p. 57.

[34] Mao Xiang, *Yingmeian yiyu*, p. 8. For the English translation of Rhapsody to the Goddess of Luo River (*Luoshen fu*), see Xiao Tong (& trans by David Knechtges), *Wen Xuan or Selections of Refined Literature*, Vol. 3, pp. 31-40.

[35] Mao Xiang, *Tongren ji*, p. 3.73b; Mao Shuyin, "Mao Pijiang qiren qishi jiqi shufa," p. 73. For more on Mao's calligraphy and his relationship with Dong Qichang, see Ju-hsi Chou, "From Mao Hsiang's Oberlin Scroll to His Relationship with Tung Ch'i-ch'ang," pp. 140-167.

[36] For more on Liu Rushi, see Kang-I Sun Chang, *The Late Ming Poet Chen Tzu-lung: Crises of Love and Loyalism*, pp. 19-37; Chen Yinke, *Liu Rushi biezhuan*.

[37] Zhou Lianggong, *Chidu xinchao*, p. 114.

[38] Mao Xiang, *Tongren ji*, p. 1.47a; Mao Guangsheng, *Mao Chaomin xiansheng nianpu*, p. 26a. For more on the Shadowy Garden poem competition, see Ōki, *Bō Jō Eibaian okugo no kenkyū*, pp. 45-67.

[39] Zhang was six years older than Mao Xiang's father, but he treated the younger Mao as a same-generation friend. His biography of Dong Xiaowan was translated and included in Pan Tzy-yen, *The Reminiscences of Tung Hsiao-wan*, pp. 133-56.

[40] On the friendship between Wang Shizhen and Mao Xiang, see Gu Qi, "Mao Xiang yu Wang Shizhen de jiaoyou," pp. 53-57.

[41] On the friendship between Li Qing and Mao Xiang, see Gu Qi, "Mao Xiang yu Li Qing de jiaowang" (Notes on the contact between Mao Xiang and Li Qing), in *Mao Xiang yanjiu*, pp. 39-47.

[42] On the friendship and contact between Mao Xiang and Yu Huai, see Gu Qi, "Mao Xiang Yu Huai jiaoyou kao" (Notes on the contact between Mao Xiang and Yu Huai), in *Mao Xiang yanjiu*, pp. 48-62; Ōki, "Mao Xiang and Yu Huai," pp. 242-248.

[43] The Early Six Gentlemen and the Later Seven Gentlemen were those Donglin scholars who were prosecuted to death by eunuch chief Wei Zhongxian during the Tianqi era. The six, who all died in prison in 1625 were Yang Lian (b. 1571), Zuo Guangdou (b. 1571), Wei Dazhong (b. 1575), Gu Dazhang (b. 1567), Zhou Chaorui, and Yuan Huazhong. The seven, who died in 1626-27, were Gao Panlong (1562-1626), Zhou Shunchang (1584-1626), Zhou Qiyuan (1571-1626), Miao Changqi (1562-1626), Li Yingsheng (1593-1626), Huang Zunsu (1584-1626), and Zhou Zongjian (1582-1627). The year of death of Zhou Zongjian is disputable. For more on the politics of that era, see John Dardess,

Blood and History in China: The Donglin Faction and Its Repression, 1620-1627, pp. 72-125.

[44] Lu Yongqiang, *Chen Weisong nianpu*, pp. 131-248.

[45] Zhang Chao, *Yuchu xinzhi*, p. 395; Chen Weisong, *Jialing ci quanji*, p. 26.3; You Tong, *Genzhai zashuo*, p. 101.

[46] Li Qing, preface to *Tongren ji*, p. 743.

[47] Hou failed the provincial examination in 1651 and was placed on a waiting list (*fubang*). Des Forges writes in his article, "Toward Another Tang or Zhou? Views from the Central Plain in the Shunzhi Reign" (p. 88), that Hou failed the Qing examinations on purpose. Xu Zhinong and Zhao Yuxia, collators of *Hou Chaozong wenxuan*, claim that Hou was initially recommended for first place in the 1651 examination but was eventually given a *fubang* status due to objections from some other examiners. See "Preface to *Hou Chaozong wenxuan*," p. 5.

[48] Although Mao did not like the Manchu conquerors, he gradually realized that the Qing rule in fact was not as bad as he had previously thought. So he gave up the idea of resisting the Manchu régime and in fact encouraged his sons to take the civil service examinations in the early Qing period.

[49] Mao Xiang, *Chaomin wenji*, pp. 7.25a-36b; Mao Guangsheng, *Mao Chaomin xiansheng nianpu*, pp. 5b, 11b, 14b, 56b.

[50] The English translation of *Wenxuan* was done by David R. Knechtges, and was published as *Wen Xuan or Selections of Refined Literature* by Princeton University Press in 1982, 1987, and 1996 in three volumes.

[51] Chen Weisong, *Jialing wenji*, p. 5.21a; Mao Xiang, *Tongren ji*, pp. 3.45a-47b.

[52] Chen Weisong, *Huhailou wenji*, p. 4.13; Mao Xiang, *Tongren ji*, pp. 3.48a-49b.

[53] Mao Guangsheng, *Mao Caomin xiansheng nianpu*, pp. 52b-53a.

[54] Mao Xiang, *Tongren ji*, pp. 12.70a.

[55] Wang Limin, Ding Fusheng, and Gu Qi, *Mao Pijiang yu Dong Xiaowan*, p. 196.

[56] For more on Cai Han's life and paintings, see Tang Shuyu, *Jintai huashi*, pp. 66-67; Yasushi Ōki, *Bō Jō Eibaian okugo no*

kenkyū, pp. 365-393; Xie Li, "Cai Han de shanshuitu shangxi," p. 43.

[57] Mao Xiang, *Tongren ji*, p. 12.75b; Ruan Yuan, *Guangling shishi*, p. 130. For this practice, see Mark Elvin, "Female Virtues and the State in China," pp. 118-123; Yu Genzhe, "Gegu fengqin yuanqi de shehui Beijing: Yi Tangdai wei zhongxin," pp. 87-95; Fang Yan, "Songdai nüxing gegu liaoqin wenti shixi," pp. 210-212.

[58] Li E, *Fanxie shanfang ji*, p. 7.3b.

[59] Mao Xiang, *Tongren ji*, pp. 7.79b-80b; Zhang Geng, *Guochao huazheng xulu*, p. 2.16a.

[60] Yasushi Ōki, "Mao Xiang and Yu Huai," p. 242, note 24.

[61] Marsha Weider, *Views from Jade Terrace: Chinese Women Artists, 1300-1912*, pp. 114-115.

[62] Han Tan, *Youhuaitang wengao*, p. 16.bb; Mao Guangsheng, *Mao Chaomin xiansheng nianpu*, pp. 54a-b, 56a.

[63] The other seven were Ma Xianglan (1548-1604), Gu Mei (Hengbo, b. 1619), Kou Baimen (b. 1624), Li Xiangjun (b. 1624), Bian Yujing (ca. 1603-65), Liu Rushi (1618-64), and Chen Yuanyuan (1623-1681).

[64] Her given name, Bai, was certainly given by her parents, but her courtesy names, Qinglian and Qinglian nushi, would have been her own choice.

[65] Wu Qi, *Lin Huitang ji*, p. 17.8a.

[66] Yu Huai, *Banqiao zaji*, p. 17.

[67] The same, p. 17.

[68] Mao Xiang, *Mao Pijiang quanji*, p. 1515.

[69] Mao Xiang, *Yingmeian yiyu*, p. 40.

[70] The same, p. 32.

[71] However, in his post-script of a poem Mao wrote for Li Zongkong (1620-89) in 1689, Mao writes that "Xiaowan left Nanjing for Suzhou when she was 13 *sui* and she lived in Bantang (of Suzhou) for six years." Mao Xiang, *Mao Pijiang quanji*, 1515; Meng Sen, "Dong Xiaowan kao," p. 172.

[72] Zhang Dai, *Tao'an mengyi*, p. 47.

[73] Mao Xiang, *Mao Pijiang quanji*, p. 1515.

[74] Yasushi Ōki writes in "Mao Xiang and Yu Huai" (p. 237) that Dong's "'employer' (the courtesan house) raised her 'ransom'".

In fact, Dong was working alone at her house in Suzhou managed by her "parents". The debts she owed were not the ransom demanded by her employer, but those she and her "parents" borrowed from various debtors as she ceased working after deciding to become Mao's concubine in the spring of 1642 and her "father" was notoriously extravagant with his numerous hobbies and reckless with money. See Mao Xiang, *Yingmeian yiyu*, p. 42; Zhang Mingbi, *Maoji Dong Xiaowan zhuan*, p. 3.

[75] Ray Huang, *Taxation and Governmental Finance in Sixteenth-Century Ming China*, p. 276.

[76] Sun Chengze, *Chunming mengyu lu*, p. 425. Qian's action was partly due to his generosity toward friends, but it was also related to his stunning ability to earn money by selling his essays and calligraphy: he was once commissioned in early Qing to compose three essays at a staggering rate of 1,000 silver taels. See Jie Zhao, *Brush, Seal and Abacus: Troubled Vitality in Late Ming China's Economic Heartland, 1500-1644*, p. 29.

[77] Mao Xiang, *Yingmeian yiyu*, p. 44.

[78] Meng Sen notes in his "Dong Xiaowan kao" that "this old man's romantic connection with beautiful women was indeed quite wide," p. 209.

[79] Qian was widely admired and followed by many talented young men in the late Ming. The chief reason obviously was his scholarly and artistic accomplishment, but his generosity towards others was certainly another factor. For more on Qian and his literary and historical achievements, see Lawrence Yim, *The Poet-Historian Qian Qianyi*; Kang-I Sun Chang, "Qian Qianyi and His Place in History," pp. 199-220; Pei Shijun, *Sihai zongmeng wushinian: Qian Qianyi zhuan*.

[80] Mao Xiang, *Yingmeian yiyu*, p. 68.

[81] Jin Sifen, *Banqiao zaji bu*, p. 165; Daria Berg, "Courtesan Editors: Sexual Politics in Early Modern China," p. 180.

[82] Berg identifies *Ranzhi ji* as a poetry collection in her article "Courtesan Editor," p. 185. This is not the case as the collection contains a variety of works written or edited by Chinese women before Wang's times. For the contents of *Ranzhi ji*, see Wang Shilu, *Ranzhi ji li*, pp. 1a-15a; He Qin, "Wang Shilu zhushu xinkao," p. 62.

[83] He Qin, "Wang Shilu zhushu xinkao," p. 62; Hu Wenkai, *Lidai funü zhuzuo kao*, p. 688.

[84] Ruan Yuan, *Guangling shishi*, p. 131. For the eleven poems written by Dong on a fan, see *Zhongguo meishu quanji*, p. 37; For a painting of Dong's, see Marsha Weider, *Views from Jade Terrace*, p. 98; For her poems, see Xu Shichang, *Wanqingyi shihui*, p. 8128; Gu Qi, "Dong Xiaowan he tade shi," pp. 87-91; Wu Dingzhong, *Dong Xiaowan huikao*, pp. 18-20.

[85] Daria Berg, *Women and the Literary World in Early Modern China, 1580-1700*, p. 155.

[86] Chen Weisong, *Furen ji*, pp. 3-4. Mao does not give Chen Yuanyuan's full name in *Yingmeian yiyu*; instead he addresses her as Chen Ji, meaning Lady Chen. She had a brief romantic encounter with Mao Xiang before she was kidnapped and taken to Beijing by the men of Tian Hongyu in 1642. After Tian's death in late 1643, she was brought to the house of the powerful general Wu Sangui (1612-78) as his concubine. When the Ming was overthrown by the Li Zicheng rebel forces, it was rumoured that she was taken by Li's right-hand man Liu Zongmin (d. 1645), and the kidnapping is considered by some historians as one of factors contributing to Wu's defection to the Qing. For more on the life of Chen, see Li Hanlin and Li Xinfu, *Chen Yuanyuan zhuan*; Chen Shengxi, "Chen Yuanyuan qiren qishi," pp. 120-137.

[87] For more on the *yiyu* writings of the Qing period, see Kang Zhengguo, "Daowang yu huiyi," pp. 353-384; Wai-yee Li, "Romantic Recollections of Women as Sources of Women's History," pp. 337-338.

[88] Shen Fu's memoir was translated into English as *Six Chapters of a Floating Life* (1935) by Lin Yutang, *Chapters from a Floating Life* (1960) by Shirley Black, *Six Records of a Floating Life* (1983) by Leonard Pratt and Chiang Su-hui, and *Six Records of a Life Adrift* (2011) by Graham Sanders.

[89] For more information on the earlier editions of *Yingmeian yiyu*, see Wei Ran, "*Yingmeian yiyu* banben yuanliu kao," pp. 27-31.

[90] Pan Tzy-yee, *Reminiscences of Tung Hsiao-wan*; Vallette-Hémery, *Mao Xiang: La dame aux pruniers ombreus*; Yasushi

Ōki, *Bō Jō* Eibaian okugo *no kenkyū*, pp. 209-318; Rainer Schwarz, *Erinnerungen aus der Schattenaprikosenklause.*

[91] According to Pei-yi Wu, self-reproach or self-blaming was one of the methods used by writers of autobiographical works in traditional China. See *The Confucian's Progress: Autobiographical Writings in Traditional China*, pp. 222-234.

[92] Dong and Mao had sailed together from Yizheng to Mao's hometown, Rugao.

[93] Zhu Jianmang views the memoir as the most moving masterpiece. Zhu, "Collation notes," *Yingmeian yiyu*, p. 1.

Reminiscences of the Plum-shaded Convent

[94] "Magu", literally "Hemp Maiden," is a legendary Daoist immortal and a symbolic protector of females in Chinese mythology. For more on the Magu legend, see Cao Hongliang, "Magu kaobian;" Cao Guoqing, "Magu chuanshuo yu Magu xinyang."

[95] Shennü, a goddess in Chinese mythology, is said to be the daughter of either Emperor Yandi or the Queen Mother of the West (*Xiwangmu*).

[96] Xi Shi (b. 506 BCE), who lived during the Spring and Autumn Period in Zhuji, the capital of the State of Yue, is claimed to have been one of the "Four Most Beautiful Women of Ancient China." For a short biography of her, see Barbara Peterson, ed., *Notable Women of China: Shang Dynasty to the Early Twentieth Century*, pp. 27-29; Lin Huadong and Fang Zhiliang, "Xi Shi kao," pp. 122-125.

[97] Yi Guang is considered by many historians to be the earlier name of Xi Shi. Apparently Mao Xiang regarded her as another beauty of ancient China.

[98] Zhuo Wenjun (175-121 BCE) was a poet of the Western Han Dynasty. As a young widow she eloped with the renowned poet and musician, Sima Xiangru (179-117 BCE). For a short biography of her, see Barbara Peterson, ed., *Notable Women of China: Shang Dynasty to the Early Twentieth Century*, pp. 61-62.

[99] Hongdu was the courtesy name of the Tang Dynasty courtesan poetess, Xue Tao (768-831), one of the most famous female poets in Chinese literary history. She exchanged poems with some twenty prominent men of letters of her time, including Bai Juyi (772-846), Du Mu (803-852), and Yuan Zhen (779-831). For more on her life and poetry, see Su Shanyu, *Xue Tao jiqi shi yanjiu*; Jeanne Larsen, trans., *Brocade River Poems: Selected Works of the Tang Dynasty Courtesan Xue Tao*; Wilt Idema and Beata Grant, *The Red Brush*, pp. 182-189; Kang-I Sun Chang and Huan Saussy, *Women Writers of Traditional China*, pp. 59-66.

[100] The Qinhuai Pleasure Quarter was the most famous entertainment area in Nanjing during the Ming. For more on the place and the courtesans there, see Kenneth Hammond and Kristin Stephton, eds, *The Human Tradition in Modern China*, pp. 10-15; Monica Merlin, "The Nanjing Courtesan Ma Shouzhen (1548-1604): Gender, Space and Painting in Late Ming Pleasure Quarter," pp. 630-652.

[101] For more on the history of Suzhou and its economic and cultural prominence, see F.W. Mote, "A Millennium of Chinese Urban History: Form, Time, and Space Concepts in Soochow," pp. 35-65; James Ferguson, "Suzhou: A Cultural and Economic Centre of 'Southern' China," pp. 51-75; Michael Marmé, *Suzhou: Where the Goods of All the Provinces Converge*.

[102] Dong Xiaowan joined Mao Xiang's household on 6 December 1642 and passed away on 22 January 1651. They were together for slightly more than eight years by Western reckoning.

[103] It is common for China historians to use the phrase "dynastic change" to refer to the change of dynasty during the Song-Yuan and Ming-Qing transitions.

[104] Mao Xiang composed a 2,400-word, 240-rhyme dirge entitled "Wangqie Dong Xiaowan aici", bemoaning the passing of Dong Xiaowan in 1651, but he felt that an elegy of four characters per line was restrictive to the expression of his deep feeling for her. The dirge is included in Wu Dingzhong, *Dong Xiaowan huikao*, pp. 43-46; Wan Jiufu and Ding Fusheng, eds, *Mao Pijiang quanji, shang*, pp. 615-619.

[105] Meigong was the courtesy name of Chen Jiru (1558-1639), a Ming painter and calligrapher from Songjiang, Nan Zhili. His other courtesy name was Zhongchun and his literary name was Migong. For more on his life and literary accomplishments, see Jamie Greenbaum, *Chen Jiru (1558-1639): The Background to Development and Subsequent Uses of Literary Personae*.

[106] Nanjing was the primary capital of the Ming Dynasty from 1368 until 1420 when the third Ming emperor Yongle (1360-1424) moved the court to Beijing. From then until the end of the Ming in 1644, Nanjing was the secondary capital of the Dynasty retaining all the civilian, military and eunuch departments as were now introduced in Beijing, but with a reduced staff level compared with former times. For more on the history of the city, the early Ming court's decision to transfer the primary capital to Beijing, and the administrative functions of Nanjing as secondary capital, see F.W. Mote, "The Transformation of Nanking, 1350-1400;" Edward Farmer, *The Early Ming Government*; Jun Fang, *China's Secondary Capital – Nanjing under the Ming*.

[107] The provincial examination was the second of the triennial three-level examinations during the Ming-Qing period. After 1420 when the Ming court was relocated to Beijing, Nanjing was given the responsibility of holding the provincial examination (for candidates largely from the Nan Zhili region) which granted *juren* degree to successful candidates.

[108] Mizhi was the courtesy name of Fang Yizhi (1611-1671), a native of Tongcheng, Nan Zhili and one of the "Four Masters of the Late Ming." For more on his life and intellectual pursuits, see Willard Peterson, "Fang I-chih: Western Learning and 'Investigation of Things'," pp. 371-411; *Bitter Gourd: Fang I-Chih and the Impetus for Intellectual Change*; Yu Yingshi, *Fang Yizhi wanjie kao*.

[109] Dong Shuangcheng, the maid of the legendary Queen Mother of the West, in Chinese mythology, was later referred to when describing beautiful women.

[110] Dong moved from Nanjing to Suzhou in 1636, but she shuttled between the two cities to fulfill her singing-girl duties during the 1636-1642 period.

[111] Bantang, the western section of the famous Shantang Street in Suzhou, was close to the scenic spot Huqiu (Tiger Hill). See Yao Chengxu, *Wuqu fanggu lu*, pp. 59-60.

[112] The Dongting mentioned here is not the large, shallow freshwater lake in northwestern Hunan, the place where dragon-boat racing originated, but the Dongting islets in Lake Tai between Suzhou and Wuxi.

[113] Xiaowan's mother, née Chan, was probably the madam of her courtesan house, not her birth-mother.

[114] Born in 1624, Xiaowan was 15 years old in 1639 by Western reckoning.

[115] The Shadowy Garden was owned by Zheng Yuanxun (1603-1644), a *jinshi* of 1643. (*Jinshi* means *Jinshi* degree holder. *Jinshi* was the highest degree in imperial China which could be obtained by scholars who passed the national metropolitan examination.) Located in the south of Yangzhou, it was one of the activity centres of the Restoration Society in the late Ming. For more on Zheng and his tragic death, see Ji Liuqi, *Mingji nanlüe*, pp. 35-36; Chen Ruheng, "Ji Yingyuan zhuren Zheng Yuanxun," pp. 136-138.

[116] Huangshan, the Yellow Mountain, is located in southern Anhui Province. Baiyue, the White Mountain, is in the county of Xiuning, also in Anhui.

[117] Hengyue, the Heng Mountain in Hunan, is also a term used for the province as a whole. Mao Xiang's father, Mao Qizong (1590-1654), was serving as the Commissioner of the Hengyong Military Defense Circuit in eastern Hunan in 1643-44.

[118] Zhongjie was the courtesy name of Xu Zhi, a native of Rugao. After passing his *jinshi* examination in 1635, he successively served as county magistrate of Yiwu in Zhejiang Province and Huilai in Guangdong Province. He was vice bureau director of appointments at the Ministry of Personnel when he committed suicide after Beijing was captured by the rebels of Li Zicheng (1606-1645) in April 1644. See Zhang Tingyu et al., *Ming History*, pp. 6869-6870.

[119] She was the famous courtesan, Chen Yuanyuan (1624-1681), who was forcibly brought to Beijing by the men of Tian Hongyu, the notorious father of the Chongzhen Emperor's favourite

consort, Tian Xiuying. Chen was presented by Tian to the emperor, who turned her away as he was preoccupied by the grave crises in the empire. Tian then sent Chen to the house of the powerful general, Wu Sangui (1612-1678). When Beijing fell to the Li Zicheng rebels (while Wu was battling the Manchu forces in Manchuria), she was taken by Li's right-hand man Liu Zongmin (d. 1645). After Wu Sangui surrendered to the Manchu forces and helped them drive away the Li rebels, Chen rejoined him. For various records of Chen's life, see Chen Shengxi, "Chen Yuanyuan qiren qishi kao," pp. 120-137; Teng Shaozhen and Li Zhiting, *Chen Yuanyuan houzhuan*; Teng Shaozhen and Li Zhiting, "Yuanyuan wannian shenghuo shulüe," pp. 114-122; Koo Hui-lan, *No Feast Lasts Forever*, p. 153.

[120] Yiyang opera, one of the earliest forms of Chinese opera, originated in the region around the northeastern city of Yiyang, Jiangxi Province in the mid- to late 14th century and gradually spread to other areas of China. For more on the opera and its history, see Ma Huaqiang, *Mingdai Yiyangqiang chuanqi kao*; Chen Hong, *Jiangxi Yiyangqiang xiqu xintan*; Zeng Yongwen, "Yiyangqiang jiqi liupai kaoshu," pp. 39-72.

[121] The Chinese in pre-modern times separated the time from 7:00 pm to 5:00 am into five "watches" or "drums": first, 7:00-9:00 pm; second, 9:00-11:00 pm; third, 11:00 pm-1:00 am; fourth, 1:00-3:00 am; and fifth, 3:00-5:00 am.

[122] Guangfu is a town in the county of Wu (which is now the Wuzhong District of Suzhou) close to Lake Tai. It has been a popular tourist attraction known for its large area of plum trees since at least the Tang Dynasty. For more on the town, see Xu Fu, *Guangfu zhi*; Song Fengmei, "Dongtian fudi: Suzhou Guangfu zhen," p. 33; Dang Yahui, "Huguang shanse dongtian fudi," pp. 30-33.

[123] Huliu and Huqiu are used interchangeably in this memoir to refer to the same scenic spot known in English as Tiger Hill.

[124] The date was 8 September 1642.

[125] West Lake is a freshwater lake in Hangzhou, Zhejiang. It has influenced poets and painters throughout Chinese history for its natural beauty and historical relics and has also been an important source of inspiration for Chinese garden designers. For

a brief history of the lake and noted historical figures associated with it, see Zheng Yunshan et al., *Hangzhou yu Xihu shihua*; Ye Guangting, *Xihu shihua*.

[126] Xiangyang, a large urban centre in the Ming province of Huguang, was captured by the rebel force led by Zhang Xianzhong (1608-47) in early 1641.

[127] The imperial relative was Tian Hongyu (d. 1643), the father of the Chongzhen Emperor's favourite consort, Tian Xiuying (d. 1642).

[128] Changmen was a prosperous business area of Suzhou and was often used as the alternate name of the city itself.

[129] Hushuguan, a town in the District of Huqiu, is about 10 kilometers from central Suzhou.

[130] Mao Xiang's mother, née Ma (1590-1676), was 52 years old in 1642. See Fang Xiaobiao, "Maomu Ma Taigongren bashi shouxu," p. 3; Mao Guangsheng, *Mao Chaomin xiansheng nianpu*, p. 57b.

[131] The river was congested.

[132] The Respected Lady (*gongren*) was a standard title granted by the Ming court to the wife of a Grade Four official.

[133] These stanzas are Mao Xiang's "Zeng Wanfen ba jujue" which was collected in *Furen ji* edited by Chen Weisong (1625-1682).

[134] Changzhou, mentioned in the memoir by its unofficial name, Piling, is a prefecture-level city in southern Jiangsu. It borders Nanjing to the west, Zhenjiang to the northwest, and Wuxi to the east.

[135] A tael of silver weighed about 40 grams. In the late Ming a tael of silver could buy approximately 95 kilograms of grain.

[136] Huguang was one of the 13 provinces in the Ming and covered the present-day provinces of Hunan and Hubei.

[137] Wuxi, mentioned in the memoir by its unofficial name, Liangxi, is a prefecture-level city in southern Jiangsu. Split in half by Lake Tai, it borders Changzhou to the west and Suzhou to the east.

[138] Yixing, mentioned in the memoir as Yangxian, is a county-level city in southern Jiangsu and is famous for pottery products.

[139] Jiangyin, mentioned in the memoir as Chengjiang, is a county-level city in southern Jiangsu, where the infamous Jiangyin Massacre took place during the Ming-Qing transition.

[140] Beigu Hill, one of the three famous hills in Zhenjiang (the other two are Jianshan and Jiaoshan), lies on the bank of the Yangzi River. Many historical sites dating back to the Three Kingdoms period, including Sweet Dew Monastery, Soaring Clouds Pavilion, and Iron Tower, are located here.

[141] Golden Hill (Jinshan) is in the northwest of Zhenjiang. It has over thirty scenic and historical spots including the 1,600-year Jinshan Temple.

[142] The annual examination was an examination conducted by the provincial director of education for the *shengyuan* degree holders. For more on the examination, see Ichisada Miyazaki, *China's Examination Hell*, pp. 33-38.

[143] Taizhou, mentioned in the memoir as "Hailing", is a prefecture-level city in northern Jiangsu. Situated on the north bank of the Yangzi River, it borders Yangzhou to the east.

[144] The date was 8 September 1642.

[145] Peach Leaf Pier was on the Qinhuai River in Nanjing.

[146] Sanshan Gate, one of the 13 gates of Ming Nanjing's Inner City (*neicheng*), was near the Qinhuai Quarter.

[147] Jiashan, mentioned in the memoir as "Weitang", is a county in Zhejiang. It is 80 kilometers west of Shanghai and 90 kilometers south of Suzhou.

[148] Songjiang, mentioned in the memoir as "Yunjian", was a prefecture in southern Jiangsu during the Ming and is now a district of Shanghai.

[149] The date was 10 September 1642.

[150] Shaoyang, mentioned in the memoir as "Baoqing", is a prefecture-level city in southwestern Hunan.

[151] Longtan was a port in eastern Nanjing.

[152] Luanjiang is the unofficial name of Yizheng, a county-level city in northern Jiangsu. The Yangzi River and the Grand Canal run through the city from east to west and north to south, dividing it into four parts.

[153] Swallow's Ledge, Yanziji, is a scenic spot in the northern outskirts of Nanjing.

[154] The date was 30 September 1642.

[155] Candidates with the status of *fuche* or runners-up were qualified to be enrolled in the national universities in Beijing and Nanjing or to be appointed to minor positions. Mao Xiang was offered the position of prefectural judge (*sili*) in Taizhou, Zhejiang after he obtained *fubang* status in 1642, but he turned it down.

[156] Puchao was a treehouse built by Mao Xiang in the suburb of Rugao in 1634, in Rugao. It also became one of his literary names.

[157] Zhenjiang, mentioned by the author as Runzhou, is a prefecture-level city sitting on the south bank of the Yangzi River.

[158] Liu Daxing, courtesy names Yuzhong and Lüding, was a native of Zhangzhou and one of the four sworn brothers of Mao Xiang. The others were Chen Liang (fl. 1630), Zhang Mingbi (1584-1652), and Lü Zhaolong (fl. 1630). For more on Liu Lüding and his artistic talents, see Sun Zhiqiang, "Wan Ming yinren Liu Lüding," pp. 58-59; Zheng Liju, "Qian Qianyi Zhangpu Liu Fujun hezang muzhiming shuzheng," pp. 103-107.

[159] Junping was the courtesy name of Han Hong (*jinshi* 754), a poet from the Tang period. He and a girl surnamed Liu fell in love, but the latter was abducted by the nomadic chieftain Shazhali during the An Lushan-Shi Siming Rebellion (755-763). With the assistance rendered by the Zhiqing military commissioner Hou Xiyi (d. 781) and his subordinate Xu Jun, the two lovers eventually were able to become reunited. For an English translation of some of Han's poems, see Geoffrey Waters, et al., trans., *Three Hundred Tang Poems*, pp. 141, 168, 197.

[160] Xianke, whose full name is Wang Xianke, is a hero in the novel *Wushuang zhuan*. Wang and Liu Wushuang fell in love with each other, but the girl was sent to the Tang palace as a palace woman, because her father was accused of wrongdoing. Wang and Liu were able to become reunited after the girl was rescued by a prison guard surnamed Gu. For the full story, see Xue Diao, *Wushuang zhuan*.

[161] Wujiang was a county near Suzhou and is now one of the five districts of Suzhou.

[162] Muzhai was the courtesy name of Qian Qianyi. Dismissed by Emperor Chongzhen in 1638 from the post of vice-minister of rites, he was living in his hometown, Changshu, in 1642 with his concubine Liu Rushi, who was a friend of Dong Xiaowan when the two were courtesans in the Qinhuai Pleasure Quarter. For more on Qian's poetry and his social and cultural activities, see Lawrence Yim, *Poet-Historian Qian Qianyi*; Stephen McDowall, *Qian Qianyi's Reflections on Yellow Mountain*; Pei Shijun, *Sihai zongmeng wushinian: Qian Qianyi*; Kang-I Sun Chang, "Qian Qianyi and His Place in History," pp. 199-218.

[163] *Chi* is a traditional Chinese unit of length which equals approximately one third of a meter.

[164] The date was 2 December 1642.

[165] Zuocun Hall was a studio in Mao Qizong's house in Rugao. The senior Mao's posthumous collection of poetry and prose is entitled *Zuocun tang yigao* and was reprinted in 2000 by Shanghai guji chubanshe.

[166] Gu Qi believes that this Mr Zhou was Zhou Shizhang, an official at the bureau of ceremonies of the Nanjing ministry of rites. See *Mao Xiang yanjiu*, p. 150.

[167] Gu Qi believes that this Mr Li was Li Banghua (1574-1644), censor-in-chief of the Nanjing censorate from 1642 until 1644 (when he committed suicide after the fall of the Ming). See *Mao Xiang yanjiu*, p. 150.

[168] The date was 27 May 1642.

[169] Bi Jinliang was the Chinese courtesy name of Francesco Sambiasi (1582-1649), an Italian Jesuit missionary who worked in China from 1613 until his death. Sambiasi is better known in China by his (formal Chinese) name Bi Fangji. For more on his life and work, see Ann Heirman, Paolo De Troia, and Jan Parmentier, "Francesco Sambiasi, a Missing Link in European Map Making in China?" pp. 29-46; Louis Pfister, *Notices Biographiques et Bibliographiques sur les Jesuites de L'ancienne Mission de Chine, 1552-1773*, pp. 136-143; Wang Chuansong, "Wuxi Tianzhutang diyiwei bentang shenfu Bi

Fangji," p. 46; Zhang Zhongpeng, "Bi Fangji yu Nan Ming zhengquan zaji," pp. 171-173.

[170] Zhang Lihua (d. 589) was a favourite consort of Chen Shubao (553-604), the last emperor of the short-lived Chen Dynasty (557-589) during the period of the North-South Dynasties.

[171] The Xuande period, from 1426 to 1435, was noted for producing high-quality porcelain, often regarded as China's finest. For more on Xuande porcelain, see Daisy Lion-Goldschmidt, *Ming Porcelain*, pp. 86-99; Adrian Joseph, *Ming Porcelains*, pp. 18-26; S.J. Vainker, *Chinese Pottery and Porcelain*, pp. 187-191.

[172] The Restoration Society was the largest literary association that took an interest in politics in the late Ming. Mao was an active member of the society and is considered by some researchers as one of its leaders. See Gu Qi and Wang Liming, "Fushe lingxiu Mao Pijiang." For more on the society and its constituent societies, see William Atwell, "From Education to Politics: The Fu She;" Jun Fang, "Literati Statecraft and Military Resistance during the Ming-Qing Transition."

[173] Madame Gu was Gu Mei (1619-1664), one of the famed "Eight Beauties of the Qinhuai Quarters" in the late Ming. A friend of Dong Xiaowan, she married Mao's friend Gong Dingzi in 1641. Her house, Meilou, in the Qinhuai, was the place where Mao Xiang and his four friends became sworn-brothers in 1636. For more on Gu and Gong, see Meng Sen, "Hengbo furen kao," pp. 435-472; Zhang Hongsheng, "Gong Dingzi and the Courtesan Gu Mei: Their Romance and the Revival of the Song Lyric in the Ming-Qing Transition," pp. 71-85.

[174] Madame Li was Li Xiangjun (1624-1653), a well-known courtesan in late Ming Nanjing. She is also the heroine in the play by Kong Shangren (1648-1718), *Peach Blossom Fan*, written about her love affair with Hou Fangyu, one of the "Four Masters of the Late Ming." Hanxiuzhai, Li Xiangjun's house in the Qinhuai, is still a popular tourist attraction in the Fuzimiao (Confucius Temple) area in Nanjing. For more on Li and Hou, see Xu Zhinong and Zhao Yuxia, *Hou Chaozong wenxuan*, pp. 121-124; Yu Huai, *Banqiao zaji*, p. 21; Roger Des Forges, *Central Plain in Late Ming*, pp. 127-137. For Kong and his play,

see Richard Strassberg, *The World of K'ung Shang-jen: The Man of Letters in Early Ch'ing China*; Chen Shih-hsiang and Harold Acton, trans., *The Peach Blossom Fan*; Stephen Owen, "Kong Shang-ren, *Peach Blossom Fan: Selected Acts*."

[175] *Swallow's Letter* (*Yanzi jian*) was a play written by Ruan Dacheng (1587-1646), a late Ming official of unsavory reputation. It is about a love affair between scholar Huo Duliang, singing girl Hua Xingyun, and the daughter of minister Li Yunfei. The punctuated version of the play (i.e. with added punctuation as an aid to modern readers) was published by Shanghai renmin chubanshe in 1986, Heilongjiang renmin chubanshe in 1987, and Huangshan shushe in 1993. For more on Ruan Dacheng and his dramatic works, see Alison Hardie, "Self-representation in the Dramas of Ruan Dacheng," pp. 57-85.

[176] The two are the hero and heroine in *Swallow's Letter*.

[177] Wang Ruwei was Mao Xiang's friend from Yizheng, Nan Zhili Province, who was a fervent lover of tea.

[178] The date was 24 September 1642.

[179] Yanguan is a county in northern Zhejinag. Mao was invited by his sworn brother Chen Liang, a native of Yanguan, to live with his family temporarily during the difficult times of the Ming-Qing transition.

[180] Xiaosheng was perhaps not the biological sister of Dong Xiaowan, but an adopted "daughter" of their "parents".

[181] The Tower of Smoke-and-Rain is at the South Lake of Jiaxing in Zhejiang.

[182] The Tong River is an alternative name for the Qiantang River from Jiande to Tonglu in central Zhejiang. Yanling, located in the Tonglu county, is said to be the very place where Yan Guang (Yan Ziling, ca. 39 BCE-41 CE) went fishing to avoid working for Liu Xiu (5 BCE-57 CE), his former classmate and the founder of the Eastern Han Dynasty.

[183] Xin'an is a river in the province of Zhejiang.

[184] Dong Xiaowan began her life as a courtesan in 1636 at the age of twelve and most probably started to provide full services to clients in 1638.

[185] Mao Xiang had three sons. The oldest, Mao Yan (1634-38) died when he was only four years old. Mao's two surviving sons

were Mao Heshu (courtesy names Guliang and Jiasui, b. 1635) and Mao Danshu (courtesy name Qingruo, 1639-1695). They were both *shengyuan* degree holders. For more on Mao's family, see Jun Fang, "Between Resistance and Collaboration: Mao Xiang's Third Way," pp. 116-119; Mao Guangsheng, *Mao Caomin xiansheng nianpu.* pp. 1a-68a.

[186] The date was 21 February 1651.

[187] The four periods of the Tang, according to early Ming poetry theorist Gao Bing (1350-1423), were Early (618-704), High (705-770), Middle (771-835), and Late (836-907) Tang.

[188] *Pinghui* is *Tangshi pinghui*, a literary work written by Gao Bing. It uses prosodic principles in a systematic manner to classify 5,769 poems of 620 Tang poets. For Gao and his influential work, see Richard Lynn, "Alternate Route to Self-Realization in Ming Theories of Poetry," pp. 320-324; Gao Bing, *Tangshi pinghui.*

[189] (*Tangshi*) *Jishi benmo* is an extensive collection of Tang poems complied by Ji Yougong (*jinshi,* 1121) of the Song Dynasty. The 81 *juan* book includes poems of 1,132 Tang poets. For an annotated version, see Wang Zhongyong, ed., *Tangshi jishi jiaojian.*

[190] *Quan Tang shihua*, complied by You Mao (1127-1202), is an abridged version of *Tangshi jishi benmo*. It contains poems by 320 Tang poets. One of the available reprints was published by Zhonghua shuju in 1985.

[191] This book is probably the *Tang shierjia shi* compiled by Xu Zichang (1578-1623) which includes poems by Wang Bo (650-676), Yang Jiong (650-696), Lu Zhaoling (ca. 636-695), Luo Binwang (640-684), Chen Zi'ang (d. 702), Du Shenyan (ca. 645-708), Shen Qiquan (ca. 656-719), Song Ziwen (d. 712), Meng Haoran (d. 740), Wang Wei (699-759), Gao Shi (d. 765), and Cen Shen (715-770). For their poems, see Xu Zidong, *Tang shierjia shi.*

[192] Zhiyu was the courtesy name of Zhu Zhifan (1556-1624), who was the top graduate (*zhuangyuan*) of the 1595 metropolitan examination. (*Zhuangyuan* was the number one (*jinshi* degree holder) among some 100-300 successful scholars who passed the metropolitan *jinshi* degree examination once every three years in

China.) Zhu served as vice-minister of rites and of personnel in the late Wanli period, and was dispatched by the Ming court to Korea as a special envoy in 1605. His report on the mission, *Fengshi Chaoxian gao*, was reprinted in 1997 by Zhuangyan wenhua shiye gongsi and in 2003 by Beijing tushuguan chubanshe.

[193] Mr Wang of Mengjin was most likely Wang Duo (1592-1652). A native of Mengjin and a *jinshi* of 1622, Wang Duo climbed the official ladder steadily to become minister of rites at the end of the Ming. After the fall of Beijing he served in the short-lived Hongguang government (1644-45) as Grand Secretary of Eastern Hall, and surrendered to the Qing army when Nanjing was captured in 1645. He was also noted for his accomplishments in painting and poetry.

[194] Lingbao is a county in west Henan.

[195] Xiaoyuan was the courtesy name of Hu Zhenheng (1569-1645), a native of Haiyan, Zhejiang, and a *juren* of the Wanli reign. Hu served as the instructor at Gucheng county and vice-director at the ministry of war in the late Ming. He was the author of a number of books, including *Xu Wenxuan, Tangyin guichen, Tangshi tancong, Dushu zaji*, and *Haiyan xian tujing*.

[196] The *Tangshu* mentioned here was probably the *New Tang History* compiled by Ouyang Xiu (1007-1072), not the *Old Tang History* authored by Liu Xu (888-947).

[197] *Chuci* or *Verses of Chu*, is an anthology of poetry attributed to Qu Yuan (c. 340-278 BCE) and Song Yu (c. 319-298 BCE). For various English translations of the work, see J.S. Minford and J.S.M. Lau, eds, *Classical Chinese Literature: An Anthology of Translations, Volume 1: From Antiquity to the Tang Dynasty*; Geoffrey Waters, *Three Elegies of Ch'u: An Introduction to the Traditional Interpretation of the Ch'u Tz'u*; Gladys Yang and Xianyi Yang, *Chu Ci Xuan: Selected Elegies of the State of Chu*; Xu Yuanchong, *The Elegies of the South*.

[198] Shaoling was the courtesy name of Du Fu (712-770), a prominent poet of the Tang Dynasty. He and Li Bai (701-762) are often regarded as the two greatest poets of China. For more on his life and poems, see William Hung, *Tu Fu: China's Greatest Poet*; Eva Shan Chou, *Reconsidering Tu Fu: Literary*

Greatness and Cultural Context; David Young, *Du Fu: A Life in Poetry*; Stephen Owen, *The Poetry of Du Fu*.

[199] Yishan was the courtesy name of Li Shangyin (813-858), a poet from the late Tang period. For more on his life and poetry, see James Liu, *The Poetry of Li Shang-yin: Ninth-Century Baroque Chinese Poet*; Stephen Owen, *The Late Tang*, 335-526; Li Zeng, "Ambiguous and Amiss: Li Shangyin's Poetry and Its Interpretation," pp. 137-150.

[200] Wang Jian (767-830) was a Tang Dynasty poet known for writing in the rare six-syllable line, which is characterized by the presence of two cæsuras per line, dividing each line into three parts of two syllables each. He was also known for writing more than one hundred poems on the lives of court ladies. One of his poems, "A New Bride", is collected in *Three Hundred Tang Poems*, p. 186.

[201] Madame Huarui (d. 976) was the favourite consort of Meng Chang (919-965), the last ruler of the short-lived Dynasty Later Shu (934-965), and an acclaimed poet during the Five Dynasties and Ten Kingdoms period. For her life and poetry, see Kang-I Sun Chang et al., eds, *Women Writers of Traditional China: An Anthology of Poetry and Criticism*, pp. 84-86; Kenneth Rexroth and Ling Chung, trans., *The Orchid Boat: Women Poets of China*, pp. 31-33; Liu Bolun, *Huarui furen*; Cao Minggang, *Huarui furen shi zhuping*.

[202] Wang Gui (1019-1085) was a high-ranking official and a renowned *ci* poet from the Song Dynasty. For a short biography of him, see Yoshinbo Shiba, "Wang Kuei," in Herbert Franke, ed., *Sung Biographies*, pp. 1115-1117.

[203] Zhongju was the courtesy name of Chen Fan (d. 168), who served as Grand Commandant during the reign of Emperor Huan (147-167) and Grand Tutor in the first year of the reign of Emperor Ling (168-188). For more on his life, see Rafe de Crespigny, *A Biographical Dictionary of Later Han to the Three Kingdoms*, pp. 64-66.

[204] Fan Pang (137-169), once a senior assistant to Chen Fan and governor of Runan, was arrested in the First (civil official-eunuch) Faction Incident in 166 and was executed in the Second Faction Incident in 169.

[205] Guo Liang (b. 133), a former student of the Defender-in-chief, Li Gu (94-147), was admired for risking his life to collect the corpse of Li after his public execution by General-in-chief Liang Ji (d. 159).

[206] The three-*juan* collection was printed after the death of Dong Xiaowan in 1651 and was included in *Ranzhi ji* by Wang Shilu (1626-1673). Unfortunately the majority of Wang's collection of female writers' works, including Dong's *Lianyan*, is no longer extant. For more on Wang Shilu and the *Ranzhi ji*, see Fu Xianglong, "Wang Shilu *Ranzhi ji* kaolüe."

[207] Gong Dingzhi (1615-1673) passed his *jinshi* examination in 1634 and served as a supervising secretary for war in late Ming. He first surrendered to the Li Zhicheng rebels and later to the invading Manchus in 1644. In the early Qing he served as minister of rites. For his life and literary works, see Sun Keqiang and Pei Zhe, eds, *Gong Dizhi quanji*; Yan Dichang, "Jintai fengya zong shiren: Gong Dingzhi lun," pp. 4-7.

[208] This work was written by Xie Zhuang (421-466) of the North-South Dynasties and was translated into English by David Knechtges. See *Wen Xuan or Selection of Fine Literature*, vol. 3, pp. 31-40.

[209] Wenmin was the courtesy name of Dong Qichang (1555-1636), a famous poet, calligrapher, painter, and official of the Ming Dynasty. Dong appreciated Mao Xiang's literary talents and maintained a life-long contact with the younger Mao. For more on Dong's life and his achievements in painting, see Wai-kam Ho, ed., *The Century of Tung Ch'i-ch'ang, 1555-1636*; Ren Daobin, *Dong Qichang xinian*.

[210] Zhong Yao (151-230) was a calligrapher and official from the late Eastern Han and Three Kingdoms period. He was highly regarded for his calligraphy in two styles – official script (*li*) and regular script (*kai*). Together with Wang Xizhi (303-361) the two were collectively addressed as (master calligraphers) Zhong Wang. For more on his life and calligraphy, see Wang Yuchi, *Zhong Yao*; Zhong Yao, *Zhong Yao xiaokai jiuzhong*.

[211] *Ronglu biao* was a memorial written by Zhong Yao congratulating the Wei army's successful ambush of Shu general

Guan Yu (d. 220). From the third century onwards, it was one of the standard copy-books for learners of Chinese calligraphy.
[212] Emperor Guan (Guandi) was the revered name of Guan Yu, a loyal general under Liu Bei (161-223), a warlord in the late years of the Eastern Han Dynasty and the founder of the Kingdom of Shu during the Three Kingdoms period. Guan was a popular figure in Chinese folk religion and has been worshipped as one of the many protective gods in China. For more on the cult of Guan Yu, see Barend ter Haar, *Guan Yu: The Religious Afterlife of a Failed Hero*; Prasenjit Duara, "Superscribing Symbols: The Myth of Guandi, Chinese God of War," pp. 778-795.
[213] The Cao E Stele inscription is a masterpiece of calligraphy in small regular script style (*xiaokai*) by Cai Yong (132-192) on the deeds of a girl named Cao E (130-143). The girl's father, Cao Xu, was a musician and shaman who accidentally fell into the Shun River in 143 while presiding over a ceremony commemorating Wu Zixu (d. 484 BCE), a top official in the State of Wu during the Spring and Autumn period, worshipped as the god of the Shun River, during the Dragon Boat Festival. Cao E, determined to find her father's body, searched for days along the river before eventually drowning herself. In 151 a monumental stele was set up in honour of her filial conduct and her deeds are recorded in the "Biographies of Chaste Women" (*juan* 84) in the *Later Han History*. The Shun River was subsequently renamed Cao E River.
[214] Changxing is a county in northern Zhejiang, with a history dating back to the third century.
[215] A merchant and tea expert in Mao Xiang's time.
[216] Zuo Si (ca. 253-ca. 307) was an essayist and poet from the Western Jin Dynasty. He was known for his three rhapsodies on the capitals of the kingdoms of Shu, Wu, and Wei. For his life and literary works, see Michael Farmer, "Zuo Si," in *Classical Chinese Writers of the Pre-Tang Period*, pp. 327-332; "Southern Capital Rhapsody," "Shu Capital Rhapsody," "Wu Capital Rhapsody," and "Wei Capital Rhapsody," in David Knechtges, trans., *Wen Xuan or Selections of Refined Literature*, Vol. 1, pp. 311-477; "A Dainty Girl," in Anne Birrell, ed. and trans., *New Songs from Jade Terrace*, pp. 85-86.

[217] Lu Tong (795-835), a Tang poet and tea lover, claimed that a person could become immortal after drinking seven cups of tea. For more on his life and writings, see *Lu Tong ji*.

[218] Lu Yu (733-804) is the author of *Chajing*, the earliest monograph on tea in China. The treatise is widely available in Chinese and was translated into English by Francis Carpenter as *Classic of Tea*.

[219] Dongpo (East Slope) was the literary name of Su Shi (1037-1101), a renowned poet, essayist, calligrapher, and official of the Northern Song Dynasty. For more on his life and literary works, see Lin Yutang, *The Gay Genius: The Life and Times of Su Tungpo*; Ronald Egan, *Word, Image, and Deed in the Life of Su Shi*; Burton Watson, *Selected Poems of Su Tung-p'o*; Xu Yuanchong, *Selected Poems of Su Shi*.

[220] Dongguan is a county in Guangdong, which is 50 kilometers from Guangzhou to the north and 90 milometers from Shenzhen to the south.

[221] The Xuande incense burners were high-quality vessels made of fine copper and dozens of costly metals including gold and silver. According to historical records, after 3,000 Xuande burners were produced in 1428, no more were forged during the remainder of the Xuande reign. For Mao Xiang's treatise on the technological and artistic qualities of Xuande burners, see *Xuanlu gezhu*, in Wan Jiufu and Ding Fusheng, eds, *Mao Pijiang quanji, shang*, pp. 555-562.

[222] A reference to women's unhappiness at their lower social status than that of men in imperial China.

[223] Meizhou was the courtesy name of Li Suiqiu (1602-1646), a scholar from Fanyu, Guangdong. In 1640 during a trip to Jiangnan, he joined Zheng Yuanxun, Mao Xiang, and 15 other men of letters in Zheng's Shadowy Garden in Yangzhou and won the poetic competition on the subject of the yellow peony. His poem was rated the best by the adjudicator, Qian Qianyi, who received all the poems anonymously. Li's works of poetry and prose were collectively published as *Lianxuge ji*, reprinted in 2000 by Beijing chubanshe. For more on Liu Suiqiu and the Yellow Peony poetic competition, see Wei Shengnian, "Li Suiqiu nianpu jianbian," pp. 27-33; Hu Gengtian, "Wan Ming

Yangzhou Yingyuan yu Huangmudan shihui kaolun," pp. 106-111; Ōki Yaushi, *Bō Jō* Eibaian okugo *no kenkyū*, pp. 45-67.

[224] Weizong was the courtesy name of Fan Ye (398-445), an official from the Liu Song Dynasty (420-479) of the North-South Dynasties and the author of *History of the Later Han*. The biography of Fan Ye in the *Book of Song* (*Songshu*) discusses the origins of perfumes in China.

[225] Mao's residence was separated from his gardens by about two kilometers.

[226] Mao Xiang was most likely the author of this song.

[227] Xiangli (Fragrance) Garden was part of the Mao family's Painted-in-Water Garden.

[228] Xiyi was the courtesy name of Xie Zhuang, the author of the "Rhapsody on the Moon."

[229] Changji was the courtesy name of Li He (790-816), a short-lived poet of the late Tang period. For his life and literary works, see Stephen Owen, *The Late Tang*, pp. 156-182; J.D. Frodsham, *Goddesses, Ghosts, and Demons: The Collected Poems of Li He*.

[230] Changjiang was the courtesy name of Jia Dao (779-843), a Buddhist poet of the late Tang period. For more on his life and literary works, see Red Pine and Mike O'Connor, eds, *The Clouds Should Know Me by Now*, pp. 12-42; Qi Wenbang, ed., *Jia Dao ji jiaozhu*.

[231] *Jie* tea is a quality tea produced in Yixing and Changxing in Jiangnan. In the Ming-Qing period, it was a tribute article regularly sent to Beijing for consumption by the imperial family.

[232] Buddha's Hand is a variety of citron; the fruit is segmented into finger-liked sections.

[233] The Bronze Tray was a huge hand-shaped receptacle built during the reign of Emperor Wudi (141-87 BCE) of the Western Han for the purpose of receiving sweet dew from Heaven.

[234] Jianning, a county in Fujian Province, was created in the tenth century by the court of the Southern Tang Dynasty (937-976).

[235] The date was 25 April 1644, the day when the Ming court was overthrown by the Li Zicheng rebels and the Chongzhen Emperor committed suicide by hanging himself at Coal Hill (Meishan).

[236] Gao Jie (d. 1645), formerly a rebel general under Li Zicheng, switched his loyalty to the Ming government and was awarded the title of Earl of Xingping. His unruly army was one of the leading forces in fighting against the Manchu conquest of China proper during the Ming-Qing transition. He was tricked and killed in 1645 by Xu Dingguo (d. 1647) who then surrendered to the Manchu army by presenting Gao's head as a token of his loyalty.

[237] Mao's mother and wife had previously moved only outside the walls of Rugao; now the whole family left Rugao for Yanguan.

[238] Fanhuzhou is a village in Rugao.

[239] Jingjiang is a neighboring county of Rugao in the east.

[240] One *li* equals approximately one third of a mile.

[241] Jifu was the courtesy name of Mao Bao (1645-1726), Mao Xiang's half-brother (who obtained *shengyuan* status in 1660).

[242] Mao Bao's mother, née Liu, was Mao Qizong's concubine. She passed away in late 1669.

[243] The day was the fifth of the fifth month, the day when people remember the drowning of Qu Yuan by dragon-boat racing.

[244] "The Great Army" refers to the Manchu army in the early Qing.

[245] This was the only official appointment Mao Qizong received during the short-lived Hongguan régime of the Southern Ming.

[246] In this memoir "Yanguan" refers to Haiyan, a county in eastern Zhejiang, not the town of Yanguan in the county of Haining. See Wu Dingzhong, *Dong Xiaowan huikao*, pp. 28-33.

[247] The eight were Mao's parents, Mao and his wife Su Yuanfang, Mao's two sons, his younger brother Mao Bao, and Xiaowan.

[248] Literally, "Large White Residence", the home of Mao Xiang's friend Zhang Qilin (whose literary name was Dabai xiansheng) in the Wuye Village of Haiyan county.

[249] Zuili is the unofficial name of Jiaxing, a prefecture-level city in northern Zhejiang. Lying on the Grand Canal, it borders Hangzhou to the southwest and Shanghai to the northeast.

[250] When the Manchus conquered China, the Qing rulers decreed that all Chinese men should shave their foreheads and wear a Manchu-style queue (plait) or face execution.

[251] Re Hill, also known as Yashan (Elegant Hill) and Washan (Tile Hill), is in Haiyan, Zhejiang.

[252] "Same-year friends" are those who passed the civil service examination in the same year.

[253] A number of mountains or hills in China bore the name "Ma'anshan". This particular one is in the Ganpu Town of Haiyan county.

[254] Qinxi is a village in the north of Haiyan.

[255] Tan'an was the courtesy name of Fang Gongqian (1596-1666), a *jinshi* of 1622 and a native of Tongcheng. He served as a junior supervisor of the household administration of the heir apparent in the late Ming, and was exiled to Ningguta (present-day Ningan, Heilongjiang) in 1659-1661. His book on his exile, *Jueyu jilüe*, was reprinted by Jilin wenshi chubanshe in 1993.

[256] The date was 27 October 1645.

[257] i.e. by the advancing Northern troops.

[258] Mao Xiang was accused of participating in the anti-Qing activities organized by his townsmen and friends Li Zhichun and Li Yuandan (son of Li Zhichun) in the late Shunzhi era (1644-1661), but was eventually exonerated.

[259] Taihang is a mountain range running down the eastern edge of the Loess Plateau in the provinces of Shanxi, Henan, and Hebei. It extends over 400 kilometers from north to south.

[260] The five sacred mountains are Mount Tai (Eastern Mountain) in Shandong, Mount Hua (Western Mountain) in Shaanxi, Mount Heng (Southern Mountain) in Hunan, Mount Heng (Northern Mountain) in Shanxi, and Mount Song (Central Mountain) in Henan. The pronunciation of Northern Mountain and Southern Mountain is the same, but the characters are different.

[261] Mao Xiang passed the low-level *shengyuan* examination with flying colours in 1627, but could not repeat the feat in the medium-level *juren* examination. From 1629 until the end of the Ming Dynasty in 1644, he took part five times in the *juren* examinations in Nanjing, and obtained only *fuche* status in the very last attempt.

[262] The date was 27 May 1642.

[263] Xihuamen was one of the gates of the Imperial City (*huangcheng*) of Nanjing during the Ming. For more on the physical layout of the city and its protective walls, see Jun Fang, *China's Second Capital*, pp. 2-6; Yang Guoqing, *Mingdai Nanjing chengqiang*.

[264] The seventh day of the seventh month has been a Chinese festival, celebrating the "annual meeting" of Niulang (a cowherd) and Zhinü (a weaver girl), since at least the end of the Eastern Han Dynasty. It is known as Skill-seeking Festival (*Qiqiaojie*) in Chinese and Double Seventh Festival in English.

[265] The date was 25 August 1648.

[266] Each of these two phrases refers to a devoted married couple.

[267] The Hall of Immortality was part of the Tang imperial garden in the suburb of Chang'an where the famed Huaqing Pool was located. First built in 748 for worshiping Laozi (d. 531 BCE) and the first six emperors of the Tang Dynasty, namely Gaozu Li Yuan (r. 618-626), Taizong Li Shimin (r. 626-649), Gaozong Li Zhi (r. 649-683), Empress Wu Zetian (r. 684-705), Zhongzong Li Xian (r. 684 & 705-710), and Ruizong Li Dan (r. 684 & 710-712). It was also called Hall of the Seven Augusts (*Qisheng dian*).

[268] Xuanzong was the seventh emperor of the Tang Dynasty who in 705 led a coup d'état to depose his grandmother Empress Wu Zetian. His 44-year reign, from 712 to 756, was the longest during the Tang period.

[269] Hong Du was the Daoist alchemist in Bai Juyi's long poem *Song of Everlasting Sorrow* (*Changhen ge*) who calls back the spirit of the hanged Yang Guifei to meet Emperor Xuanzong.

[270] Yang Yuhuan (719-756), commonly known as Yang Guifei (Precious Consort Yang), was the favourite consort of Emperor Xuanzong. Their love affair and Xuanzong's subsequent lack of attention to state affairs was partly blamed for the outbreak of the An Lushan-Shi Siming Rebellion (755-763) which ended the Tang as an effective empire. For more on the romantic story of the two and the death of Yang Guifei, see Paul Kroll, "The Flight from the Capital and the Death of Precious Consort Yang," *Tang Studies*, No. 3 (1985), pp. 25-53; "Recalling Xuanzong and Lady

Yang: A Selection of Mid- and Late Tang Poems," *Tang Studies*, 35 (2017), pp. 1-19.

[271] *Song of Everlasting Sorrow* was a narrative poem telling the romantic story of Emperor Xuanzong and Consort Yang. For English translations of the poem, see Dore Levy, *Chinese Narrative Poetry*, pp. 129-133; Geoffrey Waters, et al., *Three Hundred Tang Poems*, pp. 92-96. For Bai Juyi's other poems, see Arthur Waley, trans., *Waiting for the Moon: Poems of Bo Juyi*; David Hinton, trans., *The Selected Poems of Po Chü-I*; Burton Watson, trans., *Po Chü-i: Selected Poems*.

[272] *Jueju* (quatrain) is a style of Chinese poetry that grew popular among Chinese poets in the Tang Dynasty. *Jueju* poems are a matched pair of couplets with each line consisting of five or seven characters.

[273] The literary society referred to is the Restoration Society.

[274] *Dijing pian* (On the imperial capital), written by the noted early Tang poet Luo Binwang (640-684), depicts the night-life of the Tang capital, Chang'an. *Lianchang gong* (Ballad of the Lianchang Palace), written by Yuan Zhen, is a narrative poem describing the vicissitudes of the Lianchang Palace during the 100-year period from the reign of Tang Xuanzong to that of Tang Xianzong (712-819).

[275] Yuanci was the courtesy name of Wu Qi (1619-1694), a native of Yangzhou. He was highly regarded by his peers and scholars of Chinese literature for his achievements in *shi* and *ci* poems. For more on his life and poetry, see Wang Chaohong, *Wu Qi nianpu*; Wu Qi, *Linhuitang ji*; Zhu Shu, "Wu Qi yu Wu Weiye jiaoyou kao," pp. 74-75.

[276] Yuhuang was the courtesy name of Du Jun (1611-1687), a native of Huanggang, Huguang. He was noted for his poetic skills, his love for tea, and his refusal to serve the Qing rulers. His surviving works include *Bianyatang wenji* and *Bianyatang shiji*. For more on Du Jun, see Zhu Lixia and Zhou Qinggui, "Du Jun nianpu," pp. 174-187; Cai Jingquan, "Du Jun yu Qu Yuan," pp. 1-6 & 47; Zhang Daihui, "Kundun rensheng yikuan yizheng: Qingchu yimin shiren Du Jun de rensheng zhuiqiu yu sixiang gexing," pp. 130-133.

[277] Xiaowei was the courtesy name of Deng Hanyi (1617-1689), a native of Taizhou, Nan Zhili. He was an active member of the Restoration Society in the late Ming, and a secretariat drafter in the early Qing. He was the editor of the 40-*juan Shiguan* which collects approximately 15,000 poems of more than 1,800 Qing poets. The work was reprinted in 2000 by Beijing guji chubanshe. For more on his life and literary achievements, see Wang Zuohua, "Deng Hanyi shiji kaolüe," pp. 78-83; "Deng Hanyi shige bieji kaolüe," pp. 59-63; "Deng Hanyi yu Wang Shizheng Kong Shangren jiaoyou kao," pp. 209-211; "Deng Hanyi shishiguan jiqi shixue yiyi," pp. 133-137; "*Shiguan* jiqi wenxianxue yiyi," pp. 156-159; Lu Lin, "Deng Hanyi de xinlu lichen yu *Shiguan* de shixue jiazhi," pp. 34-46.

[278] Xinfu was the courtesy name of Huang Chuanzu (d. 1670), a native of Xishan and the editor of *Fulun ji, Fulun xuji, Fulun guangji*, and *Fulun xinji*. The book series collects poems of more than 1,000 poets from the late Ming to the early Qing. For more on his compilation of Qing poems, see Deng Xiaodong, "Qingchu Qingshi xuanben de shidai tezheng," pp. 50-56.

[279] Xianqi was the courtesy name of Yao Quan (fl. 1650), a native of Xiushui, Zhejiang and the author of *Changgu shijian*. His edited work, *Shiyuan chuji*, was reprinted by Beijing guji chubanshe in 2000. For more on his life and literary works, see Lu Lin, "Qingchu Yao Quan pingxuan *Shiguan* de shidai tese," pp. 116-125.

[280] Zhongmo was the curtesy name of Peng Sunyi (1615-1673), a native of Haiyan, Zhejiang. He refused to serve the Qing after 1644 by devoting his time to scholarly pursuits. Many of his works are still available with recent reprints, including *Mingchao jishi benmo bubian, Ping kou zhi, Liu kou zhi, Ming shichao*, and *Mingzhai shiyu*. For more on his life and literary activities, see Zhang Yu, "Ming Qing shiren Peng Sunyi xin yuefushi kaolun," pp. 16-20; Zhang Yili, "Qing ciren Peng Sunyu jiashi kaoshu," pp. 87-91.

[281] Li Zhichun (1600-1651), whose courtesy name was Dasheng and literary name Culai, was a native of Rugao. After obtaining his *jinshi* degree in 1622, he held a number of positions in the Ming government as a messenger of the messengers' office,

secretary in the ministry of personnel, and head of the seals office. He died of fasting after being captured by the Qing government for conducting underground anti-Manchu activities in the early Qing period. For more on his life and death, see Ma Weizhong and Pan Hong, "Qingchu Li Dasheng an bianyi," pp. 92-94.

[282] Li Yuandan, son of Li Zhichun, was executed together with some forty anti-Qing activists from Rugao in 1651.

[283] Zhao Youyi was the son of Zhao Kaixin (d. 1662). The senior Zhao, who was a Yangzhou native and a *jinshi* degree holder of 1634, once served as a vice bureau director of the ministry of war in the last years of the Ming. He joined the Qing government after 1644 and was vice-minister of revenue at the time of his death. For more on his life, see his biography in Zhao Erxun, *Qingshi gao, juan* 244.

BIBLIOGRAPHY

Anonymous. *Dong Xiaowan biezhuan* 董小宛別傳 (An alternative biography of Dong Xiaowan). In *Qixiage yecheng* 棲霞閣野乘 [An unofficial history of the Qixia Studio] (Beijing: Beijing guji chubanshe, 1999), pp. 231-247.

Atwell, William. "From Education to Politics: The Fu She." In William de Bary (1919-2017), ed., *Unfolding of Neo-Confucianism* (New York: Columbia University Press, 1975), pp. 333-367.

Bai Hua 柏樺. *Shuihui xianlü Yiliusier zhi Yiliuwuyi: Mao Pijiang yu Dong Xiaowan* 水繪仙侶 1642-1651：冒辟疆 與董小宛 (The fairy couple from the Painted-in-Water Garden: Mao Pijiang and Dong Xiaowan, 1642-1651). Beijing: Dongfang chubanshe, 2008.

Bai Juyi 白居易 (772-846). Trans. Arthur Waley (1889-1966). *Waiting for the Moon: Poems of Bo Juyi*. Mount Jackson, VA: Axios Press, 2012.

Barkan, Lenore. "Forty Years of Elite Politics in a Chinese County." In Joseph Esherick and Mary Backus Rankin, eds, *Chinese Local Elites and Patterns of Dominance* (Berkeley: University of California Press, 1990), pp. 191-215.

_____. "Nationalists, Communists, and Rural Leaders: Political Dynamics in a Chinese County, 1927-1937." Ph.D. dissertation, University of Washington, 1983.

Barnhart, Richard. "Dong Qichang and Western Learning: A Hypothesis in Honor of James Cahill." *Archives of Asia Art*, Vol. 50 (1997/98), pp. 7-16.

Berg, Daria. *Women and the Literary World in Early Modern China, 1580-1700*. London and New York: Routledge, 2013.

_____. "Courtesan Editors: Sexual Politics in Early Modern China." *T'oung Pao*, Vol. 99 (2013), pp. 173-211.

_____. "Amazon, Artist, and Adventurer: A Courtesan in Late Imperial China." In Kenneth Hammond and Kristin Stapleton, eds., *The Human Tradition in Modern China* (Lanham: Rowman & Littlefield Publishers, 2008), pp. 15-32.

Bi Fangji 畢方濟 (Francesco Sambiasi, 1582-1649) & Xu Guangqi 徐光啟 (1562-1633). *Lingyan lishao* 靈言蠡勺 (A brief discourse on the soul). Liuying, Tainan: Zhuangyan wenhua shiye youxian gongsi, 1995.

Birrell, Anne. *New Songs from a Jade Terrace: An Anthology of Early Chinese Love Poetry*. London: George Allen & Unwin, 1982.

Bodde, Derk (1909-2003). *Festivals in Classical China: New Year and Other Annual Observances during the Han Dynasty, 206 B.C. – A.D. 220*. Princeton: Princeton University Press, 1975.

Bossler, Beverly. *Courtesans, Concubines, and the Cult of Female Fidelity: Gender and Social Change in China, 1000-1400*. Cambridge, MA: Harvard University Asia Center, 2013.

Brook, Timothy, Jérôme Bourgon, and Gregory Blue, eds. *Death by a Thousand Cuts*. Cambridge: Harvard University Press, 2008.

Brook, Timothy. *The Troubled Empire: China in the Yuan and Ming Dynasties*. Cambridge: Harvard University Press, 2010.

_____. *Collaboration: Japanese Agents and Local Elites in Wartime China*. Cambridge: Harvard University Press, 2005.

_____. *The Confusions of Pleasure: Commerce and Culture in Ming China*. Berkeley: University of California Press, 1998.

Bryant, Daniel (1942-2014). "Syntax, Sound, and Sentiment in Old Nanking: Wang Shih-chen's 'Miscellaneous Poems on the Ch'in-huai'." *Chinese Literature: Essays, Articles, Reviews*, Vol. 14 (1992), pp. 25-50.

Bush, Susan and Christian Murck, eds. *Theories of the Arts in China*. Princeton: Princeton University Press, 1983.

Cai Changrong 蔡昌榮. "Zuowei xijujia de Ruan Dacheng" 作為戲劇家的阮大鋮 (Ruan Dacheng as a dramatist). *Wenshi zhishi* 文史知識, No. 1 of 2001, pp. 83-90.

Cai Dianqi 蔡殿齊 (1816-1888). *Guochao guige shichao* 國朝閨閣詩鈔 (Selected poems of Qing dynasty women poets). Shanghai: Shanghai guji chubanshe, 1995.

Cai Jingquan 蔡靖泉. "Du Jun yu Qu Yuan" 杜濬與屈原 (Du Jun and Qu Yuan). *Huanggang shifan xueyuan xuebao* 黃岡師範學院學報, Vol. 27, No. 1 (Feb. 2007), pp. 1-6 & 47.

Cai Guoqing 曹國慶. "Magu chuanshuo yu Magu xinyang" 麻姑傳說與麻姑信仰 (The legend and worship of Magu). *Wenshi zhishi*, No. 4 of 2002, pp. 34-48.

Cai Guoqing 曹紅亮. "Magu kaobian" 麻姑考辨 (A textual study of Magu). *Zongjiaoxue yanjiui* 宗教學研究, No. 1 of 2006, pp. 121-125.

Cao Minggang 曹明鋼. *Huarui furen shi zhuping* 花蕊夫人詩注評 (Annotated remarks on the poems of Madame Huarui). Shanghai: Shanghai guji chubanshe, 2004.

Carpenter, Bruce. "Ch'ien Ch'ien-I and Social History." *Tezukayama University Review*, No. 58 (1987), pp. 101-113.

Chang, Chun-shu and Shelley Hsueh-lun Chang. *Crisis and Transformation in Seventeenth-Century China: Society, Culture, and Modernity in Li Yü's World*. Ann Arbor: University of Michigan Press, 1992.

Chang, Kang-I Sun. "Qian Qianyi and His Place in History." In Wilt L. Idema, Wai-yee Li, and Ellen Widmer, eds., *Trauma and Transcendence in Early Qing Literature* (Cambridge: Harvard University Asia Center, 2006), pp. 199-218.

_____. *The Late-Ming Poet Ch'en Tzu-lung: Crises of Love and Loyalism*. New Haven & London: Yale University Press, 1991.

_____. "The Idea of the Mask in Wu Wei-yeh (1609-1671)." *Harvard Journal of Asiatic Studies*, Vol. 48, No. 2 (Dec. 1988), pp. 289-320.

Chang, Kang-I Sun, Huan Saussy, and Charles Yim-tze Kwong, eds. *Women Writers of Traditional China: An Anthologyof Poetry*. Stanford: Stanford University Press, 1999.

Chang, Kang-I Sun and Stephen Owen, eds. *The Cambridge History of Chinese Literature, Vol. II* (Cambridge: Cambridge University Press, 2010).

Chau, Timothy Wai Keung. "Searching for the Bodies of the Drowned: A Folk Tradition of Early China Recovered." *Journal of the American Oreintal Society*, Vol. 129, No. 3 (Jul.-Sept. 2009), pp. 385-401.

Chen Hong 陳紅. *Jiangxi Yiyangqiang xiqu xinta* 江西弋陽腔戲曲新探 (A new light on the Yiyang Opera of Jiangxi). Nanchang: Jiangxi renmin chubanshe, 2009.

Chen Liangwu 陳良武. "Huang Daozhou *Liu Zhao* kaolun" 黃道周《劉招》考論 (On Huang Daozhou's *In Memory of Liu Lüding*). *Yangzhou daxue xuebao* 揚州大學學報, Vol. 17, No. 2 (Mar. 2013), pp. 119-123.

Chen Mengyao 陳夢謠. "Meng Sen 'Dong Xiaowan kao' zhi Hongxue yiyi" 孟森《董小宛考》之紅學意義 (Meng Sen's "Notes on Dong Xiaowan" and its relations to the study of *Dream of the Red Chamber*). *Hongloumeng xuekan* 紅樓夢學刊, No. 1 of 2016, pp. 300-314.

Chen Ruheng 陳汝衡. "Ji Yingyuan zhuren Zheng Yuanxun" 記影園主人鄭元勳 (On the owner of the Shadowy Garden Zheng Yuanxun). *Yangzhou shiyuan xuebao* 揚州師院學報, No. 4 of 1985, pp. 136-138.

Chen Shengxi 陳生璽. "Chen Yuanyuan qiren qishi kao" 陳圓圓其人其事考 (Notes on Chen Yuanyuan and her life). In *Ming Qing yidaishi dujian* 明清易代史獨見 [Perspectives on the history of the Ming-Qing transition] (Shanghai: Shanghai guji chubanshe, 2006), pp. 120-137.

Chen, Shih-hsiang (1912-1971) and Harold Acton (1904-1994), trans. *Peach Blossom Fan*. Berkeley: University of California Press, 1976.

Chen Weisong 陳維崧 (1626-1682). *Jialing wenji* 迦陵文集 (Collected works of Chen Weisong). Shanghai: Shangwu yinshuguan, 1919.

_____. *Jialing ci quanji* 迦陵詞全集 (The complete collection of Chen Weisong's *ci* poems). Reprint. Shanghai: Shanghai guji chubanshe, 1995.

_____. *Huhailou wenji* 湖海楼文集 (Collected works from the Huhai Hall). 1735. Reprint. Shanghai: Shanghai guji chubanshe, 2010.

_____. *Furen ji* 婦人集 (Notes on famous women). Shijiazhuang: Hebei jiaoyu chubanshe, 1996.

Chen Yinke 陳寅恪 (1890-1969). *Liu Rushi biezhuan* 柳如是別傳 (Alternative biography of Liu Rushi). Shanghai: Shanghai guji chubanshe, 1980.

Chia, Lucille. "Of Three Mountains Street: The Commercial Publishers of Ming Nanjing." In Cynthia Brokaw and Kai-wing Chow, eds., *Printing and Book Culture in Late Imperial China* (Berkeley: University of California Press, 2005), pp. 107-151.

Chou, Eva Shan. *Reconsidering Tu Fu: Literary Greatness and Cultural Context*. Cambridge: Cambridge University Press, 1995.

Chou, Ju-hsi. "From Mao Hsiang's Oberlin Scroll to His Relationship with Tung Ch'i-ch'ang." *Allen Memorial Art Museum Bulletin*, Vol. 36, No. 2 (1978-79), pp. 140-167.

Clunas, Craig. *Fruitful Sites: Garden Culture in Ming Dynasty China*. Durham: Duke University Press, 1996.

Dang Yahui 黨亞惠. "Huguang shanse tongtian fudi: Suzhou Guangfu zhen jixing" 湖光山色 洞天福地：蘇州光福鎮紀行 (A trip to the blessed place Guangfu, Suzhou). *Tiejun* 鐵軍, No. 11 of 2014, pp. 30-32.

Dardess, John. *Blood and History in China: The Donglin Faction and Its Repression, 1620-1627*. Honolulu: University of Hawaii Press, 2002.

De Crespigny, Rafe. *A Biographical Dictionary of Later Han to the Three Kingdoms (23-220 AD)*. Leiden & Boston: Brill, 2007.

De Morant, George Soulie (1878-1955). Trans. Gerald C. Wheeler (1872-1943). *A History of Chinese Art: From Ancient Times to the Present Day*. New York: Jonathan Cape & Harrison Smith, 1931.

Deng Hanyi 鄧漢儀 (1617-1689). *Shiguan* 詩觀 (A comprehensive collection of Qing poetry). Beijing: Beijing guji chubanshe, 2000.

Deng Xiaodong 鄧曉東. "Qingchu Qingshi xuanben de shidai tezheng" 清初清詩選本的時代特徵 (The characteristics of the various editions of selected poetry in the early Qing).

Xibei shida xuebao 西北師大學報, No. 3 of 2013, pp. 50-56.

Des Forges, Roger. "Toward Another Tang or Zhou? Views from the Central Plain in the Shunzhi Reign." In Lynn A. Struve, ed., *Time, Temporality, and Imperial Tradition: East Asia from Ming to Qing* (Honolulu: University of Hawaii Press, 2005), pp. 73-111.

_____. *Cultural Centrality and Political Change in Chinese History: Northeast Henan in the Fall of the Ming.* Stanford: Stanford University Press, 2003.

Ding Fusheng 丁賦生, Wang Limin 王利民, and Gu Qi 顧啟. "Fushe lingxiu Mao Pijiang" 復社領袖冒辟疆 (The Fushe leader Mao Pijiang). *Wenshi zhishi* 文史知識, No. 8 of 2003, pp. 65-70.

Dong Bian 董邊 (1916-1998), Tan Deshan 鐔德山, and Zeng Zi 曾自, eds. *Mao Zedong he tade mishu Tian Jiaying* 毛澤東和他的秘書田家英 (Mao Zedong and his secretary Tian Jiaying). Beijing: Zhongyang wenxian chubanshe, 1989.

Dong Qianli 董千里 (1921-2007). *Dong Xiaowan* 董小宛. Beijing: Zhongguo youyi chuban gongsi, 1985.

Dong Qichang 董其昌 (1555-1636). *Dong Qichang shufa quanji* 書法全集 (Complete collection of Dong Qichang's calligraphical works). Beijing: Zhongguo shuhua chubanshe, 2001.

Du Dengchun 杜登春 (1629-1705). *Sheshi shimo* 社事始末 (History of late Ming societies). Reprint. Beijing: Zhonghua shuju, 1991.

Du Hong 杜紅. *Boming hongyan Dong Xiaowan* 薄命紅顏董小宛 (Dong Xiaowan: A beauty who died young). Taibei: Huatian wenhua shiye gongsi, 1999.

Du Jun 杜濬 (1611-1687). *Bianyatang wenji* 變雅堂文集 (Collected works from the Bianya Hall). Beijing: Beijing chubanshe, 2000.

_____. *Bianyatang yiji* 變雅堂遺集 (Surviving works from the Bianya Hall). Shanghai: Shanghai guji chubanshe, 1995.

Duara, Prasenjit. "Superscriing Symbols: The Myth of Guandi, Chinese God of War." *The Journal of Asian Studies*, Vol. 47, No. 4 (Nov. 1988), pp. 778-795.

Ebrey, Patricia. "Concubines in Sung China." *Journal of Family History*, Vol. 11, No. 1 (Mar. 1986), pp. 1-24.

_____. "How Dong Xiaowan Became My Concubine." In *Chinese Civilization: A Sourcebook* (New York: The Free Press, 1993), pp. 246-249.

Egan, Ronald. *Word, Image, and Deed in the Life of Su Shi.* Cambridge, MA.: Harvard University Asia Center, 1994.

Elvin, Mark. "Female Virtue and the State in China." *Past and Present*, No. 104 (Aug. 1984), pp. 111-152.

Fan Kangjie 范康捷. "Fan Shiyi yu *Shuihuiyuan buqi tu*" 范仕義與《水繪園補契圖》(Fan Shiyi and *Celebration of Double Third Festival at the Painted-in-Water Garden*). *Baoshan xueyuan xuebao* 保山學院學報, No. 6 of 2010, pp. 85-89.

Fang, Jun. "Between Resistence and Collaboration: The Third Way of Mao Xiang." In Ihor Pidhainy, Roger Des Forges, and Grace Fong, eds., *Representating Lives in China: Forms of Biography in the Ming-Qing Period (1368-1911)* (Ithaca: Cornell University East Asia Program, 2019), pp. 115-139.

_____. "The Beginning of the Zheng He Voyages: Nanjing and the Indian Ocean World, 1405-1433." *Chinese Historical Review*, Vol. 26, No. 1 (Mar. 2019), pp. 1-19.

_____. *China's Second Capital – Nanjing under the Ming, 1368-1644.* Abingdon and New York: Routledge, 2014 & 2017.

_____. "Literati Statecraft and Military Resistance during the Ming-Qing Transition: The Case of the Possibility Society (Jishe)." *Chinese Historical Review*, Vol. 19, No. 2 (Dec. 2012), pp. 87-106.

Fang Gongqian 方拱乾 (1596-1666). *Jueyu jilüe* 絕域紀略 (Record of remote land). In *Jilin jilüe* 吉林紀略 (Records on Jilin). Changchun: Jilin wenshi chubanshe, 1993.

Fang Liang 方良. *Qian Qianyi nianpu* 錢謙益年譜 (A chronological biography of Qian Qianyi). Beijing: Zhongguo shuji chubanshe, 2015.

Fang Shengliang 方盛良 and Zhou Jianguo 周建國. "Mao Xiang yanjiu shuping" 冒襄研究述評 (A review of studies on Mao Xiang). *Jilin shifan daxue xuebao* 吉林師範大學學報, No. 4 of 2014, pp. 37-40.

Fang Xiaobiao 方孝標 (1617-1697). "Maomu Ma Taigongren bashi shouxu" 冒母馬太恭人八十壽序 (Congratulatory message on the occasion of the eightieth birthday of Mao Xiang's mother the Respected Lady Ma). In Shi Zhongyang 石鍾揚 and Guo Chunping 郭春萍, eds., *Fang Xiaobiao wenji* 方孝標文集 [Collected works of Fang Xiaobiao] (Hefei: Huangshan shushe, 2007), pp. 3-5.

Fang Yan 方燕. "Songdai nüxing gegu liaoqin wenti shixi" 宋代女性割股療親問題試析 (A preliminary analysis of the practice of cutting one's flesh to cure one's ill parents by the Song dynasty women). *Qiusuo* 求索, No. 11 of 2007, pp. 210-212.

Farmer, Edward. *Early Ming Government: The Evolution of Dual Capitals*. Cambridge, Mass.: East Asian Research Council, Harvard University, 1976.

Farmer, Michael. "Zuo Si." In Curtis Dean Smith, ed., *Classical Chinese Writers of the Pre-Tang Period*. (Detriot: Gale, 2011), pp. 327-332.

Feng Menglong 馮夢龍 (1574-1646). *Jingshi tongyan* 警世通言 (Stories to caution the world). Shanghai: Shanghai guji chubanshe, 1998.

Ferguson, James. "Suzhou: A Cultural and Economic Centre of 'Southern' China." *Culture Mandala: The Bulletin of the Centre for East-West Cultural and Economic Studies*, Vol. 3, No. 2 (Aug. 1999), pp. 51-75.

Fisher, Tom. "Loyalist Alternatives in the Early Ch'ing." *Harvard Journal of Asiatic Studies*, Vol. 44, No. 1 (June 1984), pp. 83-122.

Fong, Grace. *Herself an Author: Gender, Agency, and Writing in Late Imperial China*. Honolulu: University of Hawaii Press, 2008.

Franke, Herbert (1914-2011), ed. *Sung Biographies*. Wiesbaden: Franz Steiner Verlag, 1976.

Frodsham, J.D. *The Collected Poems of Li He*. New York: Review Books, 2016.

_____. *Goddesses, Ghosts, and Demons: The Collected Poems of Li He*. Berkeley: North Point Press, 1983.

Fu Xianglong 傅湘龍. "Mao Xiang Shuihuiyuan yu Chen Weisong *Furen ji* zhi jizuan" 冒襄水繪園與陳維崧《婦人集》之集纂 (Mao Xiang's Painted-in-Water Garden and the compilation of Chen Weisong's *Collected Works of Women Writers*). *Zhongguo wenhua yanjiu* 中國文化研究, No. 1 of 2014, pp. 102-110.

_____. "Wang Shilu *Ranzhi ji* kaolun" 王士祿《燃脂集》考論 (A study of Wang Shilu's *Works by Women Writers in Chinese History*). *Hanxue yanjiu* 漢學研究, Vol. 30, No. 3 (Sept. 2012), pp. 135-165.

Gao Bing 高棅 (1350-1423). *Tangshi pinghui* 唐詩品匯 (Graded compendium of Tang poetry). Shanghai: Shanghai guji chubanshe, 1982.

Gao Yang 高陽 (1922-1992). *Mingmo Sigongzi* 明末四公子 (The four masters of the late Ming). Beijing: Huaxia chubanshe, 2004.

Gong Dingzhi 龔鼎孳 (1616-1673). *Gong Dingzhi quanji* 全集 (Complete works of Gong Dingzhi). Beijing: Renmin wenxue chubanshe, 2014.

Greenbaum, Jamie. *Chen Jiru (1558-1639): The Background to Development and Subsequent Uses of Literary Personae*. Leiden and Boston: Brill, 2007.

Gu Qi 顧啟. "Wangshi Wenyuan xunzong" 汪氏文園尋踪 (In search of the Cultured Garden of Rudong's Wang Family). *Nantong shifan xueyuan xuebao* 南通師範學院學報, Vol. 18, No. 4 (Dec. 2002), pp. 142-145.

_____. "Mao Xiang yu Wang Shizhen de jiaoyou" 冒襄與王士禛的交遊 (On the contact between Mao Xiang and Wang Shizhen). *Nantong shifan xueyuan xuebao* 南通師範學院學報, Vo. 16, No. 2 (June 2000), pp. 53-57.

_____. "Mao Xiang yu Wu Weiye" 冒襄與吳偉業 (On the contact between Mao Xiang and Wu Weiye). *Nantong shizhuan xuebao* 南通師專學報, Vol. 14, No. 4 (Dec. 1997), pp. 21-23.

_____. *Mao Xiang yanjiu* 冒襄研究 (Collected essays on Mao Xiang). Nanjing: Jiangsu wenyi chubanshe, 1993.

_____. "Dong Xiaowan he ta de shi" 董小宛和她的詩 (Dong Xiaowan and her poems). *Nantong shizhuan xuebao* 南通師專學報, Vol. 8, No. 1 (Mar. 1992), pp. 87-91.

Gu Qi and Jiang Guangdou 姜光鬥. "Du Mao Pijiang 'Maizi Wulang oucheng jueju'" 讀冒辟疆《賣字五狼偶成絕句》 (On Mao Pijiang's five-character quatrain "Selling caligraphical work at Wulang Mountain"). *Jiaoxue yu jinxiu* 教學與進修, No. 2 of 1983, pp. 25 & pp. 31-32.

Gu Qi and Jiang Guangdou. "Tan Mao Xiang dui Kong Shangren sixiang de yingxiang" 談冒襄對孔尚任思想的影響 (On Mao Xiang's influence on Kong Shangren's thinking). *Huaibei meishiyuan xuebao* 淮北煤師院學報, No. 1 of 1983, pp. 79-86.

Guo Qing 郭磬 and Liao Dong 廖東. *Zhongguo lidai renwu xiangzhuan* 中國歷代人物像傳 (Portraits of historical figures in China). Jinan: Qi Lu shushe, 2002.

Haar, Barend ter. *Guan Yu: The Religious Afterlife of a Failed Hero*. Oxford: Oxford University Press, 2017.

Han Tan 韓菼 (1637-1704). *Youhuaitang wengao* 有懷堂文稿 (Collected works from the Youhuai Hall). Qianlong era. Reprint. Liuying, Tainan: Zhuangyan wenhua shiye youxian gongsi, 1997.

Hanan, Patrick (1927-2014). *The Invention of Li Yu*. Cambridge, MA: Harvard University Press, 1988.

Hao Lili 郝莉莉. "'Yiyuti' wenxue yuanliu xiaokao" "憶語體" 文學源流小考 (A preliminary study of the origin of the genre of reminiscence literature). *Guyuan shizhuan xuebao* 固原師專學報, Vol. 27, No. 1 (Jan. 2006), pp. 13-16.

Hardie, Alison. "Self-representation in the Dramas of Ruan Dacheng (1587-1646)." In Marjorie Dryburgh and Sarah Dauncey, eds., *Writing Lives in China, 1600-2010: Histories of the Elusive Self* (London and New York: Palgrave Macmillan, 2013), pp. 57-85.

He Fazhou 何法周 and Wang Shulin 王樹林. *Hou Fangyu ji jiaojian* 侯方域集校箋 (Annotated writings of Hou Fangyu). Zhengzhou: Zhongzhou guji chubanshe, 1992.

He Lifang 何麗芳. Review of Mao Lianquan, *Xuanan buxuan: Mao Pijiang zhu* Hongloumeng *qishisan zheng* 懸案不懸：冒辟疆著紅樓夢七十三證 (*Unsettled case is settled: Seventy-three pieces of evidence in support of Mao Pijiang's authorship of* Dream of the Red Chamber). *American Journal of Chinese Studies*, Vol. 26, No. 1 (Spring 2019).

He Qin 賀琴. "Wang Shilu zhushu xinkao" 王士祿著述新考 (A new study of Wang Shilu's written works). *Xiamen guangbo dianshi daxue xuebao* 廈門廣播電視大學學報, No. 1 of 2012, pp. 59-62.

Heirman, Ann, Paolo De Troia & Jan Parmentier. "Francesco Sambiasi, A Missing Link in European Map Making in China?" *Imago Mundi*, Vol. 61, No. 1 (January 2009), pp. 29-46.

Hinton, David, trans. *The Selected Poems of Po Chü-i*. New York: New Directions Publishing Company, 1999.

Ho, Clara Wing-chun, ed. *Biographical Dictionary of Chinese Women: The Qing Period, 1644-1911*. Armonk and London: M.E. Sharpe, 1998.

Ho, Wai-kam (1924-2004), ed. *The Century of Tung Ch'i-ch'ang*. Kansas City: The Nelson-Atkins Museum of Art, 1992.

Hou Fangyu 侯方域 (1618-1655). *Hou Fangyu quanji jiaojian* 侯方域全集校箋 (Annotated complete works of Hou Fangyu). Beijing: Renmin wenxue chubanshe, 2013. 3 vols.

_____. *Zhuanghuitang wenji* 壯悔堂文集 (Collected works from the Zhuanghui Hall). Shanghai: Shanghai guji chubanshe, 2010.

Hsieh, Bao Hua. *Concubinage and Servitude in Late Imperial China*. Lanham: Lexington Books, 2014.

Hsi, Angela. "Wu San-kuei in 1644: A Reappraisal." *The Journal of Asian Studies*, Vol. 34, No. 2 (Feb. 1975), pp. 443-453.

Hu Gengtian 扈耕田. "Wan Ming Fushe *Liudu fangkuan gongjie shijian xinyi*" 晚明復社《留都防亂公揭》事件新議 (New light on the Anti-Disturbance Poster Incident in the late Ming). *Shixue yuekan* 史學月刊, No. 8 of 2011, pp. 128-131.

_____. "Wan Ming Yangzhou Yingyan yu Huangmudan shihui kaolun" 晚明揚州影園與黃牡丹詩會考論 (On the Yellow Peony Poetry Party at the Shadowy Garden in Yangzhou during the late Ming). *Yangzhou daxue xuebao* 揚州大學學報, Vol. 15, No. 3 (May 2011), pp. 106-111.

_____. "Cong *Xie Kangle youshan shiping* kan Mao Xiang de shanshuishi guan" 從《謝康樂遊山詩評》看冒襄的山水詩觀 (Mao Xiang's view on the mountain-water poems as seen from *Xie Kangle youshan shiping*). *Xueshu jiaoliu* 學術交流, No. 5 of 2003, pp. 199-202.

Hu Jinwang 胡金望 (1952-2013). *Rensheng xiju yu xiju rensheng: Ruan Dacheng yanjiu* 人生喜劇與喜劇人生：阮大鋮研究 (Life comedy and comedic life: A study of Ruan Dacheng). Beijing: Zhongguo shehui kexue chubanshe, 2004.

Hu Wenkai 胡文楷 (1899-1988). *Lidai funü zhuzuo kao* 歷代婦女著作考 (Notes on the works by women in the dynastic period). Shanghai: Shanghai guji chubanshe, 2008.

Hu Zhenheng 胡震亨 (1569-1645). *Haiyan xian tujing* 海鹽縣圖經 (Illustrated gazetteer of Haiyan county). Liuying, Tainan: Zhuangyan wenhua shiye gongsi, 1996.

_____. *Dushu zalu* 讀書雜錄 (Reading jottings). Shanghai: Shanghai guji chubanshe, 1995.

_____. *Tangyin guichen* 唐音癸籤 (Discourse on Tang poetry). Shanghai: Shanghai guji chubanshe, 1987.

_____. *Xu Wenxuan* 續文選 (Supplement to the *Selections of Literature*). Taibei: Taiwan shangwu yinshuguan, 1973.

_____. *Tangshi tancong* 唐詩談叢 (Miscellaneous notes on Tang poetry). Shanghai: Shangwu yinshuguan, 1937.

Huang Binghui 黃炳輝. "Gao Bing *Tangshi Pinghui* shuping" 高棅《唐詩品匯》述評 (Discourse on Gao Bing's *Graded Compendium of Tang Poetry*). *Xiamen daxue xuebao* 廈門大學學報, No. 4 of 1992, pp. 23-28.

Huang, Martin. *Intimate Memory: Gender and Mourning in Late Imperial China*. Albany, NY: State University of New York Press, 2018.

_____. *Literati and Self-Re/Presentation: Autobiographical Sensibility in the Eighteenth-Century Chinese Novel*. Stanford: Stanford University Press, 1995.

Huang, Ray (1918-2000). *Taxation and Governmental Finance in Sixteenth-Century Ming Dynasty China*. Cambridge: Cambridge University Press, 1974.

Huang Yu 黃語. "Mao Xiang wenren yaji dui jiayue xiqu de yingxiang 冒襄文人雅集對家樂戲曲的影響 (Mao Xiang's collected literati writings and their influence on family music and drama). *Hebei xuekan* 河北學刊, Vol. 30, No. 2 (2010), pp. 103-107.

_____. "Shanyinzhe yu kuyinzhe de qinggan gongming: Dequantang yeyan shimo jiqi yingxiang" 善隱者與苦隱者的情感共鳴：得全堂夜讌始末及其影響 (The 1660 evening performance at Dequan Hall and its impact). *Xibei shifan daxue xuebao* 西北師大學報, Vol. 47, No. 3 (May 2010), pp. 44-49.

_____. "Lun Qingchu Dingyou shimeng gaohui" 論清初丁酉世盟高會 (On the 1657 societal gathering in Nanjing). *Shenzhen daxue xuebao* 深圳大學學報, Vol. 27, No. 2 (Mar. 2010), pp. 89-94.

Huang Zhenyun 黃震雲. "Mingdai Zhu Zhifan yong Hancheng shi canjuan" 明代朱之藩咏漢城詩殘卷 (Zhu Zhifan's incomplete poem on Seoul). *Wenxian* 文獻, No. 1 of 2009, pp. 184-185.

Hucker, Charles O. (1919-1994). *A Dictionary of Official Titles in Imperial China*. Stanford: Stanford University Press, 1985.

Hummel, Arthur W. (1884-1975). *Eminent Chinese of the Ch'ing Period (1644-1912)*. Washington: Government Printing Office, 1943.

Hung, William (1893-1980). *Tu Fu: China's Greatest Poet*. Cambridge, Mass.: Harvard University Press, 1952.

Idema, Wilt. L. *The Red Brush: Writing Women of Imperial China*. Cambridge: Harvard University Asia Center, 2004.

Jay, Jennifer W. *A Change in Dynasties: Loyalism in Thirteenth-century China*. Bellingham: Western Washington University Center for East Asian Studies, 1991.

Ji Liuqi 計六奇 (b. 1622). *Mingji nanlüe* 明季南略 (History of the Southern Ming). Beijing: Zhonghua shuju, 1984. Jiang Yixue 蔣逸雪 (1902-1985). *Zhang Pu nianpu* 張溥年譜 (Chronological biography of Zhang Pu). Jinan: Qi Lu shushe, 1982.

Jin Sifen 金嗣芬. *Banqiao zaji bu* 板橋雜記補 (Supplement to the *Miscellaneous Notes from the Plank Bridge*). 1911. Reprint. Nanjing: Nanjing chubanshe, 2006.

Joseph, Adrian M. *Ming Porcelains: Their Origins and Development*. London: Bibelot Publishers Limited, 1971.

Kafalas, Philip A. *In Limpid Dream: Nostalgia and Zhang Dai's Reminiscences of the Ming*. Norwalk: EastBridge, 2007.

Kang Zhengguo 康正果. "Daowang yu huiyi: Lun Qingdai yiyuti sanwen de xushi" 悼亡與回憶：論清代憶語體散文的敘事 (Mourning and reminiscence: On the narrative art of Qing dynasty memoirs). *Zhonghua wenshi luncong* 中華文史論叢, No. 1 of 2008, pp. 353-384.

Koo Hui-lan (1899-1992). *No Feast Lasts Forever*. New York: Times Book Co., 1975.

Kroll, Paul. "Recalling Xuanzong and Lady Yang: A Selection of Mid- and Late Tang Poems." *Tang Studies*, No. 35 (2017), pp. 1-19.

_____. "The Flight from the Capital and the Death of Precious Consort Yang." *Tang Studies*, No. 3 (1985), pp. 25-53.

Kuang Yanzi (Kwong Yim-tze) 鄺龑子. "Cong *Yingmeian yiyu* kan wenxue shuxie zhi zhen yu cheng" 從《影梅庵憶語》看文學書寫之"真"與"誠" (The truth and sincerity of literary writing as seen from *Reminiscences of the Plum-shaded Convent*). *Xinguoxue* 新國學, Vol. 10 (2014), pp. 214-244.

Lang Ying 郎瑛 (1487-1566). *Qixiu leigao* 七修類稿 (Notes on seven categories). Reprint. Beijing: Zhonghua shuju, 1959.

Levy, Dore J. *Chinese Narrative Poetry: The Late Han through T'ang Dynasties*. Durham and London: Duke University Press, 1988.

Li Bao 利寶. *Dong Xiaowan quanzhuan* 董小宛全傳 (A complete biography of Dong Xiaowan). Beijing: Guangming ribao chubanshe, 2002.

Li E 厲鶚 (1692-1752). *Fanxie shanfang ji* 樊榭山房集 (Collected works of Li E). Shanghai: Shanghai guji chubanshe, 1992.

Li Hanlin 李韓林 and Li Xinfu 李新富. *Chen Yuanyuan zhuan* 陳圓圓傳 (A biography of Chen Yuanyuan). Taibei: Guoji wenhua shiye youxian gongsi, 1993.

Li Hsiao-t'i (Li Xiaoti). "Pleasures of a Man of Letters: Wang Shizhen in Yangzhou, 1660-1665." In Lucie B. Olivová and Vibeke Børdahl, eds., *Lifestyle and Entertainment in Yangzhou* (Copenhagen: NIAS Press, 2009), pp. 131-147.

_____. "Mao Pijiang yu Shuihuiyuan zhong de yimin shijie" 冒辟疆與水繪園中的遺民世界 (Mao Pijiang and the loyalist world of the Painted-in-Water Garden). In *Lianlian hongchen* 戀戀紅塵 [Red dust] (Shanghai: Shanghai renmin chubanshe, 2007), pp. 54-102.

_____. "Rusheng Mao Xiang de zongjiao shenghuo" 儒生冒辟疆的宗教生活 (Confucian scholar Mao Xiang's religious life). In *Lianlian hongchen*, pp. 105-126.

Li Huan 李桓 (1827-1891). *Guochao qixian leizheng lu* 國朝耆獻類徵錄 (Record of noted personalities of the Qing dynasty). Taibei: Wenhai chubanshe, 1966.

Li Jintang 李金堂. "Mingdai Nanjing Jiuyuan de xingshuai yu *Banqiao zaji*" 明代南京舊院的興衰與《板橋雜記》 (The rise and fall of the Jiuyuan Pleasure Quarter in Ming Nanjing and *The Miscellaneous Notes from the Plank Bridge*). *Dongnan wenhua* 東南文化, No. 7 of 2001, pp. 52-56.

Li Qing 李清 (1602-1683). "Preface to *Tongren ji*." In Wan Jiufu and Ding Fusheng, eds., *Mao Pijiang quanji* (Nanjing: Fenghuang chubanshe, 2014), p. 743.

Li Shiqiu 李實秋, ed. *Mao Pijiang zhuzuo* Hongloumeng *huikao (Diyiji)* 冒辟疆著作紅樓夢彙考（第一輯）(Collected articles on Mao Xiang's authorship of *Dream of the Red*

Chamber). Vol. 1. Nanjing: Jiangsu Fenghuang meishu chubanshe, 2014.

Li Suiqiu 黎遂球 (Li Meizhou 美周, 1602-1646). *Lianxuge ji* 蓮鬚閣集 (Collected works from the Lianxu Hall). Beijing: Beijing chubanshe, 2000.

Li Wai-yee. *Women and National Trauma in Late Imperial Chinese Literature*. Cambridge, MA: Harvard University Asia Center, 2014.

_____. "Romantic Recollections of Women as Sources of Women's History." In Clare Ho, ed., *Overt and Covert Treasures: Essays on the Sources for Chinese Women's History* (Hong Kong: The Chinese University Press, 2012), pp. 337-367.

_____. "History and Memory in Wu Weiye's Poetry." In Wilt Idema, Wai-yee Li, and Ellen Widmer, eds., *The Trauma and Transcendence in Early Qing Literature* (Cambridge: Harvard University Asia Center, 2006), pp. 99-148.

_____. "The Late Ming Courtesan: Invention of a Cultural Ideal." In Ellen Widmer and Kang-i Sun Chang, eds., *Writing Women in Late Imperial China* (Stanford: Stanford University Press, 1997), pp. 46-73.

Li Yafeng 李亞峰. "Shilun 'Yiyuti' wenshi de shehui yuanyin yu wenxue beijing" 試論"憶語體"問世的社會原因與文學背景 (On the social and literary background of the appearance of the genre of reminiscence writing). *Xihua daxue xuebao* 西華大學學報, Vol. 26, No. 3 (Jun. 2007), pp. 33-37.

Li Yongxian 李永賢. "Lun Qingchu shige xuanben zhong de shixue fansi" 論清初詩歌選本中的詩學反思 (On the poetical thoughts reflected in the early Qing collections of Qing poetry). *Zhengzhou daxue xuebao* 鄭州大學學報, Vol. 45, No. 4 (Jul. 2012), pp. 135-139.

Lin Lilong 林利隆. *Mingren de zhouyou shenghuo* 明人的舟遊生活 (The boat travels of the Ming literati). Yilan: Mingshi yanjiu xiaozu, 2005.

Lin Yutang (1895-1976). *The Gay Genius: The Life and Times of Su Tungpo*. New York: John Day Co., 1947.

Lin Huadong 林華東 and Fang Zhiliang 方志良. "Xishi kao" 西施考 (A textual study of Xishi). *Zhejiang xuekan*, No. 1 of 1985, pp. 122-125.

Lion-Goldschmidt, Daisy (1903-1998). Katherine Watson, trans. *Ming Porcelain*. New York: Rizzoli International Publications, 1978.

Liu, James J.Y. (1926-1986). *The Poetry of Li Shang-yin: Ninth-century Baroque Chinese Poet*. Chicago: University of Chicago Press, 1969.

Liu Rushi 柳如是 (1618-1664). *Liu Rushi shiwen ji* 詩文集 (Collected works of Liu Rushi's poems and prose). Beijing: Quanguo gonggong tushuguan guji wenxian bianweihui, 1996.

Liu Shiheng 劉世珩 (1875-1926). *Guichi ermiao ji* 貴池二妙集 (Collected works of Wu Yingji 吳應箕 and Liu Cheng 劉城). Taibei: Wenhai chubanshe, 1971.

Liu Shiyi 劉士義. "Mingdai yuehu zhidu yu wenxue chuantong" 明代樂籍制度與文學傳統 (The musician registration system and literary tradition in the Ming period). *Wuyi daxue xuebao* 五邑大學學報, Vol. 15, No. 1 (Feb. 2013), pp. 58-62.

Liu Xu 劉昫 (888-947). *Jiu Tangshu* 舊唐書 (Old Tang History). Beijing: Zhonghua shuju, 1974.

Liu Yanyuan 劉燕遠. *Liu Rushi shici pingzhu* 柳如是詩詞評註 (A critical annotation of Liu Rushi's poems). Beijing: Beijing guji chubanshe, 2001.

Loewe, Michael. *A Biographical Dictionary of the Qin, Former Han and Xin Period (221 BC-AD 24)*. Leiden and Boston: Brill, 2000.

Lu Lin 陸林. "Deng Hanyi de xinlu licheng yu *Shiguan* de shixue jiazhi" 鄧漢儀的心路歷程與《詩觀》評點的詩學價值 (The intellectual path of Deng Hanyi and the poetical value of his remarks in *Poetic Views*). *Zhongshan daxue xuebao* 中山大學學報, Vol. 55, No. 5 (2015), pp. 34-46.

_____. "Qingchu Yao Quan pingxuan *Shiyuan* de shidai tese" 清初姚佺評選《詩源》的時代特色 (The characteristics of the *Selected Poems* chosen and commented by Yao Quan in the early Qing). *Wenxue yichan* 文學遺產, No. 6 of 2013, pp. 116-125.

Lu Shiyi 陸世儀 (1611-1672). *Fushe jilüe* 復社紀略 (A brief history of the Restoration Society). Shijiazhuang: Hebei jiaoyu chubanshe, 1995.

Lu Tong 盧仝 (795-835). *Lu Tong ji* 盧仝集 (Collected works of Lu Tong). Beijing: Zhonghua shuju, 1985.

Lü Xianping 呂賢平. "Shuihuiyuan zhong ji aisi: Lun Quanjiao Wushi yu Rugao Maoshi jiaoyou jiqi dui Wu Lang de yingxiang" 水繪園中寄哀思：論全椒吳氏與如皋冒氏交遊及其對吳烺的影響 (Grief from the Painted-in-Water Garden: The literary contacts between Wushi of Quanjiao and Maoshi of Rugao and their impact on Wu Lang). *Nantong daxue xuebao* 南通大學學報, Vol. 28, No. 2 (Mar. 2012), pp. 127-134.

Lu Yongqiang 陸勇強. *Chen Weisong nianpu* 陳維崧年譜 (Chronological biography of Chen Weisong). Beijing: Zhongguo shehui kexue chubanshe, 2006.

Lu Yu 陸羽 (d. 804). Trans. Francis Carpenter. *The Classic of Tea*. New York: Little, Brown & Co., 1974.

Luk, Bernard (Luk Hung-kay 陸鴻基, 1946-2016). "The Civil Service Examinations in Late Imperial China." *Orientations*, Vol. 13, No. 3 (Mar. 1982), pp. 20-29.

Luo Wanwei 羅婉薇. *Hou Fangyu yanjiu* 侯方域研究 (A study of Hou Fangyu). Hong Kong: Lunheng chubanshe, 1997.

Lynn, Richard John. "Alternate Route to Self-Realization in Ming Theories of Poetry." In Susan Bush and Christian Murck, eds., *Theories of the Arts in China* (Princeton: Princeton University Press, 1983), pp. 317-340.

Ma Huaxiang 馬華詳. *Mingdai Yiyangqiang chuanqi kao* 明代弋陽腔傳奇考 (A study of the Yiyang Opera in the Ming period). Beijing: Zhongguo shehui kexue chubanshe, 2009.

Ma Weizhong 馬衛中 and Pan Hong 潘虹. "Qingchu Li Dasheng an bianyi" 清初李大生案辨疑 (On the early Qing case of Li Dasheng). *Shehui kexue jikan* 社會科學緝刊, No. 3 of 1991, pp. 92-94.

Mao Danshu 冒丹書 (1639-95). *Furen ji bu* 婦人集補 (Supplement to *Furen ji*). Reprint. Shijiazhuang: Hebei jiaoyu chubanshe, 1996.

_____. *Zhenyantang shiji* 枕煙堂詩輯 (Collected poems from the Zhenyan Hall). *Rugao Maoshi congshu* edition.

Mao Guangsheng 冒廣生 (1873-1959). *Mao Chaomin xiansheng nianpu* 冒巢民先生年譜 (Chronological biography of Mao Xiang). Beijing: Beijing tushuguan chubanshe, 1999.

Mao Heshu 冒禾書 (b. 1635). *Hanbitang shiji* 寒碧堂詩輯 (Collected poems from the Hanbi Hall). *Rugao Maoshi congshu* edition.

Mao Jin 毛晉 (1599-1659). *Sanjia gongci* 三家宮詞 (Palace poetry of Wang Jian, Madame Huarui, and Wang Gui). Beijing: Zhonghua shuju, 1985.

Mao Lianquan 冒廉泉. *Mao Pijiang zhu* Hongloumeng *qishisan zheng* 冒辟疆著《紅樓夢》七十三證 (Seventy-three pieces of evidence which prove that Mao Xiang was the author of *Dream of the Red Chamber*). Beijing: Huaxia chubanshe, 2016.

Mao Lianquan and Mao Jun 冒俊. "Maoshi zongpu yu Maoshi laiyuan" 《冒氏宗譜》與冒氏來源 (The genealogy of the Mao families and their origins). *Xungen*, No. 3 of 2006, pp. 128-130.

Mao, Nathan (1942-2015). *The Twelve Towers: Short Stories by Li Yü*. Hong Kong: Chinese University Press, 1979.

Mao, Nathan and Liu Ts'un-yan (1917-2009). *Li Yü*. Boston: Twayne Publishers, 1977.

Mao Qingqi 毛慶耆. "Li Suiqiu de shixue he Yijingxue" 黎遂球的詩學和易經學 (Li Suiqiu's studies of poetry and *Yijing*). *Lingnan wenshi* 嶺南文史, No. 1 of 2000, pp. 37-39.

Mao Qizong 冒起宗 (1590-1654). *Zhuocuntang yigao* 拙存堂逸稿 (Collected works from the Zhuocun Hall). Shunzhi era. Reprint. Shanghai: Shanghai guji chubanshe, 2010.

Mao Shuyin 冒舒諲 (1914-1999). "Mao Pijiang qiren qishi jiqi shufa" 冒辟疆其人其事及其書法 (Mao Pijiang: His life and his calligraphy). *Shupu* 書譜, No. 31 (1979), pp. 72-79.

Mao Xiang. *Chaomin shiji* 巢民詩集 (Collected poems of Mao Xiang). Kangxi era. Reprint. Shanghai: Shanghai guji chubanshe, 2010.

———. *Chaomin wenji* 巢民文集 (Collected works of Mao Xiang). Kangxi era. Reprint. Shanghai: Shanghai guji chubanshe, 2010.

———. *Fanxue xiaocao* 泛雪小草 (Snowy grass). *Rugao Maoshi congshu* edition.

———. *Hanbi guyin* 寒碧孤吟 (Lone chantings from the Hanbi Tower). *Rugao Maoshi congshu* edition.

———. *Jiecha huichao* 岕茶匯鈔 (Selected writings on Jie tea). 1833. Reprint. Taibei: Xin Wenfeng shiye gongsi, 1989.

———. *Jimeiren mingshi* 集美人名詩 (Selected poems on beauties). 1903-23. Taibei: Xin Wenfeng shiye gongsi, 1989.

———. *Lan yan* 蘭言 (Notes on orchids). 1903-23. Reprint. Taibei: Xin Wenfeng shiye gongsi, 1989.

———. *Liushinian shiyou shiwen tongren ji* 六十年師友詩文同人集 (Collected writings of kindred spirits over the past sixty years). Kangxi era. Reprint. Liuying, Tainan: Zhuangyen wenhua shiye youxian gongsi, 1997.

———. *Xiangliyuan oucun* 香儷園偶存 (Surviving poems from the Xiangli Garden). 1902.

———. *Xuanlu gezhu* 宣爐歌注 (Notes on the incense-burners from the Xuande era). Kangxi era. Reprint. Shanghai: Shanghai guji chubanshe, 2010.

———. *Yingmeian yiyu* 影梅庵憶語 (Reminiscences of the Plum-shaded Convent). Daoguang ed. Reprint. Shanghai: Shanghai guji chubanshe, 1995.

Mao Xiang, et al. Ran Yunfei 冉雲飛 ed. *Yingmeian yiyu* 影梅庵憶語 (Reminiscences of the Plum-shaded Convent [and other nine Ming-Qing reminiscence writings]). Hohhot: Nei Menggu renmin chubanshe, 1997.

Mao Xiang, et al. Zhu Jianmang 朱劍芒 (1890-1972), ed. *Yingmeian yiyu* 影梅庵憶語 (Reminiscences of the Plum-shaded Convent [and other two early Qing reminiscence writings]). Taibei: Shijie shuju, 1959.

McDowall, Stephen. *Qian Qianyi's Reflections on Yellow Mountain: Traces of a Late-Ming Hatchet and Chisel.* Hong Kong: Hong Kong University Press, 2009.

Meng Sen 孟森 (1869-1937). "Dong Xiaowan kao" 董小宛考 (Notes on Dong Xiaowan). *Xinshi congkan* 心史叢刊 [Collected works of Meng Sen] (Beijing: Zhonghua shuju, 2006), pp. 203-236.

_____. "Hengbo furen kao" 橫波夫人考 (Notes on Gu Mei). *Ming Qing shi lunzhu jikan zhengxubian* 明清史論著集刊 正續編 [Selected essays on Ming-Qing history] (Shijiazhuang: Hebei jiaoyu chubanshe, 2002), pp. 435-472.

Merlin, Monica. "The Nanjing Courtesan Ma Shouzhen (1548-1604): Gender, Space and Painting in the Late Ming Pleasure Quarter." *Gender & History*, Vol. 23, No. 3 (Nov. 2011), pp. 630-652.

Meyer-Fong, Tobie. *Building Culture in Early Qing Yangzhou.* Stanford: Stanford University Press, 2003.

Miller, Harry. *States versus Gentry in Late Ming Dynasty China, 1572-1644.* New York: Palgrave Macmillan, 2009.

Minford, John and Joseph Lau, eds. *Classical Chinese Literature: An Anthology of Translations, Vol. 1: From Antiquity to the Tang Dynasty.* New York: Columbia University Press, 2000.

Miyazaki, Ichisada (1901-1995). Trans. Conrad Schirokauer. *China's Examination Hell: The Civil Service Examinations of Imperial China.* New Haven: Yale University Press, 1976.

Mote, F.W. (1922-2005). "The Transformation of Nanking, 1350-1400." In William Skinner (1925-2008), ed., *The City in Late Imperial China* (Stanford: Stanford University Press, 1977), pp. 101-154.

_____. "A Millennium of Chinese Urban History: Form, Time, and Space Concepts in Soochow." *Rice University Studies*, Vol. 59, No. 4 (Fall 1973), pp. 35-65.

Niu Xiu 鈕琇 (1644-1704). *Gusheng* 觚賸 (Additional historical records). 1700-1702. Reprint. Jinan: Qi Lu shushe, 2001.

Ōki, Yasushi 大木康. "Literature of the Sixteenth and Seventeenth Century World." In Benjamin Elman and Chao-Hui Liu, eds., *The "Global' and the 'Local" in Early*

Modern and Modern East Asia (Leiden and Boston: Brill, 2017), pp. 178-191.

_____. *Mao Xiang yu Yingmeian yiyu yanjiu* 冒襄和影梅庵憶語研究 (A study of Mao Xiang and the *Reminiscences of the Plum-Shaded Hut*). Taibei: Liren shuju, 2013.

_____. *Bō Jō* Eibaian okugo *no kenkyū* 冒襄と『影梅庵憶語』の研究 (A study of Mao Xiang and the *Reminiscences of the Plum-Shaded Hut*). Tokyo: Kyūko shoin, 2010.

_____. Trans. Xin Ruyi 辛如意. *Fengyue Qinhuai* 風月秦淮 (The Qinhuai pleasure quarters). Taibei: Lianjing chuban gongsi, 2007.

_____. "Mao Xiang and Yu Huai: Early Qing Romantic *Yimin*." In Wilt Idema, Wai-Yee Li, and Ellen Widmer, eds., *Trauma and Transcendence in in Early Qing Literature* (Cambridge: Harvard University Asia Center, 2006), pp. 231-248.

Ouyang Jian 歐陽健. "Yu Huai, Mao Xiang and Xu Zheng xiaoshuo jiedu" 余懷、冒襄、徐震小説解讀 (An interpretation of the literary works of Yu Huai, Mao Xiang ang Xu Zheng). *Xiaoshuo yu xiaoshuo piping* 小説與小説批評, No. 2 of 2010, pp. 4-13.

Ouyang Xiu 歐陽修 (1007-1072). *Xin Tangshu* 新唐書 (New Tang history). Beijing: Zhonghua shuju, 1974.

Owen, Stephen. *The Poetry of Du Fu*. Warsaw and Boston: De Gruyter, 2015. 6 vols.

_____. *The Late Tang: Chinese Poetry of the Mid-Ninth Century*. Cambridge: Harvard University Asia Center, 2006.

_____. *An Anthology of Chinese Literature: Beginnings to 1911*. New York: W.W. Norton, 1997.

_____. *Remembrances: The Experience of the Past in Classical Chinese Literature*. Cambridge: Harvard University Press, 1986.

Pan Tzy-yen, trans. *The Reminiscences of Tung Hsiao-wan*. Shanghai: Commercial Press, 1931.

Pei Shijun 裴世俊. *Sihai zongmeng wushinian: Qian Qianyi zhuan* 四海宗盟五十年：錢謙益傳 (Fifty years' literary leadership: A biography of Qian Qianyi). Beijing: Dongfang chubanshe, 2001.

Peng Sunyi 彭孫貽 (1615-1673). *Ming shichao* 明詩鈔 (Collection of Ming poetry). Beijing: Airusheng shuzihua jishu yanjiu zhongxin, 2009.

_____. *Mingzhai shiyu* 茗齋詩餘 (Poems from the Tea Studio). Beijing: Zhonghua shuju, 1985.

_____. *Pingkou zhi* 平寇志 (Record of quelling bandits). Shanghai: Shanghai guji chubanshe, 1984.

_____. *Liukou zhi* 流寇志 (Record of roving bandits). Hangzhou: Zhejiang renmin chubanshe, 1983.

Peterson, Barbara Bennett. *Notable Women of China: Shang Dynasty to the Early Twentieth Century.* Armonk: M.E. Sharpe, 2000.

Peterson, Willard J. *Bitter Gourd: Fang I-Chih and the Impetus for Intellectual Change in the 1630s.* New Haven: Yale University Press, 1979.

_____. "Fang I-chih: Western Learning and the 'Investigation of Things'." In William Theodore de Bary, ed., *The Unfolding of Neo-Confucianism* (New York: Columbia University Press, 1975), pp. 371-411.

Pfister, Louis (1833-1891). *Notices Biographiques et Bibliographiques sur les Jesuites de L'ancienne Mission de Chine, 1552-1773.* Shanghai: Imprimerie de la Mission Catholique, 1932-34.

Pidhainy, Ihor, Roger Des Forges, and Grace Fong, eds. *Representing Lives in China: Forms of Biography in the Ming-Qing Period (1368-1911).* Ithaca: Cornell East Asia Program, 2019.

Pine, Red (Bill Porter) and Mike O'Connor, eds. *The Clouds Should Know Me by Now: Buddhist Poet Monks of China.* Boston: Wisdom Publications, 1998.

Qi Wenbang 齊文榜. *Jia Dao ji jiaozhu* 賈島集校注 (Annotated works of Jia Dao). Beijing: Renmin wenxue chubanshe, 2001.

Qian Qianyi 錢謙益 (1582-1664). *Liechao shiji xiaozhuan* 列朝詩集小傳 (Brief biographies of Qing poets). Beijing: Zhonghua shuju, 1959.

Qian Yong 錢詠 (1759-1844). *Lüyuan conghua* 履園叢話 (Collected talks from the Lü Garden). Beijing: Zhonghua shuju, 1997.

Ren Daobin 任道斌. *Dong Qichang xinian* 董其昌系年 (A chronology of Dong Qichang's life). Beijing: Wenwu chubanshe, 1988.

Rexroth, Kenneth (1905-1982) and Chung Ling. *The Orchid Boat: Women Poets of China.* New York: McGraw-Hill, 1972.

Ruan Yuan 阮元 (1764-1849). *Guangling shishi* 廣陵詩事 (Noted persons from the prefecture of Yangzhou). Yangzhou: Guangling shushe, 2005.

Rugao Hongyou 汝皋紅友, ed. *Mao Pijiang zhuzuo Hongloumeng huikao (Dierji)* 冒辟疆著作紅樓夢彙考（第二輯）(Collected articles on Mao Xiang's authorship of *Dream of the Red Chamber*). Vol. 2. Nanjing: Jiangsu Fenghuang meishu chubanshe, 2015.

Schwarz, Rainer trans. *Erinnerungen aus der chattenaprikosenklause.* Beijing: Foreign Language Teaching and Research Press, 2009.

Shao Zhiyu 邵志宇 and Yang Lili 楊麗麗. "Rugao Maoshi de laiyuan" 如皋冒氏的來源 (The origin of the Mao genealogy of Rugao). *Xungen* 尋根, No. 3 of 2005, 92-95.

Shen Fu 沈復 (b. 1763). *Fusheng liuji* 浮生六記. Trans. Lin Yutang 林語堂 (1898-1976). *Six Chapters of a Floating Life.* N.P., preface 1935.

____. Trans. Shirley Black. *Chapters from a Floating Life.* Oxford: Oxford University Press, 1960.

____. Trans. Leonard Pratt and Chiang Su-Hui. *Six Records of a Floating Life.* Harmondsworth: Penguin, 1983.

____. Trans. Graham Sanders. *Six Records of a life Adrift.* Indianapolis: Hackett Publishing Company, 2011.

Shen Xinlin 沈新林. *Li Yu xinlun* 李漁新論 (New light on Li Yu). Suzhou: Suzhou daxue chubanshe, 1997.

____. "Li Yu yu Mao Xiang" 李漁與冒襄 (Li Yu and Mao Xiang). *Huaiyin shifan xueyuan xuebao* 淮陰師範學院學報, Vol. 25, No. 2 (May 2003), pp. 676-681.

____. "Shuihuiyuan tanyi" 水繪園探佚 (In search of the Painted-in-Water Garden). In He Yongkang 何永康 and Chen Shulu 陳書錄, eds., *Shoujie Mingdai wenxue guoji yantaohui wenji* 首屆明代文學國際研討會文集 (Nanjing: Nanjing shifan daxue chubanshe, 2004).

____. "*Hongloumeng* yu Rugao" 紅樓夢與如皋 (*Dream of the Red Chamber* and Rugao). *Ming Qing xiaoshuo yanjiu* 明清小說研究, No. 119 (2016), pp. 118-126.

Shen Yue 沈約 (441-513). *Songshu* 宋書 (Book of the Liu Song dynasty). Reprint. Beijing: Zhonghua shuju, 1974.

Shi Yun 石雲. "Jin sanshinian Mao Xiang yanjiu shukao" 近三十年冒襄研究述考 (A review of studies on Mao Xiang in the past thirty years). *Wenjiao zhiliao* 文教資料, No. 28 of 2014, pp. 5-6.

Shu Chang 舒暢 and Zuo Shu'e 左書諤. *Zhongguo lishi shang de shida mingji* 中國歷史上的四大名伎 (Ten famous courtesans in Chinese history). Lanzhou: Gansu renmin chubanshe, 2003.

Shu Hede 舒赫德 (1710-1777). *Qinding Shengchao xunjie zhuchen lu* 欽定勝朝殉節諸臣錄 (The royally sanctioned record of the officials who died for the Ming dynasty). Taibei: Taiwan yinhang jingji yanjiushi, 1971.

Shu Mei 菽梅. "Mingdai yuehu jinchi yu yasu wenhua de hudong" 明代樂戶禁弛與雅俗文化的互動 (The tightening and relaxing of the musician household system and their impact on popular culture in the Ming period). *Hebei xuekan* 河北學刊, Vol. 24, No. 4 (Jul. 2004), pp. 165-169.

Song Fengmei 宋風梅. "Dongtian fudi: Suzhou Guangfu zheng" 洞天福地：蘇州光福鎮 (The Guangfu township of Suzhou: A blessed place). *Jianghai qiaosheng* 江海僑聲, No. 14 (1997), p. 33.

Song Haofei 宋豪飛. "*Liudu fangluan gongjie* kaolun" 《留都防亂公揭》考論 (On the Anti-Disturbance Poster). *Anqing shifan xueyuan xuebao* 安慶師範學院學報, Vol. 30, No. 11 (Nov. 2011), pp. 3-7.

Spence, Jonathan. *Return to Dragon Mountain: Memories of a Late Ming Man*. New York: Viking, 2007.

Su Shanyu 蘇珊玉. *Xue Tao jiqi shi yanjiu* 薛濤及其詩研究 (A study of Xue Tao and her poetry). Yonghe, Taibei: Huamulan chubanshe, 2008.

Strassberg, Richard. *The World of K'ung Shang-jen: The Man of Letters in Early Ch'ing China*. New York: Columbia University Press, 1983.

Sun Chengze 孫承澤 (1592-1676). *Chunming mengyu lu* 春明夢餘錄 (Miscellaneous notes about the capital city of Beijing and the central administration in the Ming dyansty). Early Qing. Reprint. Beijing: Beijing chubanshe, 2018.

Sun Chunqing 孫春青. "Mingmo de Tangshi zhengli yu Tangshixue qingxiang" 明末的唐詩整理與唐詩學傾向 (The collection and study of Tang poetry in late Ming). *Zhongguo wenxue yanjiu* 中國文學研究, No. 2 of 2009, pp. 77-81.

Sun Zhiqiang 孫志強. "Wan Ming yinren Liu Lüding kaolun" 晚明印人劉履丁考論 (On the late Ming seal carver Liu Lüding). *Meishu daguan* 美術大觀, No. 11 of 2016, pp. 58-59.

Tang, Michael. *Siren of China*. New York: Better Link Press, 2007.

Tang Shuyu 湯漱玉. *Yutai huashi* 玉台畫史 (Jade Terrace's account of female painters in China). 1837. Reprint. Shanghai: Shanghai renmin meishu chubanshe, 1963.

Tang Yuxing 湯宇星. *Cong Taoyedu dao Shuihuiyuan: Shiqi shiji de Jiangnan yu Mao Xiang de1 yishu jiaowang* 從桃葉渡到水繪園：十七世紀的江南與冒襄的藝術交往 (From the Peach-leaf Pier to the Painted-in-Water Garden: Seventeenth-century Jiangnan and its artistic communication with Mao Xiang). Hangzhou: Zhongguo meishu xueyuan chubanshe, 2012.

_____. "Mao Xiang de yimin shijie (4): Yishu shoucang" 冒襄的遺民世界（4）：藝術收藏 (The loyalist world of Mao Xiang (4): The art collections). *Rongbaozhai* 榮寶齋, No. 11 of 2011, pp. 268-271.

_____. "Mao Xiang de yimin shijie (3): Hongqiao changhe" 冒襄
的遺民世界（3）：紅橋倡和 (The loyalist world of Mao
Xiang (3): The poetic exchanges). *Rongbaozhai*, No. 7 of
2011, pp. 272-281.

_____. "Mao Xiang de yimin shijie (2): Wenhua zanzhu" 冒襄的
遺民世界（2）：文化贊助 (The loyalist world of Mao
Xiang (2): The sponsorship of cultural activities).
Rongbaozhai, No. 3 of 2011, pp. 266-277.

_____. "Mao Xiang de yimin shijie (1): Fu Ming yundong" 冒襄
的遺民世界（1）：復明運動 (The loyalist world of Mao
Xiang (1): The effort to restore the Ming dynasty).
Rongbaozhai, No. 7 of 2010, pp. 288-297.

Tao Muning 陶慕寧. "Cong *Yingmeian yiyu* kan wan Ming
Jiangnan wenren de hunyin xingai guan" 從《影梅庵憶
語》看晚明江南文人的婚姻性愛觀 (The ideas of love and
marriage of the late Ming Jiangnan literati as seen from *The
Reminiscences of the Plum-Shaded Convent*). *Nankai
xuebao* 南開學報, No. 4 of 2000, pp. 56-61.

Teng Shaozhen 滕紹箴 and Li Zhiting 李治亭. *Chen Yuanyuan
houzhuan* 陳圓圓後傳 (A biography of Chen Yuanyuan in
her late years). Changsha: Yuelu shushe, 2012.

_____. "Chen Yuanyuan wannian shenghuo shulüe" 陳圓圓晚年
生活述略 (The final years of Chen Yuanyuan). *Guizhou
shehui kexue* 貴州社會科學, No. 11 of 2011, pp. 114-122.

Vallette-Hémery, Martinne. *Mao Xiang: La dame aux pruniers
ombreux*. Paris: Philippe Picquier, 1998.

Van Gulik, R.S. (1910-1967). *Sexual Life in Ancient China: A
Preliminary Survey of Chinese Sex and Society from ca.
1500 B.C. till 1644 A.D.* Leiden and Boston: Brill, 2005.

Volpp, Sophie. "The Literary Circulation of Actors in
Seventeenth Century China." *The Journal of Asian Studies*,
Vol. 61, No. 3 (Aug. 2002), pp. 949-984.

Wakeman, Frederic, Jr. (1937-2006). "Romantics, Stoics, and
Martyrs in Seventeenth-Century China." *Journal of Asian
Studies*, Vol. 43, No. 4 (Aug. 1984), pp. 631-665.

Waley, Arthur (1889-1966). *Waiting for the Moon: Poems of Bo
Juyi*. Mount Jackson, VA: Axios Press, 2012.

Wan Jiufu 萬久富 and Ding Fusheng 丁富生, eds. *Mao Pijiang quanji* 冒辟疆全集 (Complete works of Mao Xiang). Nanjing: Fenghuang chubanshe, 2014.

Wang Bing 王兵. "Lun Qingdai Qingshi xuanben de fenqi jiqi tezheng" 論清代清詩選本的分期及其特徵 (On the periodization and characteristics of the Qing collections of Qing poetry). *Zhongguo wenhua yanjiusuo xuebao* 中國文化研究所學報, No. 52 (Jan. 2011), pp. 187-202.

Wang Chaohong 汪超宏. *Wu Qi nianpu* 吳綺年譜 (The chronological biography of Wu Qi). Beijing: Renmin wenxue chubanshe, 2012.

____. "Lun Du Jun qiren qishi" 論杜濬其人其詩 (On Du Jun and his poems). *Jianghuai luntan* 江淮論壇, No. 10 of 1998, pp. 66-68.

Wang Chuangsong 王傳松. "Wuxi Tianzhutang diyiwei zhutang shenfu Bi Fangji" 無錫天主堂第一位本堂神父畢方濟 (Francesco Sambiasi: The first priest of the Wuxi Catholic Church). *Zhongguo Tianzhujiao* 中國天主教, No. 5 of 2006, p. 46.

Wang Chunyu 王春瑜. "'Cishengyuan zaijie tashengli:' Mingmo sigongzi de shenqing houyi" 此生緣再結他生裡：明末四公子的深情厚誼 (The friendship between the Four Masters of the late Ming). In *Kanle Mingchao jiu mingbai* 看了明朝就明白 [You will understand everything after reading the history of Ming dyansty] (Hong Kong: Sanlian shudian, 2007), pp. 75-79.

Wang Enjun 王恩俊. "Shilun Fushe neibu de zhengzhi fenqi" 試論復社內部的政治分歧 (On the political differences among the Restoration Society members). *Dongbei shida xuebao* 東北師大學報, No. 1 of 2007, pp. 21-25.

Wang Limin 王利民, Ding Fusheng, and Gu Qi. *Mao Pijiang yu Dong Xiaowan* 冒辟疆與董小宛 (Mao Pijiang and Dong Xiaowan). Beijing: Zhonghua shuju, 2004.

Wang Limin and Gu Qi. "Mao Pijiang yu Dong Xiaowan de guizhong yaqu" 冒辟疆與董小宛的閨中雅趣 (The chamber life of Mao Pijiang and Dong Xiaowan). *Wenshi zhishi*, No. 1 of 2003, pp. 61-66.

Wang Ranye 王染野. "Mao Xiang kunban yanju kao ji qita," 冒襄昆班演劇考及其他 (A study on the performances of Mao Xiang's Kun Opera troupe and related issues). *Suzhou keji xueyuan xuebao* 蘇州科技學院學報, Vol. 27, No. 4 (July 2010), pp. 89-91.

Wang Shaoxi 王紹璽. *Xiaoqie shi* 小妾史 (A history of concubines). Shanghai: Shanghai wenyi chubanshe, 1995.

Wang Shilu 王士祿 (1626-73). *Ranzhi ji li* 然脂集例 (Rules for compiling *Works by Women Writers in Chinese History*). Taibei: Xin Wenfeng chuban gongsi, 1989.

Wang Shuanghuai 王雙懷, Chen Jiarong 陳佳榮, and Fang Jun 方駿. *Zhonghua tongli* 中華通典 (Comprehensive concordance of Chinese calendrical dates). Xi'an: Shaanxi shifan daxue chubanshe, 2018. 10 Vols.

Wang Shuanghuai, Fang Jun, and Chen Jiarong. *Zhonghua rili tongdian* 中華日曆通典 (Complete Sino-Western calendar). Changchun: Jilin wenshi chubanshe, 2006. 4 Vols.

Wang Xinghui 王星慧. "Cong Kangxi chunian Cao Rong zai Shanxi de weiguan zhizuo xi qi erchenxingwei" 從康熙初年曹溶在山西的為官之作析其貳臣行為 (Cao Rong's double-serving as seen from his office performance in the early Kangxi era). *Xinzhou shifan xueyuan xuebao* 忻州師範學院學報, Vol. 26, No. 1 (Feb. 2010), pp. 75-77.

_____. "Kangxi ernian Gu Yanwu zai Shanxi yu Cao Rong Li Yindu de jiaoyou kao" 康熙二年顧炎武在山西與曹溶、李因篤交遊考 (The cultural contact between Gu Yanwu and Cao Rong and Li Yindu in Shanxi in 1663). *Yanbei shifan xueyuan xuebao* 雁北師範學院學報, Vol. 22, No. 4 (Aug. 2006), pp. 35-38.

Wang Xinli 王新利. "Ming Qing shufajia Wang Duo jiaoyou jiqi shufa chuangzhuo lichen tanxi" 明清書法家王鐸交遊及書法創作歷程探析 (On the Ming-Qing calligrapher Wang Duo's social contacts and his calligraphy). *Chuancheng* 傳承, No. 6 of 2014, pp. 114-115.

Wang Yan 王燕. "Wan Ming Qinhuai mingji xianxiang chutan" 晚明秦淮名妓現象初探 (A preliminary study of the famous Qinhuai courtesans in the late Ming). *Jianghuai luntan* 江淮論壇, No. 6 of 2003, pp. 102-107.

Wang Yuchi 王玉池. *Zhong Yao* 鍾繇. Beijing: Zijincheng chubanshe, 1991.

Wang Zhonghan 王鍾翰 (1913-2007), anno. *Qingshi liezhuan* 清史列傳 (Qing dynasty biographies). Beijing: Zhonghua shuju, 1987.

Wang Zhonghe 王忠和. *Mingmo sigongzi* 明末四公子 (The four masters of the late Ming). Beijing: Dongfang chubanshe, 2010.

Wang Zhongyong 王仲鏞. *Tangshi jishi jiaojian* 唐詩紀事校箋 (Annotated record of poetical works from beginning to the end of the Tang dyansty). Chengdu: Ba Shu shudian, 1989.

Wang Zhuohua 王卓華. "Deng Hanyi shige bieji kaolüe" 鄧漢儀詩歌別集考略 (On the collected poems of Deng Hanyi). *Yulin shifan xueyuan xuebao* 玉林師範學院學報, Vol. 35, No. 1 (2014), pp. 59-63.

_____. "Deng Hanyi shiji kaolüe" 鄧漢儀事蹟考略 (On the life of Deng Hanyi). *Yulin Shifan xueyuan xuebao*, Vol. 32, No. 3 (2011), pp. 78-83.

_____. "Deng Hanyi yu Wang Shizhen Kong Shangren jiaoyou kao" 鄧漢儀與王士禛、孔尚任交遊考 (The literary contacts between Deng Hanyi, Wang Shizhen and Kong Shangren). *Zhongzhou xuekan* 中州學刊, No. 4 of 2006, pp. 209-211.

_____. "Deng Hanyi shishiguan jiqi shixue yiyi" 鄧漢儀詩史觀及其詩學意義 (Deng Hanyi's idea of historical poems and its significance). *Nanjing shida xuebao* 南京師大學報, No. 4 of 2006, pp. 133-137.

_____. "*Shiguan* jiqi wenxianxue yiyi" 《詩觀》及其文獻學意義 (*A Comprehensive Collection of Qing Poetry* and its documentary significance). *Henan shehui kexue* 河南社會科學, Vol. 15, No. 5 of 2006 (Sept. 2006), pp. 156-159.

Waters, Geoffrey (1948-2007), Michael Farman, and David Lunde, trans. *Three Hundred Tang Poems*. Buffalo: White Pine Press, 2011.

Waters, Geoffrey. *Three Elegies of Ch'u: An Introduction to the Traditional Interpretation of the Ch'u Tz'u*. Madison: University of Wisconsin Press, 1985.

Watson, Burton (1925-2017). *Po Chü-i: Selected Poems*. Columbia University Press, 2000.

_____. *Selected Poems of Su Tung-p'o*. Port Townsend, WA: Copper Canyon Press, 1994.

Wei Ran 蔚然. "*Yingmeian yiyu* banben yuanliu kao" 影梅庵憶語版本源流考 (A study on the editions of the *Yingmeian yiyu*). In *Zhongguo dianji yu wenhua* 中國典籍與文化, No. 2 of 2003, pp. 27-31.

Wei Shengnian 韋盛年. "Li Suiqiu nianpu jianbian" 黎遂球年譜簡編 (A brief chronological biography of Li Suiqiu). *Wuyi daxue xuebao*, Vol. 8, No. 1 (Feb. 2006), pp. 27-33.

Weider, Marsha, et al. *Views from Jade Terrace: Chinese Women Artists, 1300-1912*. Indianapolis: Indianapolis Museum of Art; New York: Rizzoli, 1988.

Wen Bolun 文伯倫. *Huarui furen* 花蕊夫人 (Madame Huarui). Chengdu: Ba Shu shushe, 2001.

Wu Cuncun. *Homoerotic Sensibilities in Late Imperial China*. Abingdon and New York: RoutledgeCurzon, 2004.

Wu Dingzhong 吳定中. *Dong Xiaowan huikao* 董小宛匯考 (Textual studies on Dong Xiaowan). Shanghai: Shanghai shudian chubanshe, 2001.

Wu, Nelson (1919-2002). "Tung Ch'i-ch'ang: Apathy in Government and Fervor in Art." In Arthur Wright (1913-1976) and Denis Twitchett (1925-2006), eds., *Confucian Personalities* (Stanford: Stanford University Press, 1962), pp. 260-293.

Wu, Pei-yi (1927-2009). *The Confucian's Progress: Autobiographical Writings in Traditional China*. Princeton: Princeton University Press, 1990.

Wi Qi 吳綺 (1619-1694). *Linhuitang ji* 林惠堂集 (Collected works of Wu Qi). Taibei: Taiwan shangwu yinshuguan, 1972.

Wu Weiye 吳偉業 (1609-1672). *Wu Meicun quanji* 吳梅村全集 (The complete works of Wu Weiye). Shanghai: Shanghai guji chubanshe, 1990.

Wu Xinlei 吳新雷. "Yangzhou Kunban qushe kao" 揚州昆班曲社考 (On the Kun opera societies in Yangzhou). *Dongnan daxue xuebao* 東南大學學報, Vol. 2, No. 1 (2000), pp. 88-97.

Wu Yingji 吳應箕 (1594-1645). *Loushantang ji* 樓山堂集 (Collected works from the Loushan Hall). Reprint. Beijing: Zhonghua shuju, 1985.

Xia Taidi 夏太娣. "Mao Xiang jiequ guiyin kaobian" 冒襄借曲歸隱考辨 (Mao Xiang's reclusion with music activities). *Yishu baijia* 藝術百家, No. 6 of 2006, pp. 13-16.

Xiao Tong 蕭統 (501-531). Trans. David R. Knechtges. *Wen Xuan or Selections of Refined Literature*. Vols. 1-3. Princeton: Princeton University Press, 1982-1996.

Xie Li 謝荔. "Cai Han de shanshuitu shangxi" 蔡含的山水圖賞析 (The appreciation of the mountain-water paintings by Cai Han). *Sichuan wenwu* 四川文物, No. 6 of 1986, pp. 43-44.

Xie Shaozu 謝紹祖 (fl. 1560). *Rugao xianzhi* 如皋縣志 (Gazetteer of Rugao county). 1560. Rpt. Shanghai: Shanghai guji chubanshe, 1990.

Xie Zhengguang (Andrew Hsieh) 謝正光. *Qingchu shiwen yu shiren jiaoyou kao* 清初詩文與士人交遊考 (A study of early Qing poetry, prose, and literary contact among literati). Nanjing: Nanjing daxue chubanshe, 2001.

Xie Zhengguang and Fan Jinmin 范金民. *Ming yimin lu huiji* 明遺民錄匯輯 (Collected material on Ming loyalists). Nanjing: Nanjing daxue chubanshe, 1995.

Xu Baowei 徐保衛. *Li Yu zhuan* 李漁傳 (A biography of Li Yu). Nanchang: Baihuazhou wenyi chubanshe, 2011.

Xu Chen 徐琛. *Shuihuiyuan: Mao Pijiang Dong Xiaowan chuanqi de yanyi kongjian* 水繪園：冒辟疆董小宛傳奇的演繹空間 (Painted-in-Water Garden: The space where the legendary love affairs between Mao Pijiang and Dong

Xiaowan occurred). Suzhou: Suzhou daxue chubanshe, 2013.

Xu Fu 徐傅. *Guangfu zhi* 光福志 (Gazetteer of Guangfu township). Beijing: Huaxia chubanshe, 1999.

Xu Liang 徐亮. "Gusu diyi mingjie: Shantang jie" 姑蘇第一名街：山塘街 (The No. One Street in Suzhou: Shantang Street). *Zhongguo diming* 中國地名, No. 5 of 2005, p. 18.

Xu Lingyun 徐淩雲 and Hu Jinwang, eds. *Ruan Dacheng xiqu sizhong* 阮大鋮戲曲四種 (Four dramas of Ruan Dacheng). Hefei: Huangshan shushe, 1993.

Xu Shichang 徐世昌 (1855-1939). *Wanqingyi shihui* 晚晴簃詩匯 (Collection of Qing poems). 1929. Reprint. Beijing: Zhonghua shuju, 1990.

Xu Yuanchong 許淵衝. *The Elegies of the South*. Beijing: Wuzhou chubanshe, 2012.

_____. *Selected Poems of Su Shi*. Changsha: Hunan renmin chubanshe, 2007.

Xu Zhimian 徐知免. "Mao Pijiang he ta de sange yuanzi" 冒辟疆和他的三個園子 (Mao Pijiang and his three gardens). *Nanjing ligong daxue xuebao* 南京理工大學學報, Vol. 21, No. 4 (Aug. 2008), pp. 16-20.

Xu Zhinong 徐植農 and Zhao Yuxia 趙玉霞, eds. *Hou Chaozong wenxuan* 侯朝宗文選 (Selected works of Hou Chaozong). Jinan: Qi Lu shushe, 1988.

Xu Zi 徐鼐 (1810-1862). *Xiaotian jinian fukao* 小腆紀年附考 (Additional notes on late Ming history). 1861. Reprint. Beijing: Zhonghua shuju, 1957.

Xu Zichang 許自昌 (1578-1623). *Tang shier jia shi* 唐十二家詩 (Poems of twelve Tang poets). NP: Feiyuxuan, 1603.

Xue Diao 薛調 (829-872). *Wushuang zhuan* 無雙傳 (Biography of Liu Wushuang). Beijing: Beijing chubanshe, 2000.

Xue Tao 薛濤 (768-831). Trans. Jeanne Larsen. *Brocade River Poems: Selected Works of the Tang Dynasty Courtesan Xue Tao*. Princeton: Princeton University Press, 1987.

Yan Dichang 嚴迪昌 (1936-2003). "Jintai fengya zong shiren: Gong Dingzi lun" 金台風雅總詩人：龔鼎孳論 (On Gong Dingzi). *Yuwen zhishi* 語文知識, No. 1 of 2008, pp. 4-7.

_____. *Yangxian cipai yanjiu* 陽羨詞派研究 (A study of the Yangxian School of *Ci* Poetry). Jinan: Qi Lu shushe, 1993.

Yang, Gladys (1919-1999) and Yang Xianyi (1915-2009). *Chu Ci Xuan: Selected Elegies of the State of Chu.* Beijing: Waiwen chubanshe, 2011.

Yang Guoqing 楊國慶. *Mingdai Nanjing chengqiang* 明代南京城牆 (City wall of Ming dynasty Nanjing). Nanjing: Nanjing chubanshe, 2002.

Yang Haitao 楊海濤. "Dong Xiaowan cixiu huadietu" 董小宛刺繡花蝶圖 (An embroidery work of a butterfly by Dong Xiaowan). *Shoucangjia* 收藏家, No. 6 of 2006, pp. 33-34.

Yao Chengxu 姚承緒 (fl. 1850). *Wuqu fanggu lu* 吳趨訪古錄 (In search of the history of Suzhou). Nanjing: Jiangsu guji chubanshe, 1999.

Yao Quan 姚佺 (fl. 1650). *Shiyuan chuji* 詩源初集 (The first collection of Qing poetry). Beijing: Beijing guji chubanshe, 2000.

Ye Guangting 葉光庭. *Xihu shihua* 西湖史話 (A history of West Lake). Hangzhou: Hangzhou chubanshe, 2006.

Ye Junyuan 葉君遠 and Huang Yu 黃語. "Xinjiu wenren de hexie hechang: Yisi Shangsi Shuihuiyuan xiuxie de duochong fengjing" 新舊文人的和諧和唱：乙巳上巳水繪園修禊的多重風景 (Poetic responsory of old and young men of letters: The scenery from the Double Third Festival of 1665 at the Painted-in-Water Garden), *Wenshizhe* 文史哲, No. 2 of 2011, pp. 67-75.

Yim, Lawrence C.H. *The Poet-historian Qian Qianyi.* Abingdon and New York: Routledge, 2009.

You Mao 尤袤 (1127-1202). *Quan Tang shihua* 全唐詩話 (Discussions of poetry of the entire Tang period). Beijing: Zhonghua shuju, 1985.

You Tong 尤侗 (1618-1704). *Genzhai zashuo xushuo* 艮齋雜說續說 (Miscellaneous notes of You Tong) and *Kanjian oushuo* 看鑑偶說 (Random notes of reading history). Beijing: Zhonghua shuju, 1992.

Young, David. *Du Fu: A Life in Poetry.* New York: Alfred A. Knopf, 2008.

Yu Chen 余琛. *Shuihuiyuan: Mao Pijiang Dong Xiaowan chuanqi de yanyi kongjian* 水繪園：冒辟疆董小宛傳奇的演繹空間 (The Painted-in-Water Garden: The origin of the Mao Pijiang-Dong Xiaowan legend). Suzhou: Suzhou daxue chubanshe, 2013.

Yu Genzhe 于賡哲. "Gegu fengqin yuanqi de shehui beijing: Yi Tangdai wei zhongxin" 割股奉親緣起的社會背景：以唐代為中心 (A study of the social background of the practice of cutting one's flesh to cure one's ill parents: Focusing on the Tang period). *Shixue yuekan* 史學月刊, No. 2 of 2006, pp. 87-95.

Yu Huai 余懷 (1616-96). *Banqiao zaji* 板橋雜記 (Miscellaneous notes from the Plank Bridge). 1693. Reprint. Nanjing: Nanjing chubanshe, 2006.

Yu, Pauline. "The Chinese Poetic Canon and Its Boundaries." In Jay John, ed., *Boundaries in China* (London: Reaktion Books, 1994), pp. 105-123.

_____. "Formal Distinctions in Chinese Literary Theory." In Susan Bush and Christian Murck, eds., *Theories of the Arts in China* (Princeton: Princeton University Press, 1983), pp. 27-53.

Yu Yingshi 余英時. *Fang Yizhi wanjie kao* 方以智晚節考 (On the integrity of Fang Yizhi in his later years). Beijing: Sanlian shudian, 2004.

Zeitlin, Judith. "Spirit Writing and Performance in the Work of You Tong (1618-1704)." *T'oung Pao*, Vol. 84, Fasc. 1/3, pp. 102-135.

Zeng, Li. "Ambiguous and Amiss: Li Shangyin's Poetry and Its Interpretation." *Southeast Review of Asian Studies*, Vol. 30 (Jan. 2008), pp. 137-150.

Zeng Yongwen 曾永文. "Yiyangqiang jiqi liupai kaoshu" 弋陽腔及其流派考述 (The Yiyang Opera and its subgenres). *Taida wenshizhe xuebao* 台大文史哲學報, Vol. 65 (Nov. 2006), pp. 39-72.

Zhai Guozhang 翟國璋, ed. *Zhongguo keju cidian* 中國科舉辭典 (A dictionary of civil service exmiantions in China). Nanchang: Jiangxi jiaoyu chubanshe, 2006.

Zhang Chao 張潮 (1650-1707). *Yuchu xinzhi* 虞初新志 (Selected stories by late Ming-early Qing men of letters). Reprint. Shanghai: Shanghai guji chubanshe, 2012.

Zhang Dai 張岱 (1597-1679). *Shiguishu houji* 石匱書後集 (A sequel to the Stone Cabinet Book). Reprint. Shanghai: Shanghai guji chubanshe, 2007.

Zhang Daihui 張代會. "Kundun rensheng yikuang yizheng: Qingchu yimin shiren Du Jun de rensheng zhuiqiu yu sixiang gexing" 困頓人生 亦狂亦正：清初遺民詩人杜濬 的人生追求與思想個性 (A hard life: The career pursuit and intellectual characteristics of the early Qing loyalist poet, Du Jun). *Xi'nan nongye daxue xuebao* 西南農業大學學報, Vol. 9, No. 4 (Apr. 2011), pp. 130-133.

Zhang Geng 张庚 (1685-1760). *Guochao huazheng xulu* 國朝畫徵續錄 (Sequel to the *Biographies of the Qing Painters*). Shanghai: Shanghai guji chubanshe, 1995.

Zhang, Hongsheng. "Gong Dingzhi and the Courtesan Gu Mei: Their Romance and the Revival of the Song Lyric in the Ming-Qing Transition." In Grace Fong, ed., *Hsiang Lectures on Chinese Poetry, Vol. 2* (Montreal: Center for East Asian Research, McGill University), pp. 71-85.

Zhang Mingbi 張明弼 (1584-1653). *Maoji Dong Xiaowan zhuan* 冒姬董小宛傳 (A biography of Mao Xiang's concubine Dong Xiaowan). In *Yingmeian yiyu* (Taibei: Shijie shuju, 1959).

Zhang Tingyu 張廷玉 (1672-1755), et al. *Mingshi* 明史 (The official history of the Ming dynasty). Beijing: Zhonghua shuju, 1974.

Zhang Xiaohu 張曉虎. *Qingchu sida mingji* 清初四大名妓 (Four famous courtesans in the early Qing). Taibei: Yunlong chubanshe, 1991.

Zhang Xiaoqian 張小茜. "Lun *Yingmeian yiyu* he *Fusheng liuji*" 論《影梅庵憶語》和《浮生六記》 (On *The Reminiscences of the Plum-Shaded Convent* and *Six Chapters of a Floating Life*). *Hulunbeier xueyuan xuebao* 呼倫貝爾學院學報, Vol. 11, No. 2 (Apr. 2003), pp. 55-58 & 132.

Zhang Yili 張昳麗. "Qing ciren Peng Sunyu jiashi kaoshu" 清詞人彭孫遹家世考述 (The genealogy of the Qing *ci* poet Peng Sunyu). *Zhongguo yunwen xuekan* 中國韻文學刊, Vol. 24, No. 3 (Sept. 2010), pp. 87-91.

Zhang Yu 張煜. "Qing ciren Peng Sunyi jiashi kaoshu" 明清詩人彭孫貽新樂府詩考論 (A study of the new *yuefu* poems by Peng Sunyi). *Ningxia shifan xueyuan xuebao* 寧夏師範學院學報, Vol. 39, No. 3 (Mar. 2018), pp. 16-20.

Zhang Zhongmou 張仲謀. "Quan Qing ci zuozhe xiaozhuan dingbu" 《全清詞》作者小傳訂補 (Correction of bibliographical data on eight authors of the *Complete Ci Poems of the Qing Dynasty*). *Dongwu xueshu* 東吳學術, No. 2 of 2017, pp. 85-91.

Zhang Zhongpeng 張中鵬. "Bi Fangji yu Nan Ming zhengquan zaji" 畢方濟與南明政權札記 (Notes on Francesco Sambiasi and the Southern Ming régimes). *Zhongguo shichang* 中國市場, No. 21 of 2011, pp. 172-173.

Zhao Erxun 趙爾巽 (1844-1927). *Qingshi gao* 清史稿 (Draft history of the Qing dynasty). 1928. Reprint. Beijing: Zhonghua shuju, 1977.

Zhao, Jie. *Brush, Seal and Abacus: Troubled Vitality in Late Ming China's Economic Heartland, 1500-1644*. Hong Kong: Chinese University Press, 2018.

Zhao Shaokuang 趙苕狂 (1892-1953). "*Yingmeian yiyu* kao" 影梅庵憶語考 (Notes on *Reminiscences of the Plum-shaded Convent*). In Zhu Jianmang, ed., *Yingmeian yiyu* (Taibei: Shijie shuju, 1959), pp. 1-15.

Zhao Yuan 趙園. "Guanyu Mao Xiang de *Yingmeian yiyu*" 關於冒襄的《影梅庵憶語》 (On *Reminiscences of the Plum-Shaded Convent* by Mao Xiang). *Shucheng* 書城, No. 12 of 2005, pp. 25-35.

Zhao Zhimin 趙智旻. "Qinhuai mingyuan Ma Xianglan" 秦淮名媛馬湘蘭 (The celebrated Qinhuai courtesan Ma Xianglan). In Shen Xinlin, ed., *Mingdai Nanjing xueshu renwu zhuan* 明代南京學術人物傳 [Biographies of the famous authors from Ming dynasty Nanjing] (Nanjing: Nanjing daxue chubanshe, 2004), pp. 365-72.

Zheng Liju 鄭禮炬. Qian Qianyi *Zhangpu Liu Fujun hezang muzhiming* shuzheng 錢謙益《漳浦劉府君合葬墓誌銘》疏證 (A textual study of Qian Qianyi's *Epitaph of the Liu family of Zhangpu*). *Min Tai wenhua yanjiu* 閩台文化研究, No. 1 of 2014, pp. 103-107.

Zheng Yunshan 鄭雲山, Gong Yanming 龔延明, and Lin Zhengqiu 林正秋. *Hangzhou yu Xihu shihua* 杭州與西湖史話 (A history of Hangzhou and West Lake). Shanghai: Shanghai renmin chubanshe, 1980.

Zhong Yao 鍾繇 (151-230). *Zhong Yao xiaokai jiuzhong* 小楷九種 (Nine pieces of Zhong Yao in small script). Shanghai: Shanghai shuhua chubanshe, 2011. *Zhongguo meishu quanji shufa zuanke bian Qingdai shufa* 中國美術全集 書法篆刻編 清代書法 (Complete collection of Chinese fine art, calligraphy and seals, Qing calligraphy). Shanghai: Shanghai shuhua chubanshe, 1997.

Zhou Fagao 周法高. "Dongfei yu Dong Xiaowan xinkao" 董妃與董小宛新考 (New light on Consort Dong and Dong Xiaowan). *Hanxue yanjiu* 漢學研究, Vol. 1, No. 1 (1983), pp. 9-25.

Zhou Jianguo 周建國. "Daodi shuizhi shi buxie: Lun Mao Xiang jiqi Guandi xinyang" 到底誰知事不諧：論冒襄及其關帝信仰 (Who knows that things are not harmonious: Mao Xiang and his worship of Lord Guan). *Hebei Beifang xueyuan xuebao* 河北北方學院學報, Vol. 30, No. 4 (Aug. 2014), pp. 4-6 & 21.

Zhou Lianggong 周亮工 (1612-1672). *Chidu xinchao* 尺牘新鈔 (Selected writings of recent men of letters). Early Qing. Reprint. Shanghai: Shangwu yinshuguan, 1936.

Zhu Jianmang (1890-1972). "Collation Notes." In Zhu Jianmang, ed., *Yingmeian yiyu* (Taibei: Shijie shuju, 1959), pp. 1-2.

Zhu Lixia 朱麗霞 and Zhou Qinggui 周慶貴. "Du Jun nianpu" 杜濬年譜 (The chronological biography of Du Jun). *Ming*

Qing xiaoshuo yanjiu 明清小說研究, No. 2 of 2010, pp. 174-187.

Zhu Shu 朱姝. "Wu Qi yanjiu zongshu" 吳綺研究綜述 (Studies on Wu Qi). *Heihe xueyuan xuebao* 黑河學院學報, No. 1 of 2013, pp. 135-137.

____. "Wu Qi yu Wu Weiye jiaoyu yanjiu" 吳綺與吳偉業交遊研究 (On the literary contacts between Wu Qi and Wu Weiye). *Qingnian wenxuejia* 青年文學家, No. 22 of 2013. pp. 74-75.

Zhu Yizun 朱彝尊 (1629-1709). *Jingzhiju shihua* 靜志居詩話 (Poetic talks from the Jingzhi Studio). Beijing: Renmin wenxue chubanshe, 1990.

Zhu Zhifan 朱之藩 (1556-1624). *Fengshi Chaoxian gao* 奉使朝鮮稿 (Record of my mission to Korea). Beijing: Beijing tushuguan chubanshe, 2003.

Zuo Si 左思 (ca. 253-ca. 307). "A Dainty Girl." In Anne Birrell, ed. and trans., *New Songs from a Jade Terrace: An Anthology of Early Chinese Love Poetry* (London, Boston, and Sydney: Allen & Unwin, 1982), pp. 85-86.

Zurndorfer, Harriet. "Prostitutes and Courtesans in the Confucian Moral Universe of Late Ming China (1550-1644)." *International Review of Social Hisotry*, Vol. 56, No. 1 (2011), 197-216.

INDEX

ADVANCE RESPONSES

"At last, a translation from 17th-century Chinese that captures the impossible romanticism and intense anxiety of living in those turbulent times. Whether courtesan Dong was as loving and steadfast as her memoirist-lover chooses to remember her doesn't matter. His words, elegantly and faithfully translated here, describe vividly their lives as they understood them in an age so different from our own."

—**Timothy Brook**,
Department of History, University of British Columbia,
author of *Vermeer's Hat,* Editor-in-chief, *The History of Imperial China* (6 vols).

"*The Romance of a Literatus and his Concubine in Seventeenth-century China* presents a complete, annotated English translation of Reminiscences of the Plum-shaded Convent (Yingmei'an yiyu), an important and widely circulated memoir written by the early Qing dynasty scholar-official Mao Xiang (1611-1693), in which he fondly recalls his brief life with, and deep love for, the multi-talented concubine Dong Xiaowan (1624-1651). The Fang-He translation, accompanied by an informative introduction, copious notes, the original Chinese text, and several beautiful illustrations, is faithful to the original Chinese text in every respect and reads extremely well in English. Anyone interested in moving beyond the usual stereotypes about the secondary role(s) of women in ancient China will want to read this touching and memorable account. This is because, as Mao Xiang himself remarks, 'Xiaowan was no ordinary woman of this world.'"

—**James M. Hargett**,
The University at Albany, State University of New York,
author of *Jade Mountains and Cinnabar Pools: The History of Travel Literature in Imperial China*

OTHER CHINA, HONG KONG & MACAU NON-FICTION PUBLISHED BY PROVERSE

Stuart McDouall. All Agog In China. 2014.

Jean A. Berlie. The Chinese of Macau: A Decade after the Handover. 2012.

Gillian Bickley, Ed. The Complete Court Cases of Magistrate Frederick Stewart. 2008.

Gillian Bickley. Ed. The Development of Education in Hong Kong, 1841-1898 as Revealed by the Early Education Reports of the Hong Kong Government 1848-1896. 2002.

James McCarthy. The Diplomat of Kashgar: A Very Special Agent. The Life of Sir George Macartney, 18 January 1867 to 19 May 1945. (Winner of the Proverse Prize 2013). 2014.

Major (Ret'd) Brian Finch, MCIL. A Faithful Record of the *Lisbon Maru* Incident. 2017. Translation from Chinese with additional material.

Gillian Bickley. The Golden Needle: The Biography of Frederick Stewart (1836-1889). 1997.

Lt. Cmdr. Henry C.S. Collingwood-Selby, R.N. (1898-1992). Richard Collingwood-Selby (Chile) and Gillian Bickley (Hong Kong), Eds. In Time of War. 2013.

Gillian Bickley. Ed. Journeys with a Mission: Travel Journals of The Right Revd George Smith (1815-1871) first Bishop of Victoria (Hong Kong) (1849-1865). 2018.

Gillian Bickley, Verner Bickley, Christopher Coghlan, Timothy Hamlett, Geoffrey Roper, Gary Tallentire. Ed Gillian Bickley. A Magistrate's Court in Nineteenth Century Hong Kong. 1st ed. 2005, 2nd ed. 2009.

Sophronia Liu. A Shimmering Sea: Hong Kong Stories (Winner of the Proverse Prize 2012). 2013.

Gillian Bickley. Ed. Through American Eyes: The Journals Of George Washington (Farley) Heard. 2017.

Manufactured by Amazon.ca
Bolton, ON